Shalom Yesterday, Today, and Forever

Shalom Yesterday, Today, and Forever

Embracing All Three Dimensions
of Creation and Redemption

Mark DeVine

WIPF & STOCK · Eugene, Oregon

SHALOM YESTERDAY, TODAY, AND FOREVER
Embracing All Three Dimensions of Creation and Redemption

Wipf & Stock
An Imprint of Wipf and Stock Publishers
199 W. 8th Ave., Suite 3
Eugene, OR 97401

www.wipfandstock.com

PAPERBACK ISBN: 978-1-5326-3322-5
HARDCOVER ISBN: 978-1-5326-3324-9
EBOOK ISBN: 978-1-5326-3323-2

Manufactured in the U.S.A.

For Timothy George

*who for almost four decades
has been my encourager*

He's got the whole world in his hands
He's got the whole wide world in his hands.

—FOREST HAMILTON AND ROSS STEPHENS

Contents

Acknowledgments

I WISH TO THANK Dean Timothy George and the trustees of Samford University, Birmingham, Alabama, for their granting of a sabbatical leave during which much of the research for this project was completed. I also thank Dr. Jason K. Allen, president of Midwestern Baptist Theological Seminary, who provided underserved hospitality to me in Kansas City, Missouri, during my sabbatical leave by providing housing, research assistance, and access to the seminary's library and interlibrary loan services. Thank you to reference librarian Judy Howie, who delivered patient and prompt help as my needs demanded. I also wish to thank Mindy Akright for taking care of many important tasks on my behalf.

1

Introduction: What Is Shalom?

Peace I leave with you; my peace I give to you. Not as the
world gives do I give to you. Let not your hearts be troubled,
neither let them be afraid.

—JESUS OF NAZARETH (JOHN 14:27)

IN THIS BOOK I shall employ the biblical word *shalom*[1] in a special and fairly
precise way. Shalom, for my purpose indicates the functioning and flourishing of the entire created order according to God's revealed purposes for
it. More particularly, shalom points to this divinely intended functioning
and flourishing according to three relational dimensions that supplement
and interpenetrate one another. Here they are: (1) the relationship between
God's human creatures and their creator God, (2) the relationship between
human beings themselves before their heavenly Father (*coram deo*), and
(3) the relationship of human beings with one another before God *in the
place* which is the home God the creator made for them and into which
God settled them. Disproportionate attention shall be given to this third
relational dimension of shalom because I believe it suffers from neglect,
misunderstanding, and distortion.

I am not claiming that any single occurrence of the word *shalom* in
the Bible references the full scope of these three relational dimensions. I
am making use of the word *shalom* to comprehend a larger reality than
any one instance of its use denotes. But the word *shalom* commends itself for my purposes because its semantic range includes the meanings of

1. Throughout this work I shall only italicize the word "*shalom*" when I am explicitly referencing the biblical Hebrew word. Otherwise, "shalom" shall carry the more
fully orbed special meaning for which I am employing it as I explain in this introduc-
tory chapter.

"peace," "harmony," and "prosperity" within communal settings and very often with reference to the third relational dimension to which I wish to give special attention. These meanings variously conveyed by *shalom* are crucial to the divinely intended three-dimensioned relational functioning and flourishing I shall explore.

In this book's title, "Shalom Yesterday" refers to the shalom established by the creator for his human creatures and into which he settled them in Eden. "Shalom Today" indicates that the consequences of the fall neither nullified nor altered the creator God's original intention that his human creatures enjoy the three-dimensioned shalom. "Today" refers to the time-between-the-times in which we all live—between expulsion from Edenic paradise and the arrival of the new heaven and new earth and the new Jerusalem coming down from heaven. We shall have to explore the impact of the fall upon the creator's original shalomic purposes and upon the life of humanity and the children of God in this "between time." "Shalom forever" refers to the three-dimensioned shalom promised to the children of God in the new heaven and the new earth. We shall explore elements of shalomic continuity and discontinuity prevailing between the three differentiated periods of shalom: shalom yesterday, today, and forever; shalom in Eden, shalom east of Eden, and shalom in the world to come.

Creation and Redemption

The subtitle points to the relationship between shalom, creation, and redemption. I shall argue that God the creator made the universe as the home fit for his human creatures. This fitness includes especially the creation's fitness for the functioning and flourishing of the three-dimensioned shalom I shall further define and explore. Redemption immediately signifies that the fall has occurred. Redemption is the creator's response to the fall. Though the fall results in profound and even devastating consequences for human beings and every dimension of the created order, God the creator's response to the fall ensures that sin, evil, and the consequences that flow in their wake shall not have the last word. God the creator shall have the last word by reveling himself as and by acting as not only creator but also as redeemer.

Especially important for my purposes is to insist that the entire creation is in the crosshairs of God's redemptive purposes and activity. This is so not least, and perhaps mostly, because the entire created order is necessary to the full functioning and flourishing of the three-dimensioned shalom for which the universe was created. The creator's claim upon all that he has made never attenuates whatsoever. Any suggestion that human sin or spiritual evil or anything else shall result in even the slightest divine relinquishment of the original shalomic purposes in creation is rejected. The God of Abraham, Isaac, and Jacob does not dial back the full scope of his shalomic purposes and settle for something less, such as the salvation of disembodied human souls or even of bodily resurrected human beings apart from the home he made for them.

In the course of our exploration of shalom we shall note the assertion of divine interest in shalom, especially in its third relational dimension, throughout the Scriptures. We shall have to grapple with the proper role of shalomic interest given the fall in this between time in which we live. Should Christian believers pursue shalom in this life or must shalomic hopes rest entirely in the world to come? I shall argue that indeed, interest in shalom by the creator and redeemer persists east of Eden and should persist among the people of God as well.

Shalomic Settlement

I shall argue that the shalom for which the creator made human beings is characterized by settled community life as opposed to unsettled or isolated living. Thus, a whole range of states of being that are less than settled shall be seen variously as shalom-deprived, as punishment, and as the result of the fall. Biblical words indicating such unsettled states of being include "expelled," "cast out," "gathered," "wandering," "scattered," "exiled," "sojourning," and "pilgrimage."

All of these terms that involve movement rather than a settled state of affairs belong either to divine punishment or to the redemptive activity of God, or to both. What they share is their connection to the fall, as we shall see. God makes all things serve his redeeming purposes for his elect, including the less than fully and permanently settled conditions listed. But where these unsettled conditions serve the divine purposes, they do insofar as they facilitate and nurture shalom. They serve shalomic settlement, not unshalomic unsettlement. They must serve shalom—not shalom them.

Shalomic settlement is both an original purpose of God in creation, an essential and constitutive goal of redemption, and a continuing ideal notwithstanding the unsettlement brought on by the fall and made necessary by certain dimensions of redemption. The word "gathered" is especially useful to illustrate what I mean because to be gathered is to be rescued from wandering or from having been scattered or from exile. Our God as redeemer expels from Edenic shalom and scatters as punishment and prelude to gathering and resettling into shalomic flourishing. Sojourn and pilgrimage involve movement but both prize, seek, and long for the divinely intended and promised shalomic settlement I shall explore. Jesus leaves heaven in order to gather up the elect. He sends evangelists and church planters in order to gather and settle his elect into communities of faith.

Health and Wealth

I shall argue that the divinely intended shalom entails both physical health and material prosperity—not the exaltation of a simple lifestyle, much less any glamorization of poverty or of physical suffering. I shall reject the prosperity gospel and other forms of health and wealth theology as pernicious heresies, but shall argue that current evangelical critique of such heresy is weak and ineffective. The chief weakness of evangelical futility in its anti-prosperity stance is its failure to face with full seriousness the numerous passages in Holy Scripture that teach that physical health and material prosperity are indeed to be acknowledged and enjoyed as blessings of God. The result is that the prosperity and anti-prosperity factions double down on their canons-within-the-canon rather than engage seriously with the favorite passages of the other side. So they talk past one another.

I shall note that the loudest evangelical voices against the prosperity gospel emerge from affluent communities of faith. This reality results in a jarring disconnect and seeming contradiction between the prophetic rhetoric of anti-prosperity and the lifestyles of the would-be prophets. I shall explore possible reasons for this disconnect and failure on the part of the anti-prosperity side and offer suggestions for how to offer a more biblically faithful and comprehensive challenge to the prosperity gospel.

Shalom and Suffering

I shall explore the central place of suffering in the Bible. I shall explore suffering as punishment for sin, its central place in the redemptive activity of God in Jesus Christ, and its place in both common human experience and Christian experience in the time between the times east of Eden. I shall argue that suffering plays an essential role in redemption and as such in the revelation of God—thus our God is creator and redeemer from all eternity. The actual experience of suffering is restricted to "shalom today," in the time between the times. The actual experience of suffering has no place in shalom yesterday and forever. I shall argue that suffering is to be chiefly associated with punishment for sin and the willingness to suffer in order to end suffering. This second role of suffering renders it a paradoxical element of human and Christian existence east of Eden. But the paradox does not suggest any equal place for suffering beside shalomic health and prosperity. Redemptive suffering aims at and eventually kills suffering. Nevertheless, I shall contend that redemptive suffering does secure and retain a permanent place in the new heaven and the new earth, not in experience but in memory.

I shall give attention to the rise of monasticism and shall consider whether Christian asceticism and shalom are compatible. In this connection, I shall not confine my considerations to monastic ascetism but also give attention to the biblical teaching that self denial is an essential component of Christian discipleship.

Relational Worth and Inherent Worth

Let us recall that shalom refers to a three-dimensional relational reality the creator purposes in the act of creation. The relational character and dynamic shalom denies ascription of intrinsic worth or value to any part of creation and to creation as a whole. Shalom insists that intrinsic or inherent worth can be ascribed to God alone. Even there, in God, a relational dynamic inheres—the eternal relations between the three persons in the one Godhead.

This restriction of inherent worth to God alone does not deny all worth to creatures. Everything outside of God has worth (glory, value, meaning, good purpose, praiseworthiness) only in relation to the creator for whom it was made and before whom it exists (*coram deo*) It is not only noteworthy but theologically crucial that, though God is inherently worthy due to his perfection and sufficiency, the character of that perfection and sufficiency is relational from all eternity. That relationality includes dynamics of dependence, mutual self-giving, and especially and in a comprehensively illumining way—love. This eternal relational dynamic within the divine lies at the heart of the meaning of humanity's unique creation *imago dei*.

Humanity is, through creation, uniquely fitted to and, according to the work of the Holy Spirit, capable of reflecting the worthiness for praise of the creator. Intratrinitarian relationality, dependence, and love potentially finds appropriate reflection, as in a mirror, in humanity's shalomic three-dimensional interdependence and divinely enabled capacity for love. This potential reflection of unique intrinsic divine worthiness for praise becomes a witness to his glory. Human beings uniquely, and the rest of creation in its own mirror-like way, are made capable by the creator to become means to the glorification of God, which involves bearing witness to his worthiness for praise. And what is his worthiness for praise? Why is the triune God alone to be worshipped? To God be the glory for the things he has done.

And what has he done for which he is to be worshipped? The church across the ages, when reduced to employment of the fewest words possible, has answered that question thus: he has created and redeemed. Thus the church worships God as creator and redeemer.

This derivative and inherently relational possibility of worth in the creature undermines any notion that divine employment as means or instrument implies non-essentiality. Unwarranted diminishment or marginalization of something employed as a means, or the suggestion of the limited, temporal, discardable nature of means, is often signaled by the prefix or modifier "mere" to the words "means" or "instrument." Creation, the whole of it, is a means for, an instrument for the glorification of the creator. But to speak of it as a "just" an instrument or as a "mere" means is profoundly misleading.

It is true that the creation's worth is entirely gratuitous, dependent, and utterly devoid of intrinsic value. But it's relational, dependent worth as the creature of the one who alone is intrinsically valuable is both real and profound because of the worthiness of its maker. And this relational worthiness is permanent because of the promise of God and the content of the promise made to it, namely, its complete redemption in eternity. That its worthiness is grounded from inception in instrumentality does not diminish but rather identifies and illumines the very basis of glory or worthiness of the creature. Thus, the instrumental, witness, and dependent character of the creature's worth proves essential to God's revealed purposes for it. Human beings are valuable not due to any inherent qualities or potential usefulness apart from their relationship to God, not one whit. But that's fine. As creatures they cannot and need not bear such worth. Their worthiness as creatures is precisely in the favor the creator has shown towards them by using them as fit reflectors and proclaimers of his own inherent worthiness for praise.

Why is recognition of this relational and instrumental worth important for our purposes? Because shalom asserts that creation's power to point away from itself to the creator is not a mere means but an essential and permanent means and instrumentality that shall endure into eternity. This affirmation rejects any notion that once some component or dimension of creation serves its purpose of pointing away from itself to the creator who gave it, its job is done and it may and should fall away, making way for God to be all in all. The logic of this sort of thinking would actually leave God alone, completely without his creation, including us humans.

That the Old Testament "speaks of Jesus" and "bears witness to Jesus" does not mean that once we come to see and know and trust Jesus the Old Testament can or even should be left behind. No. The Jesus Christ to whom the word of the Old Testament bears witness is now and shall ever be the

Messiah of whom the Old Testament speaks. The enthroned Jesus Christ before whom crowns shall be thrown down shall ever be the second person of the triune God who created the world *ex nihilo*, called Abraham out of Ur, parted the Red Sea, preserved Daniel in the lion's den, and shall be worshiped as such and not otherwise. The means are retained. They do not fall away. That this is so is fundamental to the assertions of shalom.

Augustine contrasted God and all that he has made in terms of the appropriate human desire and enjoyment that is appropriate to each. Only God is worthy of being enjoyed for his own sake (*frui*) without sideways glances. Only God is an end in himself where humanity's enjoyment and love are concerned. Only God can and does make good on the unique promise held out to human beings by the command and permission to love and enjoy God. This is why God alone is to be worshipped.

Everything else in the created order, from crutches, to children, right on down to crunchy Cheetos is to be used (*uti*) as a means to the love and enjoyment of the God who bestowed such blessings.[2] These blessings must serve as pointers away from themselves to their creator. Only then, Augustine taught, does love and enjoyment flourish according to the right order established by God, the order appropriate to the nature of the actual relation between he who alone is worthy of enjoyment for his own sake (*frui*) and that which is fit to be utilized (*uti*) for that enjoyment. Only where human *frui* and *uti* rest upon their appropriate objects is concupiscence, disordered desire, avoided.

As sinners, we get our *uti* and our *frui* mixed up—futilely attempting to use (*uti*) God in order to obtain what we desire in creation so that we might enjoy (*frui*) them. The result is the idolatrous attempt to love and enjoy the gifts of God as only God is worthy and capable of satisfying upon the things he has made and to have God cooperate with us in the idolatry. At this point it is vital to note that among those created things that are to be used (*uti*) and not loved or enjoyed (*frui*) as God alone is worthy is we ourselves, yet we are not lost in the enjoyment of God, but found.

Shalom affirms Augustine's profound insights concerning the proper and distinct "love" and "enjoyment" appropriate to God but not the creature. Augustine's comprehension of this distinction and relation confirms shalom's insistence that instrumentality and means do not imply impermanence, non-essentiality, or eventual obsolescence. Were such the case, our own annihilation would follow. But the promise of the redeemer proves such fears unfounded. Ours is the creator and redeemer who loves with *khessed* love, loyal love. He remembers his promise—he redeems unto eternity his

---

2. Augustine, *On Christian Doctrine*, 9–10.

rescued ones. Our instrumentality as means of God's glorification shall never become obsolete, not because of some need for it by God, but due to the exercise of the divine freedom according to which he is pleased draw it from and receive it from us. That which is used (*uti*) for the enjoyment (*frui*) of God, namely ourselves, and the whole created order awaiting and longing for redemption (Romans 8), have a permanent place in God's plans.

The permanent place for that which is used (*uti*) is sometimes minimized, ignored, or denied. To do so is to impugn the creator, the creation he redeems, and the shalom for which we were made. We betray the divine shalom when we imagine that the gifts to be used for the enjoyment of God are meant to fall away once their pointing away from themselves is done.

The actual place of the blessing of creation and the many gifts it comprises is aptly illustrated when we consider the dynamics of gift giving that ought to prevail between human parents and children. When gifts are rightly received from parents, they point the child away from the gift to the parent who gave it, resulting in love for the parent that is both greater and of a different kind than is appropriate to the gift itself. The child loves the giver more than and differently than the gift. On the other hand, we disapprove when a child views and values the parent only as the potential source of gifts. The child uses (*uti*) the parent to gain the gifts which are the main object of their desire and enjoyment (*frui*). *Uti* and *frui* have gotten mixed up. Idolatry threatens.

But where shalom flourishes, what of the aftermath of a proper gift bestowal and reception? Let the gift be a bicycle at Christmas. Shalom does not envision a child, so taken with the superior value and quality of value of the parent, abandoning the bicycle forever to cling to the parent who gave it.

Yet this sort of idea seems to insinuate itself into much "spiritual talk" in preaching and in small group Bible study. No doubt such thinking and talk might think itself encouraged by the many scriptures encouraging of and commanding self-denial and sacrifice and others that speak of love for God alone. Did not Paul count all things as dung and loss in order to giant Christ? Did not Jesus say something about potential disciple dismemberment and eye-gouging? We shall revisit whether, how, and in what way self-denial, sacrifice, and ascetic renunciation fit with shalom. But for now, it is important to recognize that the scenario in which the child abandons the bicycle forever in order to cling to the parents does not accord with the shalom I am contending for. Rather, the child keeps and enjoys the bicycle appropriately as proper gift and blessing from the parent. The bicycle is used according to its nature, continues to point away from itself to the parent, and is to be enjoyed in its proper measure as the blessing it is. Means and essentiality are not enemies, but eternal friends.

The creation as means and instrument of the glorification of the creator no more has a clock on it than does the mediatorial role of Jesus Christ as our high priest after the order of Melchizedek.

Shalom and Hierarchy

I shall argue that faithful comprehension, pursuit, and enjoyment of shalom requires recognition that the created order comprises a divinely established hierarchy of value. "You are worth more than many sparrows," Jesus said. I shall argue that the hierarchy of value informs a sequence or priority of sacrifice-ability east of Eden in which lesser-valued goods are to be sacrificed for the sake of more-valued goods when necessary. Thus, the potential for sacrifice of one's own life remains live since God remains more and differently valuable that any creature, including human beings. I shall also contend that the deep paradox of sacrifice in Holy Scripture is that the sacrifice of goods, even our own lives, is the path to securing those goods. "For whoever would save his life will lose it, but whoever loses his life for my sake will find it" (Matt 16:25).

Within the hierarchy of values, I shall note a distinction between means and ends. I shall argue that recognition of a divinely created good as a means does not imply its dispensability. Means can be as essential as ends. And goods can function both as means and as ends. The inherently relational character of the created order along with the interdependence such relationality establishes results in the flourishing of myriad instrumentalities as permanent features of the divinely established and promised shalom. Successful identification of a good as a means does not answer the question of whether that means remains essential to the shalom for which we were made.

Hierarchy of value, far from suggesting the eventual dispensability of goods ranked lower on the scale of value, belongs to the rich beauty and goodness of the created order the creator assessed as "very good." As such, creation, in all its dimensions, should be acknowledged as the blessing of the creator. Redemption does not call for moving past or letting go or discarding dimensions of creation supposedly now obsolete or rendered permanently pernicious due to the fall. Redemption entails the salvaging, recovery, restoration, and perfecting of creation. "Just give me Jesus," proves its biblical saliency only insofar as it worships the cosmic Christ of Colossians who is all in all. The blessings and gifts of God the creator (which includes our own lives) must point away from themselves to the giver, but they do not then fall away. Rather, they reflect the creator's glory as they are enjoyed properly, according to divine ordering, rather than idolatrously.

Shalom and Place

The third dimension of shalom affirms the non-human dimensions of the created order as the home fit for human beings according to the creator's wisdom and love. As such shalom insists that the blessings of creation include enjoyment of the home prepared by the creator especially for his creatures to enjoy. Like every other dimension of the created order, human and nonhuman, the home humans inhabit has been impacted negatively by the fall.

The result is that the non-human dimensions of creation are no longer what they were meant to be and human engagement of their damaged home is not what it was meant to be. But the damaged home of human beings remains the object of the divine redemptive activity and should be treated accordingly, namely, with appropriate hope given the promise of God regarding its future restoration (Romans 8); and that parallels the hope we have for ourselves and others to whom the gospel is preached, and thus with the care, use, and enjoyment possible in this time between the times.

A Theological Exercise

What follows is an exercise in theology of a particular sort. Its first aim is to prove itself biblical. In pursuit of that aim it takes comfort from finding help and confirmation from the history of exegesis and historical theology. In the spirit most recently of Thomas Oden but more broadly of the Great Tradition, I wish to make no new contribution to theology, but to offer faithful witness to the faith once delivered to the saints. What follows opens a window into some of the musings upon Scripture and reflections upon the thoughts of revered Christian teachers of the past that gave rise to my development of the shalom hypothesis. As such, this book invites testing of the shalom hypothesis by all who read and reflect seriously and prayerfully upon Holy Scripture in order to hear what God the Holy Spirit reveals to us through that word. I begin with the renewed interest in the doctrine of creation precipitated by a fresh confrontation with the Apostles' Creed.

2

Creation First

We believe in God the Father Almighty
Maker of Heaven and Earth . . .

—THE APOSTLES' CREED, ARTICLE 1

WITHOUT WARNING AND WITH unexpected power, the first article of the oldest Christian creed arrested my attention. These opening lines seemed to illumine not subsequent articles of the Apostles' Creed, but the unity of Holy Scripture from Genesis to Revelation. Creation stood out now, not as a mere preliminary or a merely instrumental feature of divine activity and purpose, nor as a mere stage upon which the triune God would enact redemption—ostensibly the "real" show. No. Here creation stands not only at the beginning, but at the center of all God's ways. Could it be that in creation we encounter the very heart of divine glory, the fundamental feature of God's worthiness for praise?

For the first time, for me at least, God the creator emerged, in a powerful new way, as the God of the gospel of Jesus Christ. This conviction animates my purpose in what follows, the pursuit of the good news of God the creator. A pursuit culminating in a happy and wondrous confession that creation lies at the heart of the gospel of Jesus Christ, because without creation there is nothing to redeem. Creation ensures, prompts, and signals both the initiation and final shape of redemption. Redemption serves creation. The implications of this ordering of the relationship between creation and redemption for preaching, discipleship, pastoral care, and missions prove decisive, rich, and far reaching indeed.

All attempts at a comprehensive understanding of the witness of Holy Scripture must start somewhere. And starting with redemption has its advantages. But so does starting with creation and that is what I propose to do.

New and Old

My attempt is not original. It boasts a long pedigree, as the opening of the Apostles' Creed indicates. Like sermons and songs, catechisms and creeds serve to remind the people of God of ancient Bible treasures and so facilitate a triggering of regret at loss and incentive to retrieve and recover neglected riches. In this case, the riches of creation.

Slow reading of the creed serves us well. No need to rush ahead to "Jesus Christ, his only Son, our Lord" in order to have our evangelical itches scratched. No. A little lingering at the first article will actually enrich and serve the second article on the Son and the third on the Holy Spirit and the church. Indeed, rushing past creation threatens to diminishes and distort a full and faithful vision of redemption's object, achievement, application, and promise.

Centering on the first article of the creed illumines a biblically entrenched Trinitarian prolepsis within the creed itself whereby the last two articles (on the Son and the Holy Spirit) reach back and penetrate the first article on the Father. Thus, of the Son we learn, "All things were made through him, and without him was not anything made that was made" (John 1:3). "He is . . . the firstborn *of creation*. For by him all things were created, in heaven and on earth, visible and invisible . . . in him all things hold together" (Col 1:15–17). And "the Spirit was hovering over the face of the waters" (Gen 1:2). The legitimacy, indeed the hermeneutical necessity of this prolepsis proves itself by its power to make clearer and fuller sense of what the Scriptures teach about God the creator.

All three persons, Father, Son, and Holy Spirit, infuse the first article because all share in creation, in the salvaging of creation after the fall, and in the fulfilling of creation's purpose in its promised future. No aspect of redemption can be rightly or fully comprehended apart from its original, organic, and inextricable grounding in the creator who redeems his creature. No authentic settling in with God the Father and the doctrine of creation forgets, slights, marginalizes, attenuates, or neglects God the Son or the incarnation or the cross or the gospel or any essential dimension of divine being and activity. The same could be said of God the Holy Spirit who "sees to" enjoyment of Father and Son by the elect. The three persons of the one God do not compete with one another. No one person, not really, ever shines at the expense of the glory of the other two or of the three together in their essential divine unity. They are, always and perfectly, in cahoots in all they are and do, including their share in the act of creation and the redemption of creation after the fall.

Creation and Redemption

But what exactly do they do, these three persons of the triune God? The ancient church across time and geography sums up the divine activity in one compound confession: God is creator and redeemer—the triune God creates and redeems. In this book I mean to assert, explore, and celebrate an integrated comprehension of creation and redemption but also, and especially, the unique status of creation at the very heart of all God's ways. For evangelicals, redemption looms large and even dominates our thinking, our worship—our lives! And why not? Does not God himself insist on being known as the one "who brought you out of the land of Egypt, out of the house of slavery" (Exod 20:2)? Did not the eternal Son, sent by the Father in the power of the Spirit, come "to seek and to save the lost" (Luke 19:10)? Did not the apostle Paul decide to "know nothing" among the Corinthians besides "Jesus Christ and him crucified" (1 Cor 2:2)? Will not the still-visible wounds of Jesus remind us for all eternity that to know God truly is to know him as the redeemer of us blood-bought sinners?

Yes. A thousand times "Yes!" So, my effort to set God the creator and the creation itself in the center of our attention intends no reverse marginalization of redemption, salvation, or the gospel. Not at all. I mean to serve the gospel. But the gospel suffers where creation loses its proper place in the thinking and doing and worshiping of those for whom Jesus died.

If we wish to offer the most complete and full praise to God the redeemer, we must give due attention to the prominent place creation occupies in the revelation of God in Holy Scripture. It will be crucial for us to consider often that we human beings, though called to rule over creation, remain, according to God's wisdom and love, creatures ourselves. Recognition that creation includes both invisible/immaterial *and* visible/material dimensions will also prove decisive for the argument I shall advance. Yet the argument is not really mine. God makes it himself in his word, and the church across the ages hears it again and again. I am just beginning to hear it anew and with power and I seek company.

Creation, in the deepest and most comprehensive sense, is both the object and goal of redemption. Acknowledgement that this is so belongs to the continuous confession of the church. This acknowledgment is repeatedly expressed in the church's witness and worship reaching back to and through the Apostles' Creed and on into the canonical period itself—into the four gospels, into the epistles, into the Apocalypse of John, and into Luke the physician's "orderly account" in Acts.

Whatever confidence bleeds through the pages that follow arises from the conviction that what I assert is the old, tested, and continually

reconfirmed testimony of Holy Scripture. I share Thomas Oden's fear of
innovation and eschewal of creativity. Whatever smacks of novelty, idiosyn-
crasy, or innovation should evoke not surprised delight but suspicion and
resistance. Along with Oden, I am committed to making no new contribution to orthodox Christian doctrine. Whatever contribution might emerge
shall surely involve retrieval of the once-possessed but somehow lost teaching of the word of God. We seek not intriguing insights of our own conjur-
ing, but eternal truth, and relevant just for that reason.

Still, the odyssey of my own study included instances of astonishment at *seemingly* new insights. Bible teachings and connections between
teachings heretofore unnoticed now struck me as unavoidable, powerful,
and profound. Surely every lifelong reader of Scripture experiences such
bursts of fresh light. Confirmation that the Bible is the living word of God
is the common experience of Bible believers down through the ages. The
famous and perhaps apocryphal declaration of John Robinson, pastor to the
Pilgrims, rings true—"The Lord hath yet more truth and light to break forth
out of His Holy Word."[1]

Over time, as insights new to us prove faithful and true, the early experience of newness weakens and gives way to recognition of an ancient
pedigree and an initially unrecognized familiarity. What we first experience as a brand new vista opening up as we round a bend in the road turns
out to be a worn path back home stirring up a surprising sense of *déjà vu*.
The journey experienced at first as strange, far from taking us away from
familiar truth, instead reconfirms and deepens longstanding confession of
Bible truth expressed in creed, catechism, and countless spiritual songs and
hymns. In the case of shalom, these words, sung since childhood, take on
surprising new significance—"This is my father's world . . . Jesus who died
shall be satisfied, And earth and heav'n be one."[2] Creation and redemption
together, with creation first in the sequence. It is not that redemption must
not occupy first place in faithful biblical reflection. It may. But so may creation. Letting creation speak first illumines the divinely purposed shalom
this book investigates.

The long-familiar first lines of the Bible and of the Apostle's Creed
signal the possibility of a fresh but also familiar understanding of God the
creator and of the creation itself: "In the beginning God created the heavens
and the earth"; "I believe in God the Father almighty, maker of heaven and
earth." Likewise, a sentence or two from the penultimate chapter of Holy
Scripture, especially when juxtaposed with the opening of Genesis, suggests

1. Quoted in George, *John Robinson and the English Separatist*, xii.
2. Maltbie D. Babcock, "This Is My Father's World" (1901).

the same possibility: "I saw a new heaven and a new earth . . . and I saw the holy city, new Jerusalem, coming down out of heaven from God" (Rev 21:1–2). Now add to the mix the two petitions of the model prayer Jesus gave to his disciples: "Our Father in heaven . . . Your kingdom come, your will be done, on earth as it is in heaven" (Matt 6:9–10).

An outline of the recovery and reconfirmation I wish to advance begins to take real shape in this petition put by Jesus into the mouths of his disciples. "Thy kingdom come" envisions neither separation of creation and redemption nor the subsuming of one to the other, but rather their essential, permanent juxtaposition and inextricable integration in a beautiful divinely sustained reciprocity and relationship. The wondrous revelatory terrain of this relationship is what we propose to explore.

Out of Chaos and into Shalom

Only God creates. The Hebrew verb *bara*, translated "to create," is reserved in Holy Scripture exclusively for *Elohim*, the one who "was" before any and everything else was. In this sense, the creator's very being is unique. In his triune being he "is" in a special, singular, and incomparable way, so that the eternal Son of God, even in his incarnate state, can say, "Before Abraham was, I am" (John 8:58). Whatever creation of human beings *imago dei* makes possible, whatever participation with the creator, whatever sharing in the divine life—it facilitates no sharing in the divine status as the only creator. Human tending of the garden reflects the glory of the creator who made both the human tender of the garden and the garden to be tended; but it involves no *bara*, no creation, by the human keepers. Creation *imago dei* results in human reflection of the divine, not replacement of or parity with the divine. Creaturely participation and sharing with the creator in this way involves no encroachment, usurpation, or one-to-one imitation of God the Father, creator of heaven and earth, in whom we believe. Biblical *imitatio* of Father by children keeps each in their respective relation to one another.

In creation, we are told, God overcomes chaos and produces order and fruition. Shalom in its third dimension flourishes where the components and dimensions of creation function according to the creator's establishment of harmony and fruitfulness.

The Familiar Made Strange

Because of our susceptibility to forgetfulness as the people of God, it is precisely the great and familiar truths, those lying at the very heart of Christian confession, that seem uniquely susceptible to neglect, distortion, attack, and even loss. It is precisely the standard and seemingly established and secure foundations of the faith that deserved the most protection but too often receive the least. The rise and recurrence of great heresies demonstrate this. The fourth-century blow dealt to Arius' denial of the full deity of Jesus Christ wounded but did not kill that pernicious teaching. Exhibit A among contemporary evidence of Arianism's resilience—Mormonism.

Arianism crops up over and over again, necessitating fresh detection, refutation, and rejection. Arianism qualifies as a "great" heresy in three ways. First, Arius denies an essential and core doctrine, the full deity of Jesus Christ—a doctrine necessary to faithful Christian witness, obedience, and praise. Second, great heresies such as Arianism display staying power. They're never, on this side of eternity, permanently killed off and buried. Like crocodile heads popping up at a carnival kiosk, the orthodox mallet must be brought down upon them time and time again. With recurrent subtlety and strength across time and geography the great heresies insinuate themselves into the collective Christian psyche and begin to sound orthodox to Christian ears. Why such persistence? The third mark of great heresies help to explain this. Great heresies, like the devil himself, appeal to Holy Scripture in order defend and advance lies. Thus comes the question of Arius—"Didn't Jesus say 'the Father is greater than I'?"

The great heresies targeted in what follows are Gnosticism and Marcionism—the great creation-hating and creator-hating heresies. Both heresies have become parents and cousins to a plethora of additional creation-hating heresies. Like Arianism, these heresies prove themselves great by recurrently distorting, undermining, and denying a cardinal doctrine across time and geography through appeals to the Bible itself—in their case, the goodness of both the creator and the creation. Against this great heresy we must fight. Not in order to gloat triumphantly over defeated heresy, but in order to recover faithful hearing of the word of the triune God through which he gives us himself and "all things" (Romans 8).

Faithful hearing of the word of God welcomes partners, fellow listeners, both living and dead. The Apostles' Creed is a human word, not a divine word, but I have highlighted it to signal the help we all need in understanding the revelation of God in the Bible. Due modesty, when confronted with the word of God, looks for as much help from as many quarters as it can find when studying the Scriptures. Our efforts to understand the doctrine creation and its relationship to redemption, occur, by intention, in the context of the history of the church. After all, who warns us that Gnosticism and Marcionism are heresies? The original defenders of Bible truth against counterfeit orthodoxies.

Yet, the more precise context within which our study must advance is not that of the church as such—but of the church listening intently together to the Bible, the whole of the Bible. Proof-texting is fine as long as its assertions accord with the message of the Holy Scriptures as a whole. Pitting favored passages against those inconvenient to our desired result take us away from the rich vision canonical discernment promises.

Thus, our pursuit of a faithful doctrine of creation will take us to many books of both testaments. It shall require reflection upon the great storyline of God's dealings with his people stretching from creation through the "between time" we all now inhabit and on to God's revealed peeks and glimpses of the coming world—our true, final, permanent, and eternal home. Failure to test understanding of either creation or redemption by the witness of the whole of Scripture leads precisely to the great heresies of Gnosticism and Marcionism or to one of its mutant heretical children.

Shalom and Old Heresies

I shall argue that such church-imbedded canonical discernment results in a complex but still discernible vision of God's purposes in both creation and redemption. I shall employ the Hebrew word "shalom" to designate this reality and vision. I do not argue that the whole of this vision or reality is implied in any one occurrence of "shalom" in the Bible or that if one collects all the "shalom" texts, the full vison I am affirming emerges *in toto*. No one word or set of words encompasses the full scope of God's purposes in creation and redemption I wish to highlight—but meanings endemic to "*shalom*" in the Bible commend it for this use. The meaning of shalom, like any word, depends upon the context in which it is employed. In Holy Scripture, shalom is variously translated as "peace," "harmony," and "prosperity," each of which shed much needed light on the meaning of both creation and redemption and upon the relationship between them.

We shall find occasion to highlight all three of these meanings as we uncover a three-dimensioned relational reality without which God's purposes in creation and redemption cannot be fully comprehended and affirmed. As noted in the previous chapter, these three dimensions are (1) the relationship between human beings and their creator, (2) the relationship between human beings themselves as they stand together before their creator (*coram deo*), and (3) the relationship between human beings before their creator in the place, in the home, prepared for them by their creator and for which home they were made and in which home they were made to flourish.

It is this third divinely created interlocking relational dimension that the Gnostic and Marcionite heresies attack, distort, and ultimately reject. Where such resistance to and denial of God's good creation in the widest sense insinuates itself, usually undetected, into Christian preaching, teaching, and indeed into the Christian psyche itself, the gospel itself suffers. Creation-affirming texts are routinely, reflexively, and illegitimately "spiritualized." Unadulterated praise for God the creator feels less justified and less welcome. The full scope of redemption shrinks down to matters of abstract and immaterial concern. An unbiblically radical opposition between this world and the promised world works its way into our preaching, teaching, and into explicitly "Christian" speech such as in small group Bible studies, where what is "spiritual" comes to mean something like "non-physical," "non-material," or "invisible," or "having to do with the immaterial human soul and nothing else."

When this occurs, the doctrine of redemption and of salvation tends to shrink down in Christian speech and reflection to focus almost exclusively on the immaterial soul of human beings. The creator, in the face of the fall, seems to cede most of what he has made to the evil one and settle for a salvaging and rescue of only one segment of what he once called "very good," namely the immaterial dimension of human beings for whom Christ died.

In prayer and especially in behavior, we Christians rarely live up to such implied anti-material values—we do try to earn money and avoid sickness and find shelter and apply hearts and minds to a thousand other ostensibly "unspiritual" matters. We affirm and wish for the same for others, especially those about whom we care the most. But we may fail to connect those prayers and behaviors in pursuit of healing or gainful employment positively to our Bible Study discussions in small groups, or in our preaching. We may fail to connect our faith in God with the work we do or with the many other "this-worldly" concerns that characterize so much of our lives. We tend to police our public "holy talk," keeping it properly "spiritual."

Why do we do this? Part of the answer lies in the pernicious power of the heresies we have noted. That power derives great strength from the universal experience of physical suffering ending in death that is the shared destiny of all who draw breath on this planet. Clearly no one with eyes to see places trust or hope in this world—especially in this material world. Surely salvation, at its core, must involve rescue and escape especially from this fallen physical realm of corruption, disease, pain, mortality, and actual death.

Yes, all of this is true. And the church has seen and understood and taken to heart this negative message. But that's not all she has understood.

On the basis of the teaching of the Bible, the church has repeatedly affirmed that the object of redemption is not only the immaterial souls of sinners but the whole created order. The same creation, the entire created order, though slated for destruction by fire, nevertheless groans, awaiting redemption at the revelation of the sons of God (Romans 8).

Yet the global rise of another heresy, the prosperity gospel, has encouraged an intensification of reflexive "spiritualizing" of biblical texts seemingly contrary to any straightforward reading. By "prosperity gospel" I include various forms of "health and wealth" theology, preaching, and teaching that insist that God's will for his children in this world is that they be both healthy and wealthy all of the time. Absence of these blessings signals some failure of faith on the part of unhealthy and unwell would-be followers of Jesus Christ. Faithful hearers of Scripture reject such teaching as wrong, cruel, and outrageous.

But rejection of the prosperity gospel is often attended by overreaction and obscurantist hermeneutical blind spots. Anti-prosperity thinking may ignore, marginalize, or wrongly spiritualize truckloads of passages proponents of the prosperity gospel cite to support their views. We can do better. The path to that better understanding requires serious and comprehensive listening to the whole biblical plethora of passages informing and illumining the true relationship between creation and redemption. That relationship entails a three-dimensioned relational shalom that puts health and wealth and the physical dimensions of the created order generally, in their proper place. To that end, let us make attempt to start our thinking right where Scripture does, in Eden.

Eden and Beyond

Eden is not just about yesterday. It's about today and tomorrow as well. Proper interest in Eden arises not from idle curiosity about what was, but from acute interest in what is and is to come. We expect creation, and therefore Eden, to reveal essential and permanent truth for us because of God's faithfulness to himself. Jesus Christ, in whom the Godhead was pleased bodily to dwell, is the same, yesterday, today, and forever. Underlying the myriad richness, fathomless depth, and dazzling beauty of the divine being, a profound stability of character and purpose pulsates. This eternal faithfulness of the triune God to himself animates all divine activity and speech—including creation itself together with the word of God through which creation occurs.

Every act and word of God invites the question, "What of primordial, ancient, present, future, and eternal significance might we learn here?" And so, the creation of the universe, and the paradisiacal garden into which our first parents were set, beckons the children of God to look back in order see more clearly the present and future purposes of their creator. The look back to the earliest yesterday promises to unveil the God with whom we have to do today. The people of God, guided by her best teachers across time and geography, have recognized this. What matters to God, and thus should matter to us now and shall matter in the future, even in the next world, confronts us in unique ways in the events recorded in the early chapters of Genesis.

Toledot

The permanent relevance of these chapters emerges immediately with the appearance of the word *toledot* in Genesis 2:4—"these are the generations of the heavens and the earth when they were created."[3] The book of Genesis is structured by the repeated occurrence of this Hebrew word, often trans- lated "these are the generations of." The phrase "the generations of" proves misleading if we read it as signaling a mere review of archival genealogical data. Rather, *toledot* signals explanation for God's people of how their own world, after the fall into sin, came to be as it is. We may bring commonplace historical curiosity to consideration of the past. But God's preservation of the past in his holy word evidences zero divine interest in satisfying such cu- riosity. The *toledot* framing of biblical narratives, a pattern surfacing in both testaments of Holy Scripture, teaches the necessity of looking backward in order see and move forward as God's people.

This *toledot* framing calls for and facilitates a theological remembrance in order to illumine the current and future relationship of the creator and redeemer for us descendants of Eden's expelled soon-to-be parents. Our home east of Eden—the fallen, sin-stained, and sin-distorted world we all inhabit—cannot be comprehended apart from consideration of that pri- mordial world that preceded it, Eden.

Human remembering is a major theme throughout the Bible, but one sometimes noted as a problem or as unnecessary or even as an obstacle to holy living. The apostle Paul's famous "forgetting of what lies behind" (Phil

---

3. For what follows regarding the significance of *toledot*, see in Ross, *Creation and Blessing*, 69–78. The *toledot* of the heavens and the earth is followed by nine others encompassing the whole of Genesis from that of Adam (5:1—6:8) to that of Jacob (37:2—50:26).

3:13) and Jesus' "No one who . . . looks back is fit for the kingdom of God" (Luke 9:62) do not seem to invite, much less encourage remembering at all. But the Lord God repeatedly calls his people to remember and reprimands those who forget. Cursory reading of these and other such passages as hostile to remembering as such or on principle cannot be sustained.

Jesus' subject is not remembering at all but rather perseverance. Paul's "forgetting" repudiates not remembering as such but rather remembering gone wrong. Paul's "forgetting" signals how this good thing, remembering, has gone wrong. Along with work, sex, play, ritual, purchasing items with cash, the exercise of authority, and a thousand other otherwise wholesome activities, we sinners manage to put them to bad use. We've managed to do the same with remembering.

Paul critiques wrongful remembering, remembering that refuses to turn and stride into the future God has prepared for his children. Paul's "forgetting" in order to "strive forward" affirms the fundamental orientation of God and his word towards the future, not the past. The pervasive call for remembering throughout the Bible, launched by the *toledot* of Genesis, serves this fundamental present and future orientation by making remembrance serve the present and the future.

The past is capable of providing such service to the present and the future precisely because this, the only true God, who acted and spoke in the past, remains faithful to himself—and thus, his character and purposes never change. So, let us look not just back, but way back to the beginning itself, back to the creation of the heavens and the earth and to its divinely situated center, Eden, and to that tragic borderland just east of Eden.

All That Other Stuff

The Bible opens with a meticulous and ordered account of the creation of the universe. Human beings were created last. Why was this the case? Should this surprise us? Should the priority of the non-human dimensions of the universe in the order of creation surprise us? Should the enormous scope, rich diversity, stunning beauty, and temporal priority of these dimensions also surprise us? Indeed, why was anything other than human beings created at all? Only humankind would be created in the image of God, after all. When the Son of God came down from heaven to save, he became a man, not a tree or a squirrel or anything else, not even an angel. The bull's eye of redemption's target is not in doubt, is it? Not stars, not snail darters, but fallen and lost sinners, right?

So why all this other stuff? Was not the other stuff marked for destruction soon enough? First came the flood, which, though leaving destruction aplenty in its wake, did not annihilate the creation as a whole. Every species found a reserved spot on the ark. The waters subsided and the spared earth recovered. Neither the earth nor Noah and his ken enjoyed restoration to Eden, but rather to a continuance of the "east of Eden" status. And God's destruction project was not finished, was it? The flood was only a first installment. A second wave of divine destruction remains in the offing—loaded, cocked, and holstered in the divine revolver of promised punishment. Supplementing the global flood waters against which a large boat provided effective shelter, an all-consuming fire is set to reduce the earth to a smoking cinder or less on the Day of the Lord (2 Pet 3:10–12).

Aren't we meant to learn that all that "other stuff," such as "the heavens and the earth," unlike human beings, are, though perhaps of some immediate and present functional utility, also temporary, doomed, and thus, scrapable? "Lay not up treasure," our Lord admonished (Matt 6:19). "Seek not the food that perishes," Jesus said (John 6:27). Spiritual folk fix their eyes "not on what is seen, but on what is unseen," right (2 Cor 4:18)? They know their Lord's kingdom is not "of this world" and that, having been incorporated into him through baptism, their "citizenship is heaven," not in this world (Phil 3:20).

"Set you minds on things that are above," the apostle Paul admonished the Colossians, "not on things that are on earth" (Col 3:2). The "everything" that must count as excrement in order to gain Christ Jesus would seem to encompasses a lot (Phil 3:8), but that is just what Paul did, and, by implication, commends to us. Stop clinging to that which perishes, to that which is temporary, to the corruptible things, to all that is doomed. Ought we not face up to the full consequences of the fall? No going back. The Lord's angel brandishes a flaming sword east of Eden. Milton got it—Paradise Lost!

Does that primordial expulsion of our first parents from the paradisiacal garden limit to two the sets or categories of all that really matter—namely, to God and humanity? Other than God, only human beings belong, potentially at least, to the "not-doomed things," right? The triune God, eternal by nature, and human beings, offered and promised eternal life by him, are all that really matter. What is worthy of love, fit for enjoyment, fit to defend, safe for the setting of our hearts upon, because they do or might last forever? God and human beings?

The case for such a limited and hierarchical scale of value and prioritizing of concern seems very strong. It seems to find deep biblical anchoring and widespread biblical sanction. But note well, the most impressive and famous champions of such construals of biblical teaching are also among the worst or perhaps actually the worst heretics ever confronted by the church across the ages. The Gnostics for one. And also, perhaps the greatest, by which I mean the worst heretic ever, Marcion!

We'll come back to the sources, heterodox and otherwise, of creation-despising reading of the Bible in due course. But first let's consider another potential surprise Genesis might evoke from some readers.

Blighted Bodies

What about the human body? Did not the flood and shall not the coming fire threaten human bodies? Are not human bodies the targets of plente-ous warning, put-downs, and even divinely encouraged nonchalance throughout Holy Writ? In the New Testament, at least, it would seem so. Don't worry about your body or clothes or houses to shelter the clothes and protect the body (Matt 6:25-33). Don't even worry about those who can kill the body (Matt 10:28)! Did not Peter and the apostles articulate holy insight and spiritual priorities fresh from their body beatings at the hands of the Sanhedrin, rejoicing that they "were counted worthy to suffer for the name [of Jesus]"—*in their bodies* (Acts 5:41)? The apostle Paul dismisses the deterioration of his "earthly tent" and brags about the marks of Jesus borne in his own dying body (1 Cor 4:16—5:5; Gal 6:17).

Does not the whole history of honored and divinely required sacrifice reach its culmination in the voluntary laying down of the body of the spot-less lamb of God at Calvary? Did not Paul's own body provide the crown jewel of that "everything" of which he was prepared to consider as dung and to suffer its loss in order to gain Christ Jesus? "By faith they were stoned, sawn in two, they were killed with the sword" seems to place little value on the preservation of the human body where the following of Jesus Christ is concerned (Heb 11:37).

So does the human body also belong to all that "other stuff," to the doomed stuff ever prone to distract, captivate, and draw the attention and affections of God's children away from the truly valuable things, the non-doomed stuff—you know, the eternally valuable, truly spiritual stuff such as the God who is spirit and the disembodied human soul?

Ultimately, is not deliverance from this "other stuff," the non-human dimensions of creation and these troublesome mortal bodies, a fundamen-tal aim of divine redemption and a key feature of Christian hope? Is not deliverance from all this "other stuff" prerequisite to reception of the new spiritual life and spiritual world promised to the children of God?

Remember that our God wants us to know that he himself is spirit and so neither suffers hunger nor lives in houses made by human hands (Acts 7:48). So it seems two questions cry out for answers—why create all this non-human stuff and why imprison the human soul/spirit in a body liable to corruption and mortality in the first place?

Separating truth from falsehood in the long history of creation-hostile teaching requires a careful sifting of wheat from chaff indeed. A fair measure of sobering negativity regarding the material dimensions of the created order will survive such a sifting. But the basic negativity of this stream of teaching toward the material world, including the human body, deserves and has regularly drawn condemnation from the church. The most robust and insightful haters of material creation recognized how inhospitable most of the Bible was to their convictions. Rather than accommodate the Bible to their views through tendentious hermeneutical backflips and tortured reinterpretations, they eventually "manned up" and flew their Bible-dissatisfied and Bible-hostile flags boldly.

Gnostics, Manichees, and Marcionites, each variously nurtured upon the platonic tradition, inserted bias and sometimes hostility to the human body. They all reject God the creator and their blatant and subtle repeated emergence among Christian believers is striking. Their thoughts gain undeserved traction in the Christian psyche through appeal to a vast range of passages either distinguishing between or even pitting against one another the visible versus the invisible or the spirit against the flesh or this world versus the next. Like all four principle heresies condemned in the fourth-century christological debates, these creation-hostile heresies are driven by what Peter Brown has aptly called a "desperate piety towards the Divine Being."[4] Where zeal for God implies hostility to what he has made, fatal departure from the biblical witness has occurred.

For this stream of sub-biblical thinking, creation is so obviously and deeply and irretrievably evil that God could not have been involved in its inception and so our concept of God must eschew even the slightest suggestion of any connection, involvement, or tainting of God's character with the created order. On closer inspection however, talk about the corrupt creation often targets the material creation only, while treating the "things invisible" differently, in a separate category all its own, especially the human mind using reason or the human spirit, or the soul. The argumentation of the creation-hostile heretics seems to play down or even forget that the created order includes both the visible and the invisible dimensions of the universe. Where such heretically creation-hostile notions find root in the

---

4. Brown, *Augustine of Hippo*, 47.

church, asceticism tends to gain in admiration. The Old Testament is variously marginalized, ignored, viewed as a mere stage in progressive revelation now obsolete. Or the Old Testament might be interpreted according to a material-hostile allegorizing aimed at a "spiritualizing" reading incompatible with orthodox affirmation of creation, redemption, and the incarnation. The body, matter, the physical universe even come to be treated as an enemy to spiritual life.

The Manicheans sang, "I have known the soul and the body that lies upon it, they have been enemies since the creation of the worlds."[5] Without making body and soul enemies, Origen could still say, "By human beings I mean souls placed in bodies."[6] Shalom prefers to such construals of the relationship between body and soul Karl Barth's designation of the human being as "the soul of his body."[7]

The human body has fallen and now suffers pain. But it remains the object of the redeeming work of the creator. And the human being created by the triune God, though comprising both physical and non-physical dimensions, is not himself without both.

The first account of creation in Genesis 1:1—2:3 makes no mention of any distinction between the physical and non-physical or "spiritual" components of the human creature. But in Genesis 2:7 we do have this—"then the Lord God formed the man of dust from the ground and breathed into his nostrils the breath of life, and the man became a living creature [nehesh]." Though some translations render nephesh "living soul," this phrase is misleading. It imports a central concept of Greek philosophy as shaped by Plato, the greatest of philosophers, into a text where it has no business. Importation of the Greek preoccupation with the distinction between body and soul rarely aids faithful interpretation of the Bible.

Christian theologians, including the writing apostles themselves, would make much happy use of the great platonic philosophical and linguistic inheritance of which they and we are beneficiaries. Divinely inspired deployment of the already ancient, historically mature, and philosophically freighted logos appears right there in the prologue of John's gospel. Note also the apostle Paul's plea to Colossians believers:

> . . . having been "raised up with Christ" to "seek the things that are above, where Christ is seated at the right hand of God. Set your minds on things that are above, not on things that are on earth. For you have died, and your life is hidden with Christ in

5. Brown, *Augustine of Hippo*, 49.
6. Origen, *On First Principles*, 186.
7. Barth, *Doctrine of* Creation, 366–93.

God. When Christ, who is your life appears, then you also will
appear with him in glory. (Col 3:1-4)

The conceptual, cosmogonic, and linguistic machinery employed in
this passage is inconceivable apart from the platonic tradition. We shall have
to examine these and other passages bearing the unmistakable footprints
of Plato and his philosophical progeny along with the multiple permuta-
tions of the platonic tradition snaking its way through the very word of
God itself. And we shall readily acknowledge the help that ancient heritage
afforded to apostolic witness and should to us as well. Sober reading of the
New Testament compels the offering of due praise to Plato and his ideologi-
cal offspring.

Due praise, yes. Unadulterated praise? No. Not by a long shot. Basil
the Great, as Georges Florovsky insightfully noted, "did not so much adapt
Neoplatonism, as overcome it."[8] Of the thought of Gregory Nazianzen, another of the Greek Cappadocian fathers—"the idea which he expresses in
Platonic language is not itself Platonic." Well we can safely assert that, unlike
the language of many early fathers of the church, and unlike much of the
New Testament, the language of Genesis is not in any way "itself platonic."
All the more reason to question importation of platonic ideas into the warp
and woof of our reading of its message.

Alertness to distortive influence of Greek thought need not and, in
my view, ought not derive from the reduction of hermeneutical interest to
either author intention or some wider (but not too wide!) consideration of
the *sitz im leben* of biblical texts. The difficulties of keeping Plato out of Genesis and indeed out of the Old Testament are many. First is the depth of the
shaping of Western thought and indeed of the popular Western psyche by
Greek philosophy. The great Greek thinkers have insinuated themselves into
our very brains, smoothing out paths down which our thoughts "unthinkingly" travel. Who among us does not reflexively and unthinkingly read the
divine breathing into Adam's nostrils the joining of a soul to a body? Only
effort opens up other possible readings. A little more effort discovers the
indifference of the Greek body/soul distinction to a reading of Genesis. But
only unusual effort recognizes this Greek reading as an enemy to faithful
interpretation.

How can we exert this unusual effort. What provides an antidote to the
Greek poison that lies within us? We must privilege through long acquain-
tance and use the Hebraic conceptual and linguistic tradition embodied in
the Old Testament ahead of and differently than we do its periodic Greek
nemesis. As the Greek inheritance has had its way with us, so ought our

8. Quoted in Pelikan, *Christianity and Classical Culture*, 8.

efforts seek to allow the Hebraic inheritance to approximate so as to at least compete with the inertial advantages enjoyed by the little Plato within.

What would such a privileging of the Hebraic inheritance teach us? Not that the human creature lacks these two such distinguishable dimensions; just that the Genesis accounts do not mean to address the matter. Instead, critical relational realities into which human beings are set from the beginning are identified—relational realities necessary to the divine declaration "very good." Three relational dimensions receive attention—human relation to the creator as male and female, to one another as male and female, and to the rest of creation as lords and keepers. These relationships constitute humanity's creation *imago dei*. Take note that no mention of humanity's creation as body and soul, or body and spirit or as including visible and invisible or material and non-material dimensions is needed to affirm humankind's unique *imago dei* status. Thus, no clarifying notice that only the invisible component was created *imago dei*. The man and the woman, as they are, body and soul, are the perfect creation *imago dei* among the other creatures. Their creatureliness, including their bodies, belong necessarily to their unique and exalted status.

No mention or acknowledgment of the existence of soul as such. No mention of a non-material dimension of human being. Instead the man Adam is called a man as flesh. The man comes alive, not with the addition to or insertion into a physical and not-yet-human body of a human soul that either makes him human or supersedes his physical body in value. God breathes into the already human man's nostrils the breath of life. The contrast depicted is between a non-yet-living and a living human being, not that between a soulless and therefore lifeless body and an ensouled and therefore truly human and living being.

Subsequent attention in Holy Scripture to a distinction between invisible and visible or material and non-material components of humanity may necessitate and encourage much reflection prove edifying in various ways, but to import such concerns into the creation accounts obscures their meaning and departs from legitimate canonical reading of these passages.

Irenaeus Versus Valentinus

Adherents of the teaching of the Gnostic Valentinus argued that the immaterial souls inhabiting bodies created by the Demiurge would be saved for eternity by virtue of their spiritual substance, their immaterial nature. Against such teaching Irenaeus objected:

For if nature and substance are the means of salvation, then all souls shall be saved; but if [salvation comes by] righteousness and faith, why should not these save those bodies which, equally with the souls, will enter into immortality? For righteousness will appear, in matters of this kind, either impotent or unjust, if indeed it saves some substances through participating in it, but not others.

For it is manifest that those acts which are deemed righteous are performed in bodies. [Thus] bodies too, which have participated in righteousness, will attain to the place of enjoyment, along with the souls which have in like manner participated, if indeed, righteousness is powerful enough to bring thither those substances that have participated in it. And then the doctrine concerning the resurrection of bodies which we believe, will emerge true and certain.[9]

Thus, Marcion rejected the whole of the Old and most of the New Testament and the Gnostics took to writing their own scriptures to fit the God and the world they favored. The Bible engenders that dissatisfaction and stirs up that hostility from the get-go. So let us turn to the creation accounts and the emergence of Eden to find out why.

9. Irenaeus, *Against Heresies*, 402–3.

3

God the Homemaker

Father of the fatherless and protector of widows
is God in his holy habitation.
God settles the solitary in a home;
he leads out the prisoners to prosperity.

—Psalm 68:5–6

And if I go to prepare a place for you, I will come again
and will take you to myself, that where I am
you may be also.

—John 14:3

Why was all that other stuff created? And why, in the order of creation, must humankind wait in the cue behind earth, sky, sea, and sea turtles before taking the stage? Because human beings need a home, a material home, a physical home—that's why. They need it because the creator, in his love and wisdom, made them to need it. What the creator brings into existence by the word of his mouth dazzles the imagination. It stirs wonder in the human heart and mind. Where sin has yet to cloud and distort human vision, creation points away from itself to the creator and evokes worship of the triune God. To God be the glory for the things he has done. And what has he done. He has created the heavens and the earth as the home fit for his human creatures made in his image.

Reduction of the non-human dimension of creation and the physical dimensions of creation both human and otherwise, to their potential to evoke worship, fails to comprehend a fundamental dimension of that praise.

The role extra-human and physical creation play is essential and, as we shall see, permanent. These dimensions of creation belong, by divine design to the fit and essential home for human beings.

God introduces himself to us in Holy Scripture as the creator, yes, but more, as the homemaker. The introduction of human beings into the created order evokes not only the divine "good," but his "very good," something the creation of humankind by itself could not do. Why? Because God, from the beginning, did not envision and thus did not produce human beings apart from their created home. Homelessness is indicative of the fall and redemptive activity always aims ultimately at its abolishment. Pilgrims and resident aliens are headed home. They are not content with their current plight apart from the promise that arrival at home is coming. Whatever contentment avails for them along the way includes trust in the revelation of their creator and redeemer as a homemaker and as the promiser of their ultimate settling by him of them into the home they were meant to inhabit.

The atmosphere permeating meticulous preparation of a home for the welcoming of a beloved child imbues the sequenced creation account of Genesis with the creation of Adam and Eve held in abeyance until their home is fully furnished. Yes, God is spirit and does not dwell in houses made by human or any other hands—but his human creatures require a home prepared by the original homemaker. Yes, God lives from himself and depends not at all upon anyone or thing outside himself—such independence is grounded in the positive and incommunicable divine attribute of the divine aseity—his "from-himself-ness." But we creatures do so depend upon much that lies outside of ourselves, including upon proper habitat.

Completion of our home drew from the creator the repeated assessment "good" as each successive component of that home was completed. But the settling into that home of human beings could draw the higher praise, praise expressive of deep divine satisfaction, "very good." These gradations of divine assessment and satisfaction illumine gradation of value but not, as we shall see, of essentiality. It took both the home and the settling into that home of its intended chief inhabitants and occupants to draw the higher praise.

Scripture against Scripture

Luther says that "God created all things in order to prepare a house and an inn, as it were, for the future man . . . then after everything that belongs to the essence of a house is ready, man is brought, as it were, into his possession that we may learn that the divine providence for us is greater than all our anxiety and care"[1] God's purpose and achievement in creation was to settle his human creatures, made in his image, into a three-dimensional shalom. This shalom was characterized by not less than three dominant relational dimensions—(1) that between God and his human children, (2) that between his children and each other *coram deo* (before the face of God), and a third relational dimension, the one I wish to highlight in this book, the one I believe is variously neglected or misconstrued in certain parts of the church, (3) that between human beings before their God with each other in their divinely prepared home.

The creation assessed by the creator as "very good" is the one that comprises this three-dimensioned shalom and not otherwise. Nothing in the text suggests the "very goodness" of component parts of the created order apart from their integration into the whole of the created order. On the contrary, the ordering of and highlighting of differentiation within creation specifically teaches the incompleteness of anything less than the entire three-dimensioned shalom God desires through the denial of his "very good" until human beings are introduced into their fit and necessary abode. We could speculate whether and how human beings might enjoy some sort of being apart from the rest of the created order and from their own bodies. But if we do so, surely the best sort of human existence then possible would be merely "good," not "very good."

But nothing in the text really welcomes such speculation. Such speculation really proves alien to the content, context, and momentum of the text. Does not speculation about human being apart from the rest of the created order actually smack of both misunderstanding and ingratitude? Encouragement to speculation is offered to us, not in Holy Scripture, but by Marcionites and Gnostics. They hate creation and the creator. They boldly reject the creator's "very good."

In varying degrees, reflexive negativity concerning the physical body and the rest of the material universe eventually took root in both Jewish and Christian discourse. Such developments should be recognized as an alien and false incursion into Christian thinking and should be opposed.

For now, it is important to note that in Eden prior to the fall, nothing but praise of God and grateful enjoyment of the whole of what God had made seems either possible or appropriate. Prior to the fall, ought not the very notion of a human being without a body or a material home strike us as completely alien? An intrusion? A party-pooping irrelevance? An ungrateful insult to the creator of that body and of that home?

---

1. Luther, *Luther's Works*, 1:47.

But let pain and mortality afflict and threated the body and then the attraction of escape from both the body and the material creation does arise and
gain traction. That is exactly what transpired in the mind of the Gnostics and
Marcion after them. Acknowledgment that the body and this physical world
after the fall prompts yearning for rescue is affirmed in the Bible. Thus the
apostle Paul's anguished cry "who will deliver me from this body of death?"
(Rom 7:24). But unlike platonic longing for some permanent escape, Paul,
anticipating just this misunderstanding, rejects it. In its place Paul articulates
the Christian quest to be "further clothed" (2 Cor 5).

And what about the rest of the created order? Is there the slightest
suggestion of a future state in which this "very good" but ostensibly preliminary "material" stage might be discarded and left behind, giving way to
some purely non-material or falsely so-called spiritual and therefore superior state? No. Rather our longings are directed to a new heaven and a new
earth—to a new Jerusalem. Should we consider the possibility of human
beings in relation to their creator apart from either their physical embodi-
ment or their embeddedness with the rest of creation?

The worst way to understand these and many other like passages is
also the worst way to read any passage—in isolation, apart from the witness
of the whole Bible, torn away from the storyline running from Genesis to
Revelation. When we do that we confront truckloads of scripture siftable
into two baskets—one positive and one negative, where the physical dimensions of creation come into view. Heresies and alien norms galore encourage
us to let the negative basket interpret the positive basket. Or to let the ostensibly spiritual basket impugn or render dangerous or at least to marginalize
the material basket.

The test of orthodox viability demands that whatever we think we hear
from the positive treatment of the rest of creation and of the human body,
we must eventually face up to the negative ones as well. These seemingly
contrary passages must be allowed to have their say. They must be set beside one another, kept together, and serious attempts to discern a synthesis
sought. Leaving seemingly incompatible teachings in intractable opposition
often involves a failure of theological nerve. However fashionable retreats
into the categories of balance or tension or paradox become, where synthesis is possible, it is also usually preferable. Enamorment with enduring
tension often smacks less of faithful hearing of the word of God than of a
cop-out driven by a prior preference for the one or the other competing
teachings imagined within the text.

One possible antidote to illegitimate intrusion of such hermeneutical
alien norms is to go against our instincts and let the passages we find most
uncomfortable speak to us with force. For those wary of what we might

term especially creation-friendly passages, serious confrontation with these passages is needed if the doctrine of creation and the divinely intended shalom are to gain appropriate affirmation. We who are so at home with the negative basket or passages, those that survey the damage done to the physical creation and warn of blind, unduly sanguine, and idolatrous attachment to the material world do well to expose ourselves perhaps for the first time to the seemingly contrary passages that are so prevalent throughout Holy Scripture. Creation-celebrating scriptures abound. We need to listen to them with fresh openness. When we consider the corruptibility of the material world after the fall, we do well to remember that our physical bodies are included in that world, and yet are not without hope.

Where the gospel of the redeemer is proclaimed, liability to corruption does not render hopeless and thus does not render scrapable, at least not ultimately, any fallen dimension of the creation targeted by redemption. Expressions of divine satisfaction with his completed works did not wait for the inclusion of Adam and Eve. The earth and the gathered waters—"good"! The greater and lesser lights to rule day and night—"good" again. God continued to give himself successive A-grades after completion of each successive component piece of creation. Until the creation of human beings. No grade was assigned exclusively for them. Instead this: ". . . and God saw everything that he had made, and behold, it was very good" (Gen 1:31a).

God's pattern-breaking pronouncement following the creation of humankind speaks eloquently of humanity's unique significance compared to the rest of creation; only with the creation of humankind and his inclusion into the created order can creation as a whole draw the superlative "very good" from the creator. This speaks to humanity's uniqueness within the created order, a uniqueness that includes a position of superiority and unique value within the universe. No other creature is created *imago dei*. No other creature exercises dominion over the lower forms of creation. And no other creature is valued so highly as humankind and none so privileged as the redeemed ones of Yahweh—"you" Jesus said, "are worth more than many sparrows" (Matt 10:31//Luke 12:7). "You" are kings. "You" shall judge the nations. "You" shall reign with Christ for thousand years. The angels are jealous of you.

But none of these "flatterings," if you will, of humankind portend any compromise or attenuation of humanity's creaturely status. Instead these passages affirm the fact and goodness of that status. Whatever comprises the uniqueness of humanity's creation in the image of God (*imago dei*) it does not include any disparagement of humanity's creatureliness. No suggestion of the need for humanity's escape from creaturely status appears. Not now and not ever. In fact, just the opposite. Humanity alone is created from a previously existing component of creation, the earth. Humankind, as *imago dei*, enjoys a unique relationship with God and a unique and superior relationship with and status above the rest of the created order.

By his creation "from the dust of the earth" he also enjoys a unique creaturely bond with the rest of creation. It is precisely *as creature* that humankind is *imago dei* and that humanity's inclusion within the rest of the created order draws the divine superlative "very good."

The Fall

The content and dynamics of humanity's temptation and fall further affirm the original goodness and sufficiency of humanity's creaturely status and divinely imposed need for a physical home. Three attractions, we are told, prompted Eve to take and eat from the forbidden tree; it "was good for food," it "was a delight to the eyes," and it promised to "make one wise" (Gen 3:6). But take note that neither the serpent prior to the fall nor the "Lord God" after the fall makes any mention of or shows the slightest interest in any but the third of these enticements—the one that included the promise that upon eating Eve would "be like God." So nothing in the account critiques consumption or enjoyment of food or delight in beauty.

What is critiqued is the desire to "be like God." This desire displays undue dissatisfaction with the creaturely status the creator called "very good" and led to an attempt to escape that status in some measure. The text indicates that, upon eating of the forbidden fruit, some opening of the eyes of our first parents did indeed occur. Furthermore, the Lord God acknowledges, albeit with biting irony, that "man has become like one of us" (Gen 3:22). Without exploring directly the character of the "knowledge of good and evil" that made humanity like God and precipitated the fall, it is crucial to recognize the profound affirmation of creation as a whole and of humanity's creatureliness taught in these first three chapters of Holy Scripture. The fall involved a foolhardy and doomed attempt to escape the confines of creatureliness and to encroach upon forbidden divine terrain.

These early chapters of Genesis have been repeatedly and universally acknowledged by the historic church as foundational for discernment of both the divine purpose in creation and the fundamental character of human sin. The seriousness of this acknowledgement is evidenced in the prominence the doctrine of creation occupies in the entire history of the church's creedal and confessional history, and in the sustained attention the book of Genesis and especially the first three chapters of Genesis has received, producing a continuous output of commentaries across the centuries.

That no critique of enjoyment of the consumption of food or delight in beauty is found here suggests certain features of shalom that shall bear upon proper and improper resistance to health and wealth teaching. The crux of the fall involved neither hedonism nor avarice but rather distrust of God's word. Had God's word been trusted and obeyed, our first parents would have spent their time enjoying their creator, each other, "all the trees of the garden" available to them, and the "keeping" of the garden which was their proper charge. Instead they succumbed to the false promise that they could, without threat to their divinely intended shalomic enjoyment of life, become like God through the gaining of the knowledge of good and evil.

Instead, their attempted encroachment upon divine turf spoiled their shalom, damaging each of the three relational dimensions of shalomic bliss. Alienation from God, their wise, loving, sustaining, and providing creator and heavenly Father. Alienation from one another. And alienation from the place, the home perfectly designed for their inhabitance. What the fall did not reveal was that all that really matters is the creator and not the creation. Or that once the creation's power to point human beings away from itself to the creator, its job is done and thus its spiritual usefulness is satisfied, completed and now obsolete.

Yes, the created order and all that it comprises (including our own lives!) provides opportunity for idolatrous use by us sinners. But it is highly significant and important to remember that the creation did not tempt Adam and Eve; the serpent did. The consequence of the sin that followed was loss of the divinely intended enjoyment of the both the creator and the created order, and thus, also the home into which God had settled Adam and Eve.

But what will be the status of creation east of Eden? What of the relationship of redemption to creation? Clues to the answers appear in the first chapters of Genesis and more comprehensive answers emerge in the rest of the canon.

Humanity's embeddedness within the created order informs humanity's creation *imago dei*. Only with the introduction of humankind, made in the very image of God, can God's own work draw from God himself the greatest satisfaction, "very good," and the highest grade, A+. Humanity's last spot in the creative que signals no subordination of humankind within the created order but rather the completion of creation itself. Indeed, humankind sits atop the scale of value within the created order. We alone are created *imago dei*, in the image of God. We alone are installed, under the creator, as lords (lowercase!) over and stewards of the rest of creation. Thus, no leveling of value within the created order is implied. "You," Jesus said, "are of more value than many sparrows" (Matt 10:31//Luke 12:7). To torture or even to neglect a dog is wrong. But if one or many threatening dogs or gorillas must be put down to save one child—so be it!

Yet, man's privileged place within the created order does not and need not raise him above his status as a creature. God's "creature" is the whole of the created universe with human beings happily installed at the top. Still, the order of creation, with human beings created last, and the all-encompassing scope of celebration by the creator, do reflect fundamental realities decisive for all that follows. Crucial clues to the purposes of God, the meaning of life, and indeed, to the saving work of Jesus Christ emerge right here in the first chapter of the Bible.

Faith and the Fall

God's act of creation produces his "creature." The whole of what God the creator brings into existence is his creature. That human beings are made in the image of God in no way alters or diminishes their creaturely status. They share with the moon and stars, the rocks and trees, this creaturely status God called "very good." The unique and superior position human beings enjoy compared to and in relation to the rest of creation exists within, not above or outside, the created order. Thus, when God speaks his "very good" he affirms the whole of his creation *as* creature. The text contains no hint that creaturely status on the part of the creaturely order, including human beings, is lacking or in need of improvement. Nor is there any suggestion whatsoever that Eden and the conditions enjoyed there constitute some preliminary stage for the creation as a whole or for human beings.

In fact, as Dietrich Bonhoeffer has articulated so well, the fall of humankind into sin involved an abortive and thus doomed attempt to repudiate their creaturely status.[2] They attempted to alter or escape their creaturely status by supplementing it with a knowledge of good and evil, a knowledge reserved for God alone, a knowledge they were free from having to shoulder. Before the biting of the forbidden fruit, they knew only good. Perfect shalom flourishes best not where human beings face good and evil and chose the good rather than the evil. Shalom flourishes best where evil is absent. The fall has burdened us with the unhappy burden of having to face good and evil, but one day it shall no longer be the case.

The temptation of our first parents included two crucial aspects, a formal or epistemological dimension and a material one. The formal or epistemological dimension called into the question the trustworthiness of the word of God—"Did God say?" (Gen 3:1). This dimension of the temptation strikes

---

2. Bonhoeffer, *Creation and Fall; Temptation*, 72–76.

at the very foundation of God's trustworthy character and of the happy dependence trust should have embraced and enjoyed. There's no other way to be happy in Jesus, even in Eden, but to trust and obey. Trust in and obedience to God's word promised only satisfaction with all that God had made. Doubt in and disobedience of God's word could only bring disaster. That disaster included alienation from God. That alienation was precipitated by a doomed desire to be like God according to a non-communicable divine attribute—his divine aseity, his independence, his from-himself-ness. This abortive grasping at forbidden creator-likeness is the material dimension of the fall. Positively, the abortive grasping attempts to snatch dimensions of divinity forbidden to human beings, namely, at knowledge belonging to the divine independence and aseity. Negatively, the grasping stupidly sought escape from the creaturely dependence the creator knows to be very good.

God creates not all at once but progressively, in stages, over a period of time. That this is so teaches us much about the substance, status, and potentialities of the created order. From the beginning, creation in itself was not only not "very good" or even "good" but was quite the opposite—it was "without form and void, and darkness was over the face of the deep" (Gen 1:2). On its own, without divine shaping and management, the creation is a horror show of a certain type. Of itself creation produces chaos.

God's word not only creates the universe, it steps us through the process of creation in order to teach us what leads to the divine "very good" at its completion. Of itself creation can only exhibit and engender disorder, emptiness, and chaos, and, as we know all too well, such chaos brings all manner of human suffering and eventual death.

Creation apart from God has nothing good to offer, has no inherent or intrinsic value. Its only value comes from God's gracious creation, shaping, sustaining, governing, and guidance. Only God lives from himself (*a-se*; Ps 50:12; Acts 7:48)) and only God is good (Luke 18:18) in himself. Nothing created has value apart from its relation to its creator. Creation from the beginning depends utterly upon God for its very existence, its maintenance (Ps 104:29; Col 1:16,17), and its goodness.

For human beings, knowledge and enjoyment of the goodness of creation depend upon trust in the word of God. We are told the truth by God, that the entire created order is "very good." Here the unique status of human beings within the created order brings upon them a unique vulnerability. Unless we trust God's word we lapse into ignorance of the truth and we forfeit authentic enjoyment of the truth—including enjoyment of creation, of our own and of the rest of the created order.

This matter of the necessity of trust in God's word illumines deep continuities between the Old and New Testaments. It helps us understand better what Jesus meant when he said of the law and the prophets "they speak of me" and how "without faith no one can please God" (Heb 11:6). Faith as the sole path to pleasing God did not begin with the proclamation of the gospel post-Pentecost. Grace and faith do not emerge as fallback positions taken by the creator when works did not fly. From the beginning, right there in the garden, trust in God's word was the means by which knowledge of God and enjoyment of God and all that he has made became possible. Only through faith in God's word could human beings know and enjoy anything—God, themselves, and the rest of creation. Trust produces obedience. Doubt gives birth to transgression. Trust enjoys the gift and blessing of creation in grateful reception from the hand of the giver, the creator himself.

So doubt of God's word led to the fall. Not just any word but doubt in God's particular word to Adam and Eve—that they may and ought to enjoy one another and God himself by keeping the garden and laying hold of the fruit from all of the trees available but one. As we have seen, the name of that tree provides the clue to its prohibition.

We have already noted that, by God's creation, a hierarchy of value inheres within the created order. We shall have to speak more about this in due course. But next, let us consider an important characteristic regarding the nature of the value of creation as a whole, the component dimensions creation comprises, and the value or worth of the creator.

From Apophasis to Affirmation

Never could there have been Eden without extra-Eden? How can we say, "never could have been"? Because we are told explicitly that what God made by his word was "good" in every particular finished component and "very good" upon its completion with the introduction of humanity into creation. What the creator did *and did not do* was necessary to its perfection.

Speculation about alternative scenarios can serve us, not by suggesting real possibilities—such speculation lapses into what John Calvin called "vain speculation." But certain speculative musings regarding impossible because not pursued creation scenarios, inclusive of contents, relational order, and sequencing, can serve faithful, deeper, and more comprehensive understanding of that creation. So, for example, what if God had created only Eden, without the extra-Edenic heavens and earth? Or what if humanity were created first rather than last in the created order?

That these alternative circumstances did not prevail might illumine more clearly, more precisely, what made actual creation "good" and then "very good." Once the content, ordering, and meticulous sequencing of divine creation is both revealed and called "good" and "very good," it legitimizes and welcomes consideration of alternatives as "bad." This sort of backward and speculative hermeneutical approach belongs to the ancient theological method of apophasis—an attempted homing in on what is through exploration of what most assuredly is not. God is *not* confined by space. He is *in-finite* and so, positively, omnipresent. God is *not* dependent upon anything outside himself. He is in-dependent or, positively, *a-se*, from himself or sufficient in himself.

Such an approach opposes an apologetic privileging of extra-biblical notions brought in to test the word of God. It assumes a dogmatic hermeneutic of suspicion toward extra-biblical ideas, not the reverse. For believers, we and the world are "in the dock," not God. Thus our entertainment of speculative alternatives to biblical truth labors to affirm more clearly and deeply what God has done and said through insight into what makes rejected alternatives pernicious. Let God be true and every man a liar! Thus we labor to justify God and not ourselves.

Eden as Center and Source

The creator carved out, named, and set apart (sanctified?) a small tract of land. There he constructed a perfect and beautiful paradise habitat to serve as the home of human beings. By doing so God established Eden as a center, source, and purpose of life for the entire universe. We see this in the necessity of the creation of and introduction of humanity into created order for creation to earn and receive the highest divine approbation—"very good." But negatively, according to apophasis, it was impossible that the heavens and the earth could ever be complete and thus "very good" without the inhabiting of Eden by Adam and Eve. We gain insight into the necessity of extra-Edenic creation and the relationship between Eden and non-Eden in the prerogative of Adam to name the living creatures who shall inhabit the whole of creation. This naming belongs to humanity's dominion over creation and so to the exercise of and enjoyment of his creation in the image of God. Thus, extra-Edenic creation plays an essential role in the divine purpose in creation itself. Already something of the necessity for both Eden and extra-Eden is established.

The unique and strange river flowing within and, significantly, out of Eden into the rest of the earth illumines Eden's significance itself and its significance for the rest of the earth:

> A river flowed out of Eden to water the garden, and there it divided and became four rivers. The name of the first is Pishon. It

is the one that flowed around the whole land of Havilah, where there is gold. The gold of that land is good; bdellium and onyx stone are there. The name of the second river is Gihon. It is the one that flowed around the whole land of Cush. And the name of the third river is the Tigris, which flows east of Assyria. And the fourth river is the Euphrates. (Gen 2:10–14)

Shalomic reading of this passage looks to affirm both literal and symbolical meanings.[3] The most immediately attractive reading from the standpoint of shalom is that the river indicates that Eden provides life sustaining water to the rest of the world. Symbolically, the river, as it separates into four rivers, not something that occurs in nature, represents the settlement of the garden paradise as the spiritual center and source of the whole earth.

Thus, I do not understand the river that divides into four rivers as only watering the garden but, as symbolically, the whole earth. As such the creator makes the garden a kind of central source of life for the rest of the earth. The rest of the earth looks to the garden for life sustaining water. But what if the garden, the earth's spiritual center, is spoiled? Then what? As we shall see, redemption shall entail the establishment of a new center and source, which shall then give way to a multiplication of such "centers" that themselves shall serve the establishment once more of a single center.

3. For readings of this passage informing this section see Louth, ed., *Ancient Christian Commentary on Scripture, Old Testament*, 1:55–59; Mathews, *Genesis 1—11:26*, 207–8, and Ross, *Creation and Blessing*, 124.

4

Expulsion and Beyond

Therefore the Lord sent him out from the garden of Eden
to work the ground from which he was taken. He drove out
the man, and at the east of the garden of Eden placed the
cherubim and a flaming sword that turned every way to
guard the way to the tree of life.

—GENESIS 3:23–24

CERTAIN CONSEQUENCES OF ADAM and Eve's transgression emerged immediately, the full measure of those consequences would emerge and be felt over time. Alienation from the creator and from one another seems to have burst upon our first parents instantly. But the devastation of that alienation would play itself out in the tragic history of this world we all inhabit. No murder occurred upon the sharing of the forbidden fruit but this would come and inevitably so. Resistance of the land to human cultivation was prognosticated by the Lord, but firsthand experience with that resistance would come later and would occur elsewhere.

Scripture frequently characterizes the consequences of the fall in terms of loss. In their fullness and permanence we have lost some great multitude of namable yet incalculable "spiritual," "invisible" blessings intended for our enjoyment, such as joy, peace, and love. Though created *imago dei* we have lost a right relationship with our maker, with each other, and even with ourselves. Thus, the good shepherd Jesus Christ comes to seek and save that which was lost. The title of Milton's great work expresses the lament of the entire church across the ages as it reflects upon the wages of humanity's rebellion against its loving and wise creator—*Paradise Lost*.

That the history and full measure of loss precipitated by sin occurs elsewhere than in the place where rebellion occurred is significant. It reminds us the Adam and Eve's sin required their expulsion from Eden. Humanity sinned against the father of lights from whom all good gifts proceed. The consequences of that sin distorted, attenuated, and poisoned every gift meant for humanity's enjoyment. Just as the scope of the creation the creator called good and very good encompassed all things visible and invisible within creation, so the loss incurred through sin includes every dimension of that good and very good creation. Thus, the loss of the very good home they were meant to inhabit and to enjoy to the glory of the creator. Theoretically, the consequences of sin might have played out within a ruined Eden but they did not. Why not?

Because where they were, the actual physical location of the home prepared for them and into which the creature settled them had to be forfeited. The actual location and the home the creator made there belong as essentially to the blessings of creation and to the ends for which human creatures were made as do their very souls. No, the home into which Adam and Eve were settled is not as valuable as their very souls, but it was as essential to the blessing of God. Thus, punishment required their physical removal from it. They had to be deprived of it. The loss incurred would have been less and of a different kind had they been allowed to stay in that ruined home.

The fall brings humanity into a homelessness. A physical homelessness. The transition from home to homelessness is brought about by an involuntary expulsion. Adam and Eve are forced to move. They are evicted from the home meant for them into alien place where they will have to make do.

The expulsion of Adam and Eve from Eden draws attention to the fact that the garden paradise home into which the creator placed his special human creatures was only a tiny portion of the created order as a whole. The conditions informing David's later astonishment at the relatively miniscule slice of creation occupied by human beings prevailed from the beginning— "When I look at your heavens, the work of your finger, the moon and the stars, which you have set in place, what is man that you are mindful of him, and the son of man that you care for him?" (Ps 8:3–4).

Not only is man like an infinitesimal speck of flesh in relation to the rest of creation, but Eden was a tiny tract of land carved out from a vast geography beyond. Yet this relative smallness did not prevent Eden from securing acknowledgment as the paradise created especially for human flourishing. Clearly God's making and filling of Eden and his placing of Adam and Eve there were primordial necessities. But do we glimpse in Eden's definitively circumscribed boundaries within an infinitely larger created order a permanent feature the divine will. Do we confront here a harbinger of divine dealings with his children going forward. Are we to discern here patterns of divine will and activity meant to shape the efforts and expectations of believing communities now and forever? I believe so. This we shall test as we consider the divine will and activity in subsequent epochs of the long and continuing history east of Eden.

But for now let us take note that the paradise of God inhabited by our first parents was in fact a tiny place within a vast universe. But not just any place—Eden was at the center of the universe, the source of life for the universe, and was for the entire universe, under God the creator, its *raison d'tre*. Adam and Eve's punishing expulsion into extra-Edenic earth highlights the divine will to settle his children into specific places within whole of the created order. But it should not cast a negative light on extra-Edenic earth as such. The paradisiacal home of our first parents included the whole of extra-Edenic creation. There never was because there never could have been an Eden without heavens and the earth within which Eden was situated, and having been so situated, constituted, then and only then, the paradisiacal home of the creator's special creatures.

That expulsion from Eden is an eviction from home and, as such, a necessary dimension of divine punishment. That punishment for sin precipitated this expulsion invites reflection upon the purposes of creation and redemption. When set beside the rest of the story from Genesis 3 to the last word in the Apocalypse, this necessary expulsion and eviction informs every dimension and aspect of our lives in and outside the church. It casts light upon the content of hope and the character of obedience and love.

Expulsion and eviction stand in deliberated and profound contrast to settlement. The home for which we were made, the abundant life intended for us, was not characterized by movement as such, but permanence of place, abundance of provision, and security under the protective and providing hand of the loving, wise, and strong creator. Flourishing human existence, by divine design, is a settled existence. Settled does not mean static or motionless, but neither does it involve being scattered or living as resident aliens or even as sojourners or pilgrims. That our lives east of Eden are so characterized is undeniable, but faithful comprehension of the meaning of our variously scattered, resident alien, sojourning, and pilgrimaging lives requires faithful understanding of the lost settled state and its implications for those who have lost it through sin. What was lost informs the nature of redemption, of hope, and of obedience and love in the time between the times.

One temptation east of Eden is to flirt with a kind of glamorization of the array of unsettled states that do in fact and profoundly shape and even define human existence post-fall. But this is a mistake. Unsettled human existence is a consequence of the fall and redemption involves more but not less than the undoing of those consequences. We were not made to suffer any more than we were made to sin. Suffering is the consequence of sin. A treacherous conceptual borderland emerges in Holy Scripture that wrongly gives rise to the sort of glamorization I have in mind. Description of that borderland requires the language of paradox. He who saves his life will lose it. But he who loses his life for my sake and that of the gospel, the same shall save it. We are joint heirs with Christ, if we suffer with him. From such teaching can spring the notion of the redemption of suffering. Such a conception is well meant and not utterly wrong. But it is mainly wrong and ripe for misunderstanding and prone to mislead those who wallow to much therein.

The title of a famous J. I. Packer volume provides protection from the false suggestions pro-suffering passages sometimes stir up—*The Death of Death in the Death of Jesus*. Suffering turned into a means. Suffering is made to serve the killing of suffering.

Shalom beyond Expulsion

For my purposes the expulsion of Adam and Eve marks the first instance of scattering. Certain features of this first scattering illumine both the fundamental place of a settled existence and an unsettled existence for human beings in the divine purposes in creation and redemption. That expulsion from the garden marks one component of divine punishment among many leveled upon our first parents can teach us much about the will of God for human beings. The creator means for human beings to live settled lives, not scattered ones.

Divine punishment deprives sinners of divine blessings. The blessing of human existence within the safe and fruitful habitat divinely designed for their flourishing is now denied to Adam and Eve. Have Adam and Eve been abandoned by their creator? Is there no hope east of Eden? Is human enjoyment of every divine blessing now and forever ripped away? No, because the only true God loves with khessed love from all eternity in himself and then in relation to his creature.

But the lesson Adam and Eve are meant to learn, and the lesson we are meant to learn as their progeny, is not that the garden never really mattered, that settlement into geographically circumscribed homelands were only a temporary accommodation until we were better taught to value only spiritual things where spiritual means non-material. The proper assessment of the new situation east of Eden is not, "So what! We can flourish even better out here if we just recognize the material and physical blessings that prevailed in the garden were just temporary accommodations to our temporary physical existence." It is not the case that those material blessings were meant to give way to a purely "spiritual" as in non-material set of blessings. It is not that what we initially saw as punishment in our expulsion we now see paradoxically as a blessing, teaching us not to set our hearts on physical health and material well-being.

If your spiritual formation and education resembles mine, such an anti-material take on the meaning of the expulsion from the garden into the valley of the shadow of death east of Eden might seem somehow plausible. The conflict is between how proper such "spiritual" talk rings in our ears and how ridiculous such a reading of Genesis 3–4 appears to us on its face.

Expulsion did not reveal the home so personally and intricately prepared for Adam and Eve as non-essential to ultimate divine creative purposes or even as a danger to true spirituality. Expulsion was meant to bring instructive suffering. Expulsion belongs to the chastening by God of those he loves. It teaches that the only way to enjoy the blessings endemic to human life is to receive them from the hand of the creator and to use them as he intended. We sinners are not meant to view the suffering brought on by disobedience as resulting in the transformation of the suffering into a spiritual good, as such. God makes suffering serve redemption. But redemption ends with the killing off of suffering and death. Shalom encourages frequent remembering of the necessary but limited and temporally bounded good use of suffering to bring about its own demise. Enjoyment of the shalom of Eden was proper enjoyment just as enjoyment of the shalom of the new heaven and the new earth shall be.

Suffering becomes necessary because of sin. Suffering is necessary because punishment of sin is necessary. The love of God, rather than settling for a universal unleashing of eternal punishment deserved by his rebellious human creatures, instead becomes, in the second person of his triune nature, incarnate in Jesus Christ in order to redeem human life and take punishment himself in the place of those he came to save.

The necessity of suffering and the inexorable path redemption must take to the cross of Jesus Christ given the khessed love of God does not transform suffering into a "good" as some evangelical language sometimes suggests. We speak of God in Jesus Christ "redeeming suffering." We seize upon Joseph's "you meant evil against me, but God meant it for good" (Gen 50:20) to suggest some sort of fundamental transformation in the meaning of suffering. We point especially at the suffering and death of Jesus to prove the redeeming power of suffering. Yes, yes, yes! Suffering wins salvation for us! Jesus' suffering exposes the ultimate impotence of suffering in the face of the omnipotent love, mercy, and grace of God. But take note, the goal of Jesus' suffering is not to glamorize it, or to teach us to accept suffering in the lives of others, or to habituate ourselves to suffering, but to end suffering forever.

Temptation toward glamorized assessments of suffering thinks it finds support in certain streams of biblical teaching, such as the honoring of those who suffer for the sake of others. But the honor of that sacrificial suffering includes its quest to protect others from or deliver others from suffering. Then there is Paul's boasting about and defense of his suffering as attributes not detriments to his apostolic credentials. He does this especially in the second epistle to the Corinthians, but also in his pointed rebuke at the end of Galatians—"From now on let no one cause me trouble, for I bear on my body the marks of Jesus" (Gal 6:17). Here again, though, that suffering is hardship is hardly denied. Indeed, its burdensome character is highlighted as of a piece with that of the Lord Jesus Christ who suffers to end suffering.

Blessings Denied

The divine response to human rebellion in the garden is to punish human beings. But that punishment is neither absolute nor final. The punishment is loving divine warning, discipline, and correction aimed at forestalling ultimate, final, absolute punishment. Creation, in all its dimensions, both human and extra-human is divine blessing, a fact embedded in that exclamatory divine assessment of all that the Lord had made once human beings were settled into their proper home—"very good!"[1] Every component of divine punishment leveled in the wake of our first parent's sin involves deprivation of divine blessing. Childbirth that might have been only joyous shall now bring pain. The land that should have yielded delicious and nutritious sustenance with ease shall now resist human efforts at cultivation. The relationship between man and woman designed for reciprocal love, service, and joy shall now provide fertile ground for all manner of relational discord and social pathology. Most tragic, and the fountain of all other deprivations was the immediate enmity sin brought to the relationship between humanity and its creator.

The punitive feature of expulsion from the Garden was its deprivation of the divine blessing of the perfectly fit home for their habitat. God the homemaker now kicks the kids out of the house and locks the door! Why? Because he means for them to remain homeless forever? Not at all. More perfectly than but nevertheless parallel to a loving earthly parents' withdrawing of a gift meant to serve as a blessing to a child—say a knife or

1. See Ross, *Creation and Blessing*.

an automobile, either of which may bring benefits or injury or death—the ultimate purpose of punishment includes eventual regaining of the blessing. The parent knows that misuse of the gift already alters its reception as blessing to that of potential or actual curse, even if the child cannot see this. Love prompts withdrawal of blessing. After the fall the garden cannot be accessed and enjoyed as a blessing because Adam and Eve are no longer fit to lay hold of the gifts and their benefits properly. Their receptors are damaged. So out they go! For their own good.

A bit more milking of this analogy can illumine the meaning of the expulsion from that Garden and the place of shalomic flourishing east of Eden generally. Proper reception of the gift of a knife or an automobile should include the revelation to the child of the love the parent has for them. That revelation should prompt responsive love to the parent. If this occurs it is right to recognize that the resultant bond of love between the child and the parent is a higher, a more valuable benefit resulting from the bestowal and reception of the gifts than any benefit bound up with actual use of the car or the knife themselves. It is also true that where such loving gift bestowal and reception fails to nurture such a bond of gratitude and love in the recipient, that reception has failed to fully accomplish its divinely intended end.

But it is just at this point that a plethora of false deductions emerge sourced not from the word of God but, albeit unwittingly, from the ancient swirling vat of creator-hating, creation-hating, matter-hatting, and body-hating heresies. Oh, yes, the material creation is blessing, but its main and ultimately only goal that really matters or matters eternally and is therefore of true "spiritual" significance, is its usefulness to bond us in love with the creator. The material creation is "mere" means to this spiritual benefit. Once the material dimensions of creation have served this purpose their significance is exhausted, their use no longer required—they may and ought to then fall away so that all that is left is us and God, us and Jesus. Just give me Jesus!

No! This line of thinking is rampant among Bible-believing Christians but it is wrong. Back to the parents dolling out cars and knives. The result of the bestowal and reception of the gifts should include both enjoyment of the benefits proper to the use of cars and knives and nurturing the bond of love proper to loving and providing parents and grateful obedient and responsible children. The healthy flourishing of the parent-child relationship includes enjoyment of both sets of enjoyments. The enjoyments are meant to and, when the full blessings of shalomic flourishing occur, actually do interpenetrate, overlap, and mutually reinforce one another. They are not in competition with one another. They are friends who belong together.

The parents aim is not for the child, after some period of proper driving and cutting, to eventually abandon both car and knife, run home (no car now), throw arms around Mom and Dad with the exclamation, "All I want is you two; the great gift-givers. Who cares about those gifts now that I see you in your love and generosity! I count those gifts as dung in order to gain you. You alone are all I desire!" No. What the parents envision is that the child enjoy the benefits of gifts in the proper way. When that happens, the gifts serve to illumine the love of the parents, evoke gratitude and love for the parents, and proper use and enjoyment of benefits arising from use of the gifts themselves. This scenario paints a little picture of shalomic flourishing analogous to the biblically revealed relationship between the creator and his creations with human beings as his special children.

It is true the higher blessing, indeed the highest blessing of all served by the bestowal, reception, use, and enjoyment of the gifts centers on that first relational dimension of shalom, the relationship between the creator and his human creatures. And of course, God is spirit and we all want to be really spiritual about all this stuff, right?

But recognition of an embedded hierarchy of value at work within the created order must not be overdrawn and then, as a result, wrongly interpreted. This happens when, once the hierarchy is recognized and acknowledged, only the highest value—God is allowed to receive full affirmation. Every other value is transformed into either a temporary means to the recognition of God or even a threat or at least a potential threat to the highest value, which is God. So everything below the highest spiritual value must be let go so that God alone shines forth as the only one worthy of praise.

Perhaps the quickest unmasking of such highfalutin, ostensibly spiritual thinking is to note that we, the would-be spiritual ones, the would-be worshipers of God as the only blessing we desire—we are but creatures too! Why do we get to stay? Is God so needy that he needs us to acknowledge his glory? No he does not. He has us because it pleased him to create, yes us, and yes especially us, but not us as some disembodied souls, or slated eventually to become (Plato!) disembodied spiritual souls. He made us for himself to belong to each other before him to whom we all belong in the home fit for us to inhabit. Identification of a component or dimension of the created order that ranks, in some substantive sense, below another component or dimension, does reveal something very significant that we shall mention in a moment. But what such recognition of lower relative rank does not reveal is its non-essentiality in the creator's original, ongoing, and ultimate eternal plans.

Did Aron Ralston, the hiker who dismembered himself to save his life after pinning his arm in a Utah canyon, act wisely? Would it have been just as well to have stabbed himself in the heart rather than face life without his forearm? No. Would it be great if he could have the removed member successfully reattached? Yes. If he was a believer, will he have all his members in the new body promised to him. Yes.

Hierarchy of value informs many decisions that confront us in this life. Particularly when it comes to what we might call the order of sacrifice and or potential sacrifice. A subject explored more fully in chapter 6.

But for our purpose here, it is important to note that divine punishment included withdrawal of the full blessings of home through expulsion from the garden. Punishment through temporary denial of enjoyment of the full blessings of shalom serve the divine redemption which aims at more, but not less than restoration of that shalomic plan in all three relational dimensions. Yet, expulsion from Eden does mark a profound distancing of humanity from the original shalomic home once enjoyed by our first parents. Discontinuity between the Eden they inhabited before the fall and the land east of Eden we now inhabit is easier to discern than any prevailing continuities. The Great Tradition of the church affirms that the entire universe retains the imprint of its maker and still bears witness to him. But John Calvin, who affirms this continued witness, is surely right that apart from new acts of the Holy Spirit to illumine the word of God and open the eyes of faith in us, the rays or revelation emitted from those witnessing imprints shine in vain, benefiting no one. Though the fall has not obliterated the seed of region (*semen religionis*), that sense of divinity (*sensus divinitas*) persisting in every human being according to their creation in the image of God (*imago dei*) that makes us all worshipers, apart from the redeeming activity of the spirit, it makes us a factory of idols rather than the grateful obedient children of God.

So expulsion marks a profound break from what ought to be and lands us in a dark place, east of Eden. Discernment of continuities between Eden and the land east of Eden requires revelation no less definitively than does any truth from which sin blinds us. We should bring real sympathy to Marcion, the Gnostics, and the Manicheans even as we reject their refusal to worship the creator and to estimate aright the value of all the he has made notwithstanding the fall. The opening of the Apostles' Creed appropriately makes clear that belief in the creator is always a confession of faith: "We believe in God the Father almighty, maker of heaven and earth" (Barth). But alas, God the Holy Spirit does indeed, according to his wisdom and timing, illumine his word and draw from us that confession and so illumine both discontinuities and continuities between Eden and east of Eden.

From that first bite into the forbidden fruit, human history becomes the history of the consequences of the fall of humanity into sin and the creator's response to that fall. It's easy to produce a long list of such consequences. Some entries identify disruptions and disorder within nature. The ground now resists humanity's necessary cultivation of the earth for food. Child-birth brings great pain and risk. Flood, drought, fire, hurricanes, tornadoes, and earthquakes threaten human life. Other entries identify distinguishable sins, like the so-called seven deadly ones—pride, envy, gluttony, lust, anger, greed, and sloth. But those seven have lots of company—jealousy, hate, mal-ice, covetousness, deceit, and idolatry just for starters. One result of the fall that showed itself right there at the headwaters of humanity's fall into sin is a particular act of divine punishment, punishment that deprives humanity of the divine blessing of settlement. It's the divine scattering.

Noah

Humankind multiplied and spread out over the earth east of Eden, settling and building communities, as they were meant to do. But "the Lord saw that the wickedness of man was great in the earth, and that every intention of the thoughts of his heart was only evil continually. . . . So the Lord said, 'I will blot out man whom I have created from the face of the land, man and animals and creeping things and birds of the heavens. . . . But Noah found favor in the eyes of the Lord" (Gen 6:1–8). The wickedness of human-ity was so great and so pervasive that no scattering of them could satisfy the needed divine punishment. But like scattering, the divine punishment leveled upon sinful humanity would deny to them the lands upon which they were gathered and settled and making themselves at home. Once again loss of shalomic flourishing, including especially and pointedly in its third dimension, the settled-at-home dimension, defines divine punishment. The entire earth shall be engulfed in a global flood.

But the destruction shall not prove absolute. Indeed, the destruction will serve the divine salvaging of all that he has made and end in the reemer-gence of the earth. In every constituent component of this new-old earth, wonders have been preserved and restored to their east-of-Eden condition and potential with the Lord's favored ones, Noah and his family—gathered, protected, and resettled into the fallen but still mercy-targeted land. Neither the deprivation nor the destruction of the flood and its aftermath shall be the last word on the prospects for the shalomic intentions of God in creation any more than expulsion from the garden was.

Babel

Conditions for a fruitful settlement of humanity seemed to be in the offing after the great flood. But just as the reach to "be like God" by laying hold of the knowledge of good and evil failed to deliver what the serpent promised, so the attempt to lay hold of a kind of shalomic settlement apart from the creator met with the divine displeasure and resulted in the opposite of settlement. Yahweh scattered the would-be city planners and city builders. Their sin was not the desire to settle and build a city. Settlement, city-building, and indeed kingdom-building proceeded apace through Noah's offspring at Erech, Accad, and Calneh in the land of Shinar. These settlings and buildings drew no divine punishment, no confusion of language or scattering. Neither did Nineveh or Resen (Gen 10:1–12). Just Babel.

It's true that the builders of Babel wished to forestall their dispersal "over the face of the earth" (Gen 11:4) and it is true that this dispersal was central to the divine will and activity. But the filling of the earth Yahweh commanded and facilitated through Noah's offspring was already taking place and its fulfillment involved settlement and building. Babel itself is listed as one of these points of settlement comprised within the divinely initiated spread, populating, and settling in order to achieve the "filling of the earth" the Lord desired (Gen 10:10). Genesis 10 sketches out numerous tentacles of the populating of new lands and settlement within those lands by the progeny of Noah. So Babel was one of many sites designated for settlement.

The sin was not the desire to settle and build a city. The sin was to "build *ourselves* a city and a tower with its top in the heavens and let us *make a name for ourselves*" (Gen 11: 4; emphasis mine). The goals of the builders reach beyond both the proper sphere and capabilities designated for them by the creator. Their desires give rise to foolish imaginings that encroach upon divine prerogatives, namely to settle and bless them himself and cause them to flourish as he sees fit. Yahweh is already deep into the settling and building business and indeed, he initiates and prospers human embrace of and participation in this work of his. But make no mistake about it, the work is his to determine, initiate, and govern.

The creator shall go on to be the great city and nation builder himself. In fact the divine settling and building remains yet incomplete. Jesus Christ is up to it as I type—"I have told you that I go to prepare a place for you. And if I go and prepare a place for you, I will come again and take you to myself, that where I am, you may be also" (John 14:2–3). The settling and building the creator accomplishes east of Eden is not for himself but for his human creatures, just as his creation of the heavens and the earth and the special preparation of Eden itself was prepared as the fit home for Adam and Eve.

The pattern east of Eden is that Yahweh puts his own name on the settlements populated by his gathered people. There, in the divine settlements, he makes his name to dwell. Why? Because just as the heavens and the earth and all that dwell therein belong to him, so especially do his human creatures made in his image, honored with special privileges and responsibilities, happy duties with respect to the rest of earthly created order. The creator's claim is upon all that he has made including human settlement that does not fully recover what was lost in the expulsion from Eden, not by a long shot, but they do point back to what was lost and forward to what is promised—settlement by God of his people into shalomic homes where he dwells with his people. The conditions that characterize appropriate settlement in this world are grounded in the created ordering of the world fitted for the human flourishing intended by the Lord.

Order is a key concept in the Bible. Every dimension of the created order is fitted for flourishing in certain ways in relation to the creator, to other human beings, and to the non-human dimensions of creation. Human beings occupy pride of place above the rest of creation but also of course, below, happily below their creator, their wise and loving and providing and sustaining heavenly father. They are, from creation, his dependent children, called to listen to and obey his word and to receive all good gifts from his hand and to use those gifts for their intended enjoyment to the glory of God. Among those gifts was the "keeping of the garden." East of Eden, "garden keeping" survives in connection with the divine settling of his people, the building of cities and kingdoms in places where they are gathered by Yahweh. It is the desire of Yahweh to "makes his name to dwell" in Zion.

The settlement at Babel stands over against settlement by God. The would-be builders of Babel sought to make themselves a city and "name for themselves." Because of this, the nascent settling and building of Babel was disrupted and destroyed by Yahweh.

It is a mistake to consider the scattering of the people of Babel first of all as part of the divine insistence that human beings "be fruitful and multiply" and thus "fill the earth" (Gen 1:28). The confusion of language and the resultant scattering was not needed for the achievement of the divine will to see the earth populated. The confusion of language and the scattering were divine punishment for sins associated with the settlement and building of Babel unrelated to the ongoing spread of human beings in the earth.

The tragedy of Babel is not that they longed to live in a settled, citified, kingdom-aspiring condition against the determination of God to scatter them and keep them more or less in an unsettled state on this earth. The tragedy is that they refused to lay hold of the divinely intended gathering and settling of them into cities and kingdoms flourishing by his blessings and fit to make his name dwell. They, wittingly or not, took a page from their and our first parents and sought in their own way to "be like God" in a sphere only God can occupy. Our first parents thought that knowing good and evil

"like God" would work out wonderfully. The first Babylonians thought building themselves a city to make their name great would as well.

The Lord's response to the sins of both Adam and Eve and to the
thwarted builders of Babel drips with divine sarcasm. In the garden: "Then
the Lord God said, 'Behold, the man has become like one of us in knowing
good and evil'" (Gen 3:22), implying "How's that new knowledge working
out for you?"

At Babel:

> "Behold, they are one people, and they have one language, and
> this is only the beginning of what they will do. And nothing
> they purpose to do will be impossible for them. Come let us go
> down and confuse their language, so that they may not under-
> stand one another's speech." So the Lord dispersed them from
> there over the face of the earth, and they left off building the
> city. (Gen 11:6–8)

This divine frustration of human aspiration and effort belongs to a
pattern of such thwartings that demonstrate again and again how easy the
scuttling of human pretentions is for the creator and Lord of this world. As
the nations conspire, Yahweh laughs (Psalm 2). Joseph's divinely induced
dream scuttle's Herod's attempt to kill the infant Messiah (Matt 2:7–15).

Just as fruit-eating, *per se*, was not the problem in Eden, neither was
settling and city-building the problem at Babel. Where shalom takes hold,
fruit-consumption and city-building abound. Medicinal use of Pomegranates reaches back at least to Egypt in 1500 BC. From ancient times this
delicacy has served as a symbol of fertility, abundance, and prosperity in
the Middle East and beyond. Their symbols adorned the pillars fronting
Solomon's temple (1 Kgs 7:13–22). It should not surprise that through Moses' cataloguing of components of prosperity awaiting the people of Israel,
they learn that it shall be a land flowing not only with milk and honey, but
also with pomegranates (Deut 8:8). My younger son's development (how I
do not know) of a taste for this expensive fruit prompted a family meeting
to make everyone aware that "we are not a pomegranate family."

And of course, cities are a God-thing throughout the Bible, including in prophecies and promises that describe the coming kingdom, the new
heaven and new earth with the city of Jerusalem at its center. Divine punishment of cites by destroying them and by scattering its surviving inhabitants
arises not from divine hostility to the gathering, settling, and building from
which cities arise, but from his own claim upon them. God's claim upon cities in Holy Scripture is no less certain than his claim upon the human body.
The misuse of the body in adultery is of a piece with wrongful settlement

and city-building as a platform for human pride and pretention rather than the glory of God. Both misuses encroach upon divine turf, upon the divinely established three dimensioned relations of shalom.

Divine scattering at Babel came as punishment bringing suffering just as did Adam and Eve's expulsion from Eden. But neither these nor subsequent divine scatterings signal divine abandonment of the shalomic purposes in all three dimensions. It signaled no divine resignation resulting in a pared-down vision of the scope of redemption—a redemption ready to settle for the salvaging of some ostensible "spiritual" (non-material) achievement in the lives of his chosen people. Far from it. Faithfulness to the fully shalomic purposes emerges again and again in the establishment and re-confirmation of the covenants made with Adam, Noah, Abraham, and David and finally fulfilled and yet to be consummated in Jesus Christ.

Abraham

The shift within the Pentateuch from Genesis 11 to Genesis 12 is dramatic and profound. Prior to the call of Abraham in Genesis 12, the narrative is concerned with Yahweh, the creator's dealings with the whole human race. But with Abraham's call to leave his home in Ur for a land that the Lord "will show" to him, the narrative narrows down to the lives, children, and times of the patriarchs of Israel—Abraham, Isaac, and Jacob—the chosen people of God. But this zooming-in upon the birth and trajectory of the people of Israel entails no shrinking of the scope of divine claim or concern; both remain universal.

The call of Abraham is to the privilege and responsibility of the one in whom "all the families of the earth shall be blessed" (Gen 12:3). Here as so often in the story line of the Bible from Genesis to Revelation, particularity and universality impinge upon one another. The whole human race is implicated in the fall of Adam and Eve. The faith of Abraham shall stand as an enduring model of the faith that saves. Jesus Christ died once for all. At the center of the so-called scandal of the gospel is the disturbing but clear biblical teaching that our sins, committed almost two millennia after the fact, implicate us in the first century crucifixion of a Jew named Jesus outside the gates of Jerusalem.

The creator and redeemed is pleased to deal with and reckon with many through his special dealings and reckonings with a few. So it would prove with Abraham. Yahweh's dealings with Israel would contribute to the Lord's witness of himself to the nations. Foundational to God's witness to himself is that he is the creator. Over and over again, that the Lord is God and beside him is no other is demonstrated and proven by his creation of the universe together with his continued power over all that he has made. But the creator makes Israel too! His calling forth of Israel in the calling of Abraham bears witness to God to both Israel and to the nations. The significance and destiny of the entire world is implicated in the Lord's dealings with Israel—the universe is caught up in the divine election of and dealings with the particular nations birthed in the calling of Abraham. Jesus was a Jew. He never did become a Christian! He never converted. Jesus' Bible, the Old Testament, against Marcion the creator-hater, is the Bible for everyone who would be saved. Paul, in order to distinguish what the law can do verses what faith can do, references Abraham to teach the character and necessity of faith in Jesus Christ.

But along with the usual and appropriate use of the call and life of Abraham to illumine the nature and necessity of faith in order to please God, God's dealings with Abraham reveal other features of redemption that support our exploration of shalom. Yahweh's first words to Abram require that he get up and go because he and his family together with all their possessions (and he was wealthy) to a promised land.

The faith of Abram held up as a model in the book of Romans required that he *not* sell all that he had and give it to the poor. Instead the call was to cooperate with the Lord's intention to make of him "a great nation." And it could not happen just anywhere either. It had to happen in a certain place, on divinely designated land, promised land.

Let that fact sink in. Yahweh somehow did not realize, as some of us think we do, that where you are on the earth matters not. You and I may have been encouraged to believe that since our God enjoys the attribute of omnipresence that, "spiritually" speaking, no one place is better or worse than another where dealings with God are concerned. Virtually nowhere in Scripture will we find evidence to support such a notion. Places matter. Already we have encountered Eden situated with minute personal intention and care and from which Adam and Eve had to be expelled to "elsewhere," east of Eden. The builders of Babel were not allowed to stay put. Yahweh wanted them scattered and so they were. Now here's Abram and his clan minding their own business in Ur. But can they stay? No. They must go.

Once you alert yourself to the significance of place in the Bible you will recognize that Yahweh's establishment of and revelation of the differentiated significance of place runs through the whole of Scripture. Certainty that place matters "spiritually" will become a truism in biblical interpretation for you so that any passage that seems to suggest otherwise will appear suspect and the burden will be upon that passage on confrontation with the massive and pervasive counter passages such as the one in Genesis 12. We shall have to reckon with a couple of such passages in due course.

What Yahweh promises to do with Abram in the promised land is also significant. He is going to settle Abram and his family there and make of them a great nation. The gestation of this grand divine vision and promise will prove to be very long indeed. Abraham will settle in Canaan but he will die with the promise not yet fulfilled. But the content of the promise displays the divine interest in land and settlement and what we might call civilization, the settled organized, healthy, productive flourishing of human communities. And all the nations of the world shall be blessed through what Yahweh does with Abram. Yahweh's dealings with Abram bear witness to all the nations concerning the true God with whom they too have to do. The settlement of Israel into the promised land required the conquest of nations previously settled there.

And why, if the rescue of souls is the goal of the gospel did Jesus not head straight to Golgotha? Why all the dilly-dally if what we really need is just for Jesus Christ to die on the cross for us, winning forgiveness of sins, reconciliation with God and others, adoption into the family of God, resurrection from the dead and eternal life? Shalom answers thus: everything that the creator and redeemer did and said prior to the death of Jesus on the cross was necessary for the cross to be saving. No time is wasted by the redeemer. No word of his proves superfluous. No deed was dispensable. It was all necessary, revelatory, and predictive.

There had to be the raising up of the nation of Israel, settled into that particular land, and boasting exactly the long and tortuous history for Jesus of Nazareth to receive as his birthright and inheritance. Jesus had to be able to point to the temple on Mount Zion and declare—"There will not be left here one stone upon another" (Mark 13:2). Oh yes, everything happens for a reason, you better believe it. And what has happened in the history of salvation retains its relevance, even though certain features of its teachings do not apply directly to us on this side of the cross and Pentecost. The words and deeds of the Lord never become obsolete in that sense: "Now these things took place as an example, but they were written down for *our* instruction" (1 Cor 10:11; emphasis mine). "For whatever was written in former days was written for our instruction, that through endurance, and through encouragement of the Scriptures we might have hope" (Rom 15:4).

We turn now to the Psalms. The Psalter offers a unique window into the character and scope of shalom because it opens us to the worshiping community of Israel. Here we meet head-on the longings, fears, petitions, and laments proper to the creator who redeems and promises to redeem.

5

Shalom in the Psalms

Old men and old women shall again sit in the streets of Jerusalem, each with staff in hand because of great age. And the streets of the city shall be full of boys and girls playing in the streets.

—THE LORD THROUGH THE PROPHET
ZECHARIAH (ZECH 8:4–5)

IN THIS CHAPTER WE shall muse upon selected psalms with special alertness to shalom generally and to shalom in its third dimension in particular. Thus, we shall be especially interested in the language of physical health, home, city, land, refuge, stronghold, dwelling, harvest, and of course shalom.

The Psalms are uniquely fitted to open up the place of shalom for both the individual Christian life and the life of the church because it teaches us what divinely approved worship entails. As such it helps us identify the proper content and place of shalom in petition, longing, enjoyment, gratitude and praise. And it offers insight into the relationship between shalom and suffering, sacrifice, and other dimensions of what we might deem non-shalomic dimensions of life in this between time.

Psalm 23

"The Lord is my shepherd." These best-known words from the Old Testament open perhaps the most beloved psalm. But before we think about this word shepherd and other comforting images and metaphors contained in the psalm, let us reflect a little on those most foreboding words from verse 4—"I walk through the valley of the shadow of death." I use the phrase "valley of the shadow of death" and variations of it often throughout this book. I also make frequent use of the phrase "vale of tears" or "valley of tears" which traces back to many early Bible translations of Psalm 84:6. Both phrases capture something fundamental to the Scripture's teaching about what human beings, including worshipers of the true God, should expect in this world, tears and death, death and tears.

Psalm 25

In this lament psalm David pleads with the Lord "let me not be put to shame," a dominant preoccupation by the people of God in many parts of Holy Scripture. He begs for guidance that he might walk in the paths of the Lord, so that he might walk in the paths pleasing to the Lord and for forgiveness of sins, the sins of his youth, not on the basis of any personal merit but because of the Lord's own character, namely his *khessed*, which Alan Ross translates, rather than as "steadfast love," as "loyal love," which has the advantage of highlighting the personal character of this love that lies at the very heart of the divine nature and of the divine promise to his people. That loyalty is first of all to God's self. God is the original promise keeper who has entered into covenant relationship to his people, a covenant he shall eventually maintain my fulfilling both the divine and human sides of in Jesus Christ.

That the loyalty of God to himself encompasses the covenant promises legitimizes petitions to the Lord for a vast array of blessings: not to be put to shame, mercy and pardon for guilt, divine guidance in the ways of the Lord, the ways of truth, and many more. Once one belongs to the people known by the name of the Lord, appeal for a stunning array of blessings is legitimized and welcomed by the Lord himself, not on the basis of anything outside of the Lord, but on the basis of the Lords on character and promise such that his own reputation is at stake.

And those blessings include for David that he may here in this psalm, as he does in many Psalms and as others of the covenant people of God do throughout the Old Testament, hope "that his soul shall abide in well-being, and his offspring shall inherit the land." Ross, along with many translations, renders *shalom* in verse 13 as "prosperity." Grammatically, "land" serves here, as it does hundreds of times throughout the Bible, as a synecdoche for the whole of physical, material life or even the whole of life. The meaning of "land" falls within the semantic range of "shalom" as I am employing it in this study.

Here as elsewhere in the Psalms and in the rest of the Old Testament, one encounters not the slightest need to treat material blessings, such as prosperity in the land and deliverance from enemies, as somehow of different class from non-material blessings, such as pardon for guilt. But how many evangelical preachers will reflexively either pass over the material blessings prominent in the psalm or find some way to spiritualize it? Yet that same preacher will pray for an unemployed congregant to find a good paying job and raise money to help a family whose house has burned to the ground (after enough folks involved have insisted that what burned was "just stuff" and really does not matter).

The contradiction between the psalm's straight forward and unabashed inclusion of so-called spiritual blessings along with material ones and the seemingly congenital need of Christian preachers and teachers to separate them, ignore the material ones or perhaps pit them against one another and find a way to rehabilitate the material references by making them non-material in meaning is a gnostic move that violates the biblical witness. It is telling and brilliantly instructive that when physical and material concerns foist themselves upon us, our prayers tend to follow far more faithfully biblical paths than does our teaching, preaching, small group discussions, and routine devotional practices. We pray and act better than we preach, teach, and engage in self-conscience Christian talk.

We feel justified, indeed compelled to pooh-pooh the material and physical dimensions of life partly because we think the anti-world and spirit-versus-flesh language of the New Testament demands it. But is this so? The answer is no. But a nice and very Jesus-loyal preparation for recognizing that the answer is no is to immerse ourselves deep and long in the Old Testament first, Jesus' Bible, the one he said "bears witness about me" (John 5:39).

Psalm 37

As much as any of the psalms, this one touches on multiple components of shalom. The word *shalom* occurs in verse 11. There it mainly denotes that absence of hostility and flourishing of harmony that we so reflexively associate with the word shalom. But the psalm as a whole casts a vision of divine deliverance and blessing that encompasses other components of the three-dimensioned shalom Yahweh promises and produces for his people.

Claus Westermann notes that this psalm so exhibits the character of wisdom literature that it could be included in the Proverbs. The Lord through the psalmist means to teach his people how they should respond when wicked people hold sway in the land, live in prosperity and oppress the righteous. The heart of the teaching addresses the problems that arise when the wicked flourish in the land and oppress the righteous. Admonition to the oppressed righteous ones parallels divine instruction to the people of God throughout the Bible—"fret not . . . be not envious . . . trust . . . do good . . . commit your way to the Lord . . . be still . . . wait patiently . . . refrain from anger." All of these admonitions strike the ears of serious students of the Bible as utterly commonplace. Every one of these admonitions fit nicely into Gnostic, anti-material, and so anti-shalomic readings of the psalm.

The typical use of this psalm in my spiritual formation, and I suspect, in the spiritual formation of many evangelicals, demonstrates brilliantly such Gnostic, and thus anti-shalomic, interpretive reflexes at work among us. Verse 3 receives disproportionate and often exclusive attention: "Delight yourself in the Lord, and he will give you the desires of your heart." Ripped completely from its context and made to stand entirely on its own, the verse allows for Gnostic readings prized by some evangelicals. It is true that the close association in this verse between taking delight in the Lord and the promise that the heart's desires of God's people will be satisfied rules out any notion that the Lord promises to grant any and all of their petitions. No, those who delight in the Lord bring righteous petitions issuing from righteous desires.

But the Gnostic reading is impossible. It imagines that the verse promises that those who delight in the Lord will receive in return righteous desires. The language actually teaches that those who take delight in the Lord already have righteous desires and these give rise to righteous petitions. The word translated "desires" may be and probably would be better rendered "petitions." But beyond this, the desires or petitions slated for granting are not in doubt in the psalm. The psalmist does not take a time out from the subject matter of the psalm between verses 2 and 4 for a brief excursion into general musings about the connection between delight in the Lord and the satisfaction of holy desires. The petitions teed up by the psalm for divine granting are enumerated in the psalm. The Lord will act on behalf of his people who trust him and wait expectantly. He shall see to the fading of the wicked like grass. He shall cut them off. He shall not let his righteous ones be put to shame in times of famine but will give generously to them. He shall see to their inheritance of the very land the wicked now strut triumphantly upon. His people shall dwell upon the land forever. In short, those who delight in the Lord shall see the Lord act on their behalf in these ways explicitly. To spiritualize the psalm is to gut it of its force and truth. The reach of the arm of the Lord who made heaven and earth is not shortened to some ostensibly "spiritual" realm with which he and his people must learn to settle.

That Gnostic reading scratches two itches at once—(1) it avoids the third dimension of shalom that affirms material, this-worldly blessing as integral to redemption, and (2) it supports the "Just Give Me Jesus," "All I Need Is Jesus" feature of Gnostic construal of the faith. "Delight yourself in the Lord," in such unwittingly Gnostic readings, means to delight ourselves in the Lord *rather than*, for example, some promise that we shall "inherit the land" or that "evildoers shall be cut off" or that we shall "delight ourselves in abundant peace"—a shalom that includes more than some internal calm but refers emphatically to peace "in the land" where we shall dwell forever with one another and the Lord.

In context, the Gnostic reading of the psalm as a whole and of verse 3 becomes not just impossible but preposterous. The delight in the Lord encouraged in verse 3 turns explicitly on the certain expectation that the promises that punctuate the entire psalm shall be fulfilled. The wicked shall be cut off from the land and shalom shall ensue in all three of its dimensions. The psalm teaches the people of God to expect that the typical pattern of divine dealing with his children shall prove true for them as well. This is the pattern: The Lord makes promises to deliver his people from the distress or lack of some sort; from the suffering that now characterizes their lives. But the deliverance will not happen immediately. The deliverance shall be delayed. The people are expected to trust the word of the Lord in the meantime, continue in obedience to his law, wait with the certain expectation of actual fulfillment of the promise, and to praise the Lord in the meantime and take comfort. Then, according to the Lord's wisdom and timing, actual physical, in-this-time, three-dimensioned shalomic deliverance comes.

Take note that this is the divine pattern that has prevailed ever since expulsion from the Garden. Thus, every generation of the people of God has a history of the actual playing out of this pattern to look back to. At the center of this pattern is the deliverance of the people of Israel from Egyptian bondage and his eventual settlement of his people into the land of promise. These are constituent stages of the pattern—(1) promise of deliverance in troubled times; (2) delay in fulfillment of the promise; a time for faith and obedience and expectant waiting and bearing up; and (3) actual fulfillment of the promise in space and time in this time between the times.

That these have played out over and over again over several millennia among God's people supplements the word of God's promise with a history of the Lord's actual faithfulness as the great promise keeper. Thus the basis for our faith that the Lord shall prove true to his promise rests upon a firm foundation; his power remains unrivaled and unstoppable and his *khessed* love for his elect has not and shall never diminish.

The spirituality commended by this psalm does not support a faith that is reduceable to waiting and bearing up in this world and where fulfillment of the promises is utterly delayed until the return of our Lord. Yes, whatever deliverance comes to the people of God in the time between the times shall prove partial and temporary—things deteriorated soon after the Egyptian pursuers were drowned by the collapsing Red Sea; the people of Israel, sinners that they were, found ways to destroy whatever shalom the Lord afforded them in Canaan; and we too, us Christians of the West and especially of North America, who have enjoyed as much divinely bestowed shalom of certain types as any people who have ever lived, have managed to make pretty bad use of it. But bad reception and use of divine blessing does not alter the character of the gifts bestowed as divine blessing.

The African American church in the United States and persecuted churches around the globe today, such as the burgeoning Christian communities of faith in China, understand better how to read Psalm 37 and the Bible itself in faithful shalomic fullness. The temptation to Marcionite rejection of the Old Testament diminishes to the vanishing point when they meet with the Lord who delivers from Egyptian bondage and promises over and over again to so deliver his people in the future. Chinese Christians recognize the affluence of Christians in the West as the beneficiaries of such deliverance. We may resist such a reading of our affluence because we know ourselves to be great sinners as affluent Christians. But both insights are true—our affluence is the utterly gracious blessing of God *and* we have made bad use of it and turned the blessing into a curse. Wherever the Lord sees fit to bestow significant three-dimensioned shalomic blessing upon his people, the false pride and idolatrous tendencies Moses warned of in Deuteronomy 8 threaten and too often come to fruition. But the failure of the people of God to receive and use and enjoy shalom does not result in the divine abandonment of his shalomic purposes in creation or redemption.

If the Lord sees to a significantly shalomic deliverance of the church in China, and surely believers should pray to that end, sooner or later, the Chinese church will likely fall into the typical pride and idolatry of which sinners are prone. If history is any guide, including biblical history, the now blessed Chinees shall in significant ways convert divine blessing into a curse. But such bad use of divine blessing does not alter its character as a bestowed divine blessing any more than was Eden or the blessing of our lives or of our conversion.

Psalm 46

Far from glamorizing the unsettledness, homelessness, or resident alien status that befalls the people of God, comfort and hope in God center on him as "our refuge and strength," so that "if the earth gives way," as it sometimes does, and "though its waters roar and foam," as did the storm surge of hurricane Hugo right into my little home in Charleston in 1989, "we will not fear." Why? Because such unsettling, poverty-inflicting, and even death-threatening phenomena down here on earth really don't matter, are actually good things, blessings when seen with the eyes of faith, perhaps actually to be prayed for or even welcomed? No. Our comfort is that our God is not unstable and he dwells secure and we belong to him and he promises to keep us and rescue us from all this unsettlement and poverty and death. So, in the midst of all this evil undoing of the shalom in which God dwells and which he promised for his creatures and which he promises to restore and perfect and make permanent, we can with good reason "be still and know" that he is God, for he, the shalom dweller and maker, "will be exalted in the earth."

This psalm is also a great example of the ease with which biblical authors include both material and non-material dimensions of life on earth as the purview of God the creator and redeemer and, for that reason, the proper concern of his suffering and worshiping children.

Distinction between material and non-material dimensions of life exists and is not denied. But the psalmist evidences zero compulsion to highlight that distinction and make sure readers know to rank the non-material dimensions higher than the material ones and to be hyper-alert constantly of the danger of prizing the material concerns too much. That compulsion must be brought to this text and to most of the Bible. It should be recognized as an alien norm nurtured on the philosophical soil of the platonic tradition and exploited from of old by Gnostics, Marcionites, Manicheans, and others.

Psalm 62

"For God alone my soul waits in silence," the psalm opens. Then in verse 5, David, as Dr. Martyn Lloyd Jones admonished all believers to do, preaches to himself: "For God alone, O my soul, wait in silence." Activity dominates the pages of Holy Scripture—the recounting of activity, of God and of humanity and of angels and demons. God also promises to act in the future and commands much action by is people—go, leave, give, proclaim, pray, make haste, flee, resist, rebuke, be kind, love. The Bible is more a book of action than not. It's a happening book.

But another emphasis punctuates its pages as well, a counterpoint to the dominance of doing; the divine call for his people to wait as David does in this psalm. Waiting emerges in the Psalms as so necessary and so rich in spiritual depth that it feels like an activity. It is a deliberate waiting, a focused, content-full waiting, as though one awaited the arrival of a beloved friend long absent or one's father, as I did as a child. The whistle blew from the tower at the Southern Railway boxcar shop Monday through Friday at 4:00 pm. Alert most days in heart, mind, and ears for the sound of that whistle, once it sounded, my eyes fixed on the corner of Burnett Street and Valley Falls Road for the first sign of the blue Chevy turning, conveying my father back to me after the day's separation. Active waiting, expectant wait-ing, because a waiting upon a person, a special person, the person whom I loved and who loved me and cared for me.

But it is a real waiting. It awaits what it cannot have until the wait is over. "From him comes my salvation." He is the savior now, but there is salvation yet to come. He's not done. And that is good for the psalmist because things down here on earth still need much putting right. But he's re-ally coming as savior and Lord. He promised he would. And his love is of the *khessed* kind—"Once God has spoken: twice have I heard this: that power belongs to God, and that to you O Lord, belongs steadfast love" (*khessed*). It's not possible that he would forget or renege on the promise. Therefore, the waiting shall be requited and not only might David wait with assurance, so may and ought all his children. "Trust in him at all times, O people: pour out your heart before him: God is a refuge for us."

The putting right of things the Lord's coming brings exposes as misleading and even mistaken certain short-sighted interpretations of things as they appear now: "Those of low estate are but a breath; those of high estate are a delusion; . . . Put no trust in extortion; set no vain hopes on robbery; if riches increase, set not your heart on them." David does not gainsay riches or the increase of riches as such. He does not deny the power of riches to provide real and valid earthly goods. He does not impugn as evil the increase of riches. He emphasizes that the blessings of riches gained are short-lived, ephemeral, unsecured and unsecurable. Riches boast of much more than they can deliver. What riches seem to promise—power, comfort, security, joy, hope—only the coming Lord is able to provide. Riches are not idols of themselves. We make them idols by attributing to them powers residing only in the Lord. Setting the heart on increased riches is foolhardy. Waiting on the Lord is wise because the Lord shall deliver what we imagine riches can provide.

Psalm 47

The word "all" signals a key shalomic feature of this short psalm, namely, the universal scope of the divine claim not just upon Israel, but upon all— "Clap your hands *all* peoples!" The Lord is a great king "over *all* the earth." In fact the Lord is not just *a* king, but "*the* King over *all* the earth." Thus, all peoples, all nations are prompted to gather and sing, and to do so to the God who subdued the peoples under his chosen people, because, the psalmist says, "He chose our heritage for us, the pride of Jacob whom he loves." The Lord God's long special involvement with his chosen people Israel does not compete with or forestall his claim upon and prerogatives respecting "the peoples," "the nations." Instead, the election of Israel is the foundation and revelation of that universal claim.

The hope of the nations is bound up with the creator and Lord of heaven and earth's dealings with Israel. Karl Barth once said that in a real sense, the history of the Jews is the history of us all. I stole from a professor of patristics this pithy, somehow jolting but true observation—"Jesus was a Jew. He never did become a Christian. He never converted!"

The Jews so often forgot or misunderstood or failed to embrace the universal scope of the use the Lord who made them a people promised to make of them. But the forgetting and misunderstanding and failing not only did not prevent that universal divine use, it contributed to it. Israel's failings are somehow paradigmatic and so are recorded for our benefit (1 Cor 10:11).

But in this psalm the positive interrelation of Yahweh's particular, gracious, electing ways and the universal scope of his claim and his love shine forth in the worship of Israel—"God reigns over the nations; God sits on his holy throne. The princes of the people gather as the people of the God of Abraham."

Psalm 65

On what basis is praise due to "God in Zion"? Why especially and uniquely to him ought "vows be performed"? Is it because "when iniquities prevail" against David, and we who appropriate David's experience when they sing his song in worship, he "atone[s] for our transgressions"? Yes. But also because he brings his chosen ones near where they "shall be satisfied with the goodness of [his] house." He also answer the cries and petitions of his people "by awesome deeds" as the God "of salvation."

Why is the "God in Zion," "the hope of all the ends of the earth and the farthest seas"? Is it because "when iniquities prevail" he will "atone for our transgressions"? Yes! But also because of what he does to and on the earth that was made the proper home of his human creatures: "You visit the earth and water it; you greatly enrich it; the river of God is full of water, you provide their grain, for so you prepared it." And this divine watering aims at much more than "neither much nor little," and does not have in view in the first instance the commending of contentment in whatever state one finds oneself. That such an admonition and such a work of the spirit belongs to the will of God and must find its place in faithful pastoral care and preaching must not be allowed to mute, drown out, or even exclude the many instances of divine intention and actual production of abundance for his people. We ought to let ourselves hear with utterly receptive ears the song of David to the Lord: "You water [the earth's] furrows abundantly, . . . blessing its growth. You crown the year with your bounty; your wagon tracks overflow with abundance. The pastures of the wilderness overflow, . . . the valleys deck themselves with grain, they shout and sing together with joy."

Psalm 66

Why to God ought the people of Israel "shout for joy" and "sing the glory of his name"? Because of his "awesome deeds." What awesome deeds? He kept their soul among the living, did not let their feet slip, tested them, tried them like silver, brought them into the net, laid a crushing burden on their backs, let men ride over their heads so that they "went through fire and through water." Is that all? Is that the end? He kept them alive and then led them through profoundly hard experiences and that's it? He enabled them to be content with all the testing and feet slipping and crushing burdens on their backs and being drug through the water and fire? No. The glory of the God of Israel does not stop with such testing but gives way to the justification and goal of the testing—"yet you have brought us out to a place of abundance." This ending is essential to the glory, to the worthiness for praise of our God. This ending in abundance, in this case not an abundance in the next world but in this one, proves his steadfast love (v. 20).

Psalm 68

As is so often the case, here in Psalm 68 "scattering" belongs, not to divine favor, but to divine opposition or punishment. The Lord scatters not the righteous, not the faithful, but "his enemies" (v. 1). The blessing of God runs in the opposite direction. As the "Father of the fatherless and protector of widows is God in his holy habitation." From that "habitation" God "settles the solitary in a home." The association of settlement with God is evident. He is not scattered, in exile, on pilgrimage, a resident alien, but "dwells" in his "holy habitation." And when he blesses his people, he settles them into the land, the home he prepared for them. And there he does not teach them to despise material prosperity but rather "leads out the prisoners to prosperity" leaving "the rebellious" to "dwell in a parched land."

Oh yes, being scattered, being on exile, living as resident aliens and pilgrims on this earth; the fall into sin of humanity results in all these anti-shalomic experiences and burdens. No doubt about it. Even God in the second person of his Godhead shall let go of some of the prerogatives of his deity, become an exile himself, emptying himself in sacrificial love, making himself poor and ending up with no place to lay his head. All of this arises from sin, the fall, and its consequences, especially that only by such an emptying and making poor can shalom be restored, perfected, and made permanent.

But in the meantime, the Lord, displaying his steadfast love, blesses his people with glimpses and foretastes of the shalom to come: "Rain in abundance, O God, you shed abroad; you restored your inheritance as it languished; your flock found a dwelling in it; in your goodness, O God, you provided for the needy." The default reading of many affluent believers in the West of "provided for the needy" is that it commends to us acts of charity by which the immediate physical needs of those who are poor are met from their abundance. While such charitable acts are indeed commendable and find abundant support in Holy Scripture, this and many other passages throughout the Bible do not have such conditions and such a scenario in view. What is happening here is that those who were poor are made "not poor." They are delivered from having been poor to material prosperity. When God does this, he supplies not a single millibar of energy for that glow of satisfaction that may rightly well up in the breast of a middle-class church group fresh from its once-a-month service at the downtown soup kitchen. But when God does this, the poor are made not poor.

The answer to two questions is knowable by anyone who wants to gain the knowledge: (1) By what means have the most poor folks in history been lifted out of poverty? And (2) on account of what circumstance have the most people who would likely have been poor, instead, not been poor? The answer is the rise of capitalism. Without claiming that capitalism came down on plates from on high in upstate New York or denying that sinful human beings make capitalism worse than it might be, why would any believer deny the providence of God in the rise of something achieving unprecedented deliverance from poverty on a global scale. Later I shall offer a few suggestions as to why many do so.

Psalm 85

The Lord is credited and praised for his favor to his "land." "The land" here, as often elsewhere, comprehends the whole life of the people of Israel before God in the place where he has settled them much as shalom comprehends the three-dimensioned relational reality guiding our reflection. So how did the Lord show favor to the land? He "restored the fortunes of Jacob," which entailed his speaking "peace to his people," bringing his "salvation near" so that "glory may dwell in the land." Such divine favor expresses the khessed of the Lord so that righteousness and shalom "kiss each other" and "faithfulness springs from the ground." "Yes, the Lord will give what is good, and our land will yield its increase."

The notion that the psalm paints a picture of settlement that pits the so-called spiritual against the physical does violence to the plain reading of the text and forfeits the truth of peace and prosperity encompassing the whole of human existence, material and non-material, a human flourishing before the creator and Lord of the people. Any attempt to impose a reading of the psalm that it means to teach, namely, that the original divine will of God for his creature and all of creation involves a comprehensive shalom and his redeeming work, does as well. Such illegitimate spiritualizing also undermines the full scope of both legitimate petition, thanksgiving, and ultimately worship.

Psalm 95

Again and again, we are taught in Holy Scripture to identify the deity and glory of God with his two great acts, of creation and redemption. We are taught by God himself that we must acknowledge his "God-ness," if you will, in the fact that he created the universe and that his steadfast love for all that he has made continues in spite of the sinful rebellion of his human creatures. Thus, the second great act demonstrating the reality and character of his deity—he redeems what he has made from the consequences of its fall. All other pretenders to deity are exposed as imposters because they did not create and cannot redeem.

But the second element, the glory, also proves crucial. To say that God deserves glory is to say that he is worthy of praise. It is not to suppose that in "giving glory" human beings provide to God what he lacks, but rather they acknowledge what he already has, worthiness for praise, precisely as the one who creates and then redeems what he has made. Thus, Psalm 95:

> Let us make a joyful noise to the rock of our salvation! Let us come into his presence with thanksgiving. . . . for the Lord is a great God, a great king above all gods. In his hands are the depths of the earth; the heights of the mountains are his also. The sea is his, for he made it, and his hands formed the dry land. Oh come let us worship and bow down; let us kneel before the Lord, our Maker! For he is our God, and we the people of his pasture, the sheep of his hand.

Really!? Should such be sung in the times between the times? In this vale of tears? In the fallen, corrupt world once destroyed in the flood and now set for permanent holocaust not long hence? Surely such joyous thanksgiving for the creation must wait. Likewise if we sing, "This Is My Father's World." Really? How can it be? Yet it be. That hope for the entire created order in all its shalomic substance and relationality is no more preposterous than our hope for our "spirits" or, though it is a term wholly incompatible with Old Testament's language and conceptual horizons, our "disembodied souls." We take it as a commonplace to rejoice in the Lord for such souls, as well we should, not because of their present or even promised future state, but because of the promises made regarding God's future blessings to be heaped upon such souls. Our faith in promises regarding the non-material dimension of human being is confirmed by glimpses and tastes of the coming completed sanctification of our souls.

Parallel promises apply to every dimension of the created order. "Say among the nations, 'The Lord reigns! Yes, the world is established; it shall never be moved . . . Let the heavens be glad, and let the earth rejoice; let the sea roar, and all that fills it; let the field exult, and everything in in it!" (Ps 96:10–11).

Psalm 97

"The Lord reigns, let the earth rejoice; let the coastlands be glad!" (v. 1) "Zion hears and is glad, and the daughters of Judah rejoice" (v. 8). The universal scope of this psalm's vision does not compete with but meshes with its designation of Zion as the special venue of rejoicing. The psalm recalls the Lord's deliverance for his people that has occurred, one attended by natural phenomena—clouds, thick darkness, and fire. That deliverance of his chosen people signals a coming deliverance of the whole earth, indeed the heavens and the earth, centered around a restored and as such a new Jerusalem. Jesus, as the Messiah of the Jews is the savior of the world. Zion as the city where Yahweh makes his name to dwell is the center from which shall extend the reign of "the most high over all the earth" (v. 9). In terms of shalom, this psalm along with many other passages affirms that the scope of both creation and redemption encompasses every dimension of creation, material and non-material alike. And it further affirms that acknowledgment, experience, and enjoyment of the creator's redeeming activity in all three shalomic dimensions are in fact not held in utter abeyance until their complete and permanent fulfillment in the eschaton. Thus, the psalm actually celebrates both an instance of redeeming deliverance in keeping with the promised future deliverance and uses it as a springboard to rejoice at the prospect of that eschatological fulfilment upon which it waits.

Psalm 104

In this descriptive praise psalm the Lord is extolled as the God of all creation. The psalmist gazes upon all that the Lord has made and finds himself stunned with the beauty, the provision for human life, and the enormous scale and diversity of the created order. The Lord is praised not only because he created the universe and all that is in it, though that alone would justify and merit praise. But the Lord continues to sustain his creation and to make it serve the needs of human beings who receive from it provision for life.

The Lord's "splendor and majesty" is displayed because he "set the earth on its foundations so that it could never be moved" (vv. 1, 5). Hmm? But was not the earth destroyed in the flood *after* the earth was so established? Well, yes, destroyed in its opposition to him, but not annihilated. The Lord's splendor and majesty is further displayed in his continuing utter control over all that he has made:

> The mountains rose, the valleys sank down
>   to the place that you appointed for them.
> You set a boundary that they may not pass,
>   so that they might not again cover the earth. (vv. 8–9)

This psalm abounds with soaring praise for the glory due to the Lord for his creation and his sustaining of all that he has made. It surveys and describes in detail features of the created order and its continuing fitness as the home for human beings. Both provide present and continuing bases for worship of the Lord who by his mighty power and deeds sustains all that he has made. All of this wonder and praise regard the present creation, after the fall. It would be difficult to exaggerate the importance of this and other such psalms as evidence for the notion of shalom I am advancing. Shalom is far from utterly lost in the time between the times. Otherwise no such psalms should find their way to worshipful lips. Praise songs for what prevailed in creation prior to the fall, perhaps; praise for the hope of the promised new heaven and earth, fine. But for this present vale of tears? No. And yet the psalmist, in surveying this present creation, is undeterred in his meticulous descriptions of creation and effusive praise for the creator here and now.

The church through the ages has followed the lead of the psalmist. Thus I was lead to sing from childhood—

> This is my Father's world, And to my listening ears
> All nature sings, and round me rings the music of the spheres.
> This is my Father's world: I rest me in the thought
> Of rocks and trees, of skies and seas—His hand the wonders wrought. . . .
>
> This is my Father's world, O let me ne're forget
> That though the wrong seems oft so strong, God is the ruler yet.
> This is my Father's world: The battle is not done;
> Jesus who died shall be satisfied, and earth and heav'n be one.[1]

The psalmist also acknowledges the utter dependence of all living creatures upon the favor of the life sustaining creator in verses 27–30. The glory of the Lord, the creator, is declared and the psalmist prays that the Lord will "rejoice in his works" (v. 31) even as the psalmist himself sets himself to "sing to the Lord as long as I live; I will sing to the Lord as long as I have being" (vv. 31, 33).

How far from despairing resignation over the lost cause of this present created order is this and so many psalms? How incompatible are this psalmist's assessments of the value of the present heaven and earth as occasion for gratitude, praise, and worship to the creator with a posture dominated by emphasis on resignation and bearing up? Oh yes, passages of despair, resignation, and mere hope for the future come to mind. But what are we to think of this psalmist? Was he carried away into delusive optimism on an especially good day at a time when life was going well and he decided to jot down his thoughts? Or are we confronted in the psalm with the divinely inspired praise of the psalmist anchored in the truth? Which is it? Is it really appropriate for the Psalms to gush as so many of them do over the state of the fallen created order when, no matter how well things might be going for

---

1. Babcock, "This Is My Father's World."

the psalmist and his loved ones and his community at the time of composition, in many places famine and disease and war and death abound?

How does my shalom idea respond to such challenges? First, it seems to me impossible to deny the appropriateness and indeed the happy duty of praise to God for this world, for the glimpses and tastes of shalom that harbinger a perfect and permanent one to come. To do so in no way excludes full-on acknowledgement of the consequences of the fall, the appropriateness of grief, and the resting of faith not in this world or in ourselves at all but in the one who is with us, sustains us, and promises to preserve and redeem us and this world eternally. So the lament psalms are kept right alongside these gushy happy ones, because both belong.

Where recovery of a biblically grounded vision of shalom yesterday, today, and forever prevails in this world, our "yes, but" talk will move in two directions, not just one. Where shalom is acknowledged in the garden and in the coming age but practically denied here and now, every attempted acknowledgment of shalom here and now is quickly followed up by, "Yes, but all of our hope is in the next world. We are in but not of this world. Our citizenship is in heaven," or some such.

Shalom yesterday, today, and forever affirms such "yes, but" patterns of Christian talk. But it affirms "yes, but" talk in the other direction as well. Like this—first speaker: "Do not set you hopes on this world. This world is the valley of the shadow of death. This world is not our home" Second speaker: "Yes, but our Lord is with us. He blesses us with good things still; he has not abandoned us. He gives to us glimpses and tastes of the good things to come. This is the day that the Lord has made; let us rejoice and be glad in it."

If our speech is to prove faithful to the biblical witness, and to psalms such this one, the "yes, but" pattern must run in both directions. In the end, the glimpses and tastes of shalom here and now win out. That is the promise. That is the hope. Let us not despise the glimpses and foretastes provided by the Lord of shalom. Let us not shake our heads at this psalm in cynicism. Let us not think ourselves deeper, more insightful, more sober and mature in our outlook than he. Let us not view him as an ostensibly naïve psalmist carried away in moments of this-worldly bliss into unwarranted this-worldly reverie in the Lord. The psalmist does not in this psalm exhaust appropriate responses to God by his people in this world, but he does model one major appropriate and divinely expected response. Woe unto us if we lose our ability to offer such wondrous praise and exalted worship ourselves.

Psalm 107

"Oh give thanks to the Lord, for he is good, for his steadfast love endures forever!" Even though generally I resists encouragements to rank things or to identify the most important this or that, if pressed, I would suggest that the most important word in the Old Testament is not *torah* (law), as many might insist, but *khessed*, often translated "steadfast love." It designates the loyal love of the Lord, which contrasts with other loves, such as ours, which may wax and wane, change its object, and even die. Not the love of Yahweh—it remains faithful, it remembers its promises, it never abandons or forsakes its beloved. In *khessed*, unlike *torah*, we are confronted directly with the good news of the gospel.

Torah belongs to the gospel as well, evidenced by its frequent appearance in the Psalms and most recently explored and celebrated by Dietrich Bonhoeffer. If *torah* opens us up to God's redeeming activity carried right through to the cross and beyond, *khessed* opens to us the character and the promise of God to his people underlying that divine activity.

So how has that steadfast love expressed itself to the people of Israel so that it had to issue in worshipful song? What did the Lord do that displayed his *khessed* towards his people? He gathered them from the lands and brought them to a city in which to dwell. He rescued them from hunger and thirst, rescued them from wandering and satiated their hunger and thirst. He delivered them from distress.

OK. But where's the spiritual stuff? You know, like forgiveness of sins or making them content to just bear up under their distresses or to even rejoice in their distresses since God uses such trouble to sanctify his children? Do you feel such tension when you read a psalm like this that seems so fixated on the things "the gentiles run after" (Matt 6:32)? Heck, it has God showing off that he provides to his people the things the gentiles run after. What gives? Are you a bit disturbed when you read such a psalm? Are you anxious to find a verse in the psalm that focuses on one of those ostensibly "spiritual" matters? Then perhaps we can treat all this concern for the flesh and rescue from danger and supplying of physical needs as mere preparation for the only really important matters, the "spiritual" (read non-material) matters. And if we find even one mention of those internal heart-and-mind matters in the psalm, then perhaps we'll bring out the heavy hermeneutical guns and reinterpret all the physical stuff "spiritually."

Why might we feel such discomfort with such a psalm? Shalom suggests that the discomfort comes not from a faithful hearing of the biblical witness, not from comprehension of the gospel, but from an alien norm. An alien norm involves the exaltation of a supposed truism or collection of truisms obtained either outside or inside the Bible that then functions, whether consciously or not, as an interpretive key (*crux interpretum*) for any passage in the Bible. Certain hermeneutical keys have periodically arisen in the history of biblical interpretation that have served the church well—so-called rules of faith (*regula fidei*) such as the Apostles' Creed or a similar shortish summary of supposed settled results of interpretation that focus on fundamental themes of biblical teaching. The bible itself offers one such *crux interpretum*. Or perhaps we should say that Jesus Christ offers one—himself. "You search the Scriptures . . . and it is they that bear witness about me" (John 5:39). Jesus Christ, then, is no alien norm but the actual norming norm (*norma normans*) of all faithful Christian interpretation of Holy Scripture, including Psalm 107.

Shalom, as a construct seeking to gather up an array of biblical teachings, could be used, but ought not to be used as such a rule of faith or key to interpretation. Rather, I wish to expose my shalom construct to the only test that matters, the Scriptures themselves. To the extent that shalom arises from a faithful reading of the Bible, it may also identify the sort of alien norm that might illegitimately disturb a straightforward reading of Psalm 107 and, quite frankly, most of the Bible. It is either the restriction of the "spiritual" to non-material matters or the severe subordination of the non-material to functioning as a mere means to the non-material or as a stage as in a theatre upon which it pleased the creator to enact the drama of a redemption that is either wholly or almost exclusively concerned with non-material dimensions of reality and of creation, namely non-material and disembodied souls. Such a posture reflexively snuggles up to Paul's longing to be delivered from "this body of death" but has more trouble understanding his pointed rejection in 2 Corinthians 5 of any "desire to be found naked." Rather, he longs to be and expects to be "further clothed."

But Psalm 107 affords little respite to such alien-norm-besotted "spiritual" ones. It just relentlessly treats those things the Gentiles run after as matters of the Lords' and his people's proper concern. Indeed, these earthly, physical, political, health-and-wealth related matters either lie at the heart of display of the divine *khessed* or Psalm 107 needs excising from Holy Writ.

What did the Lord do? Healed them by his word, delivered them from destruction, made the storm be still, hushed the sea, turned deserts into pools of water and a parched land into springs of water. He let "the hungry dwell and they established a city to live in; they sow fields and plant vineyards and get a fruitful yield. By his blessing they multiply greatly, and he does not let their livestock diminish" (vv. 36–38). I have passed over the many verses in this psalm that have the Lord exercising his steadfast love in the defeat of and deliverance of his people from their enemies but the psalm is chocked full of such. Take in the crescendo admonition arising from all this recounted *khessed* activity: "Whoever is wise, let him attend to these things; let them consider the steadfast love of the Lord" (v. 43).

This psalm touches on many aspects of shalom. It treats wandering as a suffering from which the divine *khessed* rescues by gathering in. It affirms that the scope of divine interest and the worthiness of the Lord to receive praise, his glory, his promises, concern the total person and the total life of the community of his people. The psalm does not support the notion that divine redemption intends the weaning of human beings away from desire for material well-being and the redirecting of that desire toward non-material matters.

Although disordered desire, concupiscence, is a fundamental consequence of the fall, the putting of it right does not entail the lopping off or despising of the physical dimensions of shalom, but the reordering of them, the putting of them right again.

Psalm 125

> Those who trust in the Lord are like Mount Zion,
> which cannot be moved, but abides forever.
> As the mountains surround Jerusalem, so the Lord surrounds
> Jerusalem,
> so the Lord surrounds his people,
> from this time forth and forever more. (vv. 1–2)

Really!? If shalom as I have understood it faithfully comprehends the message of Holy Scripture, then the sort of creation-hostile, material-versus-non-material, invisible-versus-visible, spirit-versus-flesh readings of the Bible must tie themselves in knots in the face of this psalm. They simply cannot abide anything like a straightforward reading of it. Mount Zion cannot be moved? Mount Zion abides forever? How so? Is it not, along with the rest of creation, including the moon and the sun and the stars, set for a fiery destruction (1 Pet 3:7–10)?

Well yes, inasmuch as we too face destruction, *in our rebellion against God!* Likewise, our mortal bodies, liable to corruption, face sure destruction, but not annihilation. No. Rather, our doomed mortal bodies, thanks to the resurrection of Jesus Christ, for those who are in Christ, are sown like seed—"sown a natural body; it is raised a spiritual body . . . the dead will be raised imperishable . . . the dead will be raised imperishable, and we shall be changed. For this perishable body must put on the imperishable and this

mortal body must put on immortality . . . 'Death is swallowed up in victory'"
(1 Cor 15:44–55).

For shalom, the language of "putting on" and "being further clothed"
(2 Cor 5) and of death being "swallowed up" teaches us that the biblical language of "destruction" is not best interpreted as "annihilation" with respect
to our mortal bodies. And Romans 8, along with the countless passages that
speak of the continuance of this world, such as this psalm, does of Mount
Zion teach us that words such as "restoration," "renewal," and "perfection" comprehend the full biblical witness to redemption with respect to
the non-human fallen creation rather than does the language of "annihilation" or even of "replacement." Shalom can speak of our own death and of
the destruction of the world and of restoration, renewal, and perfection in
terms of death and resurrection, and affirm hope in the new—but new as
the transformation, the being changed of all that has fallen, rather than an
annihilation or discarding. This means that the use of what remains is the
use of what is marked for redemption

Shalom comprehends divine warning of opposition to the world as opposition to the world *in its opposition to him and in its falleness.* That world
is indeed doomed and set for true annihilation.

Psalm 146

Our hope ought not to rest in "princes . . . in whom there is not salvation,"
but in the God of Jacob, "who made heaven and earth, the sea, and all that
is in them." Beside the many passages that impugn this world and prompt
shifting of thoughts and hearts away from this world to God and to the next
world are many other passages that turn us toward this world and, as in this
psalm, particularly to God as the creator of this world. That God made this
world and remains its creator and sustainer and Lord is a sure basis for hope
and worship. In this world too, not only in the next, the Lord reigns and acts
in the ways that reflect his *khessed*: he "sets the prisoners free," "opens the
eyes of the blind," "lifts up those who are bowed down," "watches over the
sojourners," "upholds the widow and the fatherless." This Lord "will reign
forever . . . Praise the Lord!"

Psalm 144

What sorts of petitions does the Lord welcome from his children? What is
the scope of appropriate worship? Boldly, unabashedly, David praises God
who "trains [his] hands for war, and [his] fingers for battle." That God, the

one who so trains David, is his "steadfast love" and "fortress," his "strong-hold" and "deliverer." He, the one who "subdues peoples" under David is the one of whom he says "Blessed be the Lord, my rock." Are we still able to speak of God this way and praise him for such things? Is such worship appropriate for Gentile Christian believers post-Pentecost, or does this sort of thing belong exclusively to Israel and only to them for circumscribed era now long past?

And oh what seemingly unspiritual and definitely politically incorrect petitions David unleashed—"Rescue me and deliver me from the hand of foreigners." And how far from a simple lifestyle or a settling for help to be content with a little could David's petitions stray:

> May our sons in their youth
>> Be like plants full grown,
> our daughters like corner pillars
>> cut for the structure of a palace;
> may our granaries be full,
>> providing all kinds of produce;
> may our sheep bring forth thousands
>> and ten thousands in our fields;
> may our cattle be heavy with young,
>> suffering no mishap or failure of bearing;
> may there be no cry of distress in the streets!
> Blessed are the people to whom such blessings fall!
> Blessed are the people whose God is the Lord!

For what was David really asking and prompting the whole worshiping congregation to request from their Lord? Are the granaries and the sheep and the cattle really metaphors for non-material, "spiritual" goods? Not likely. David knew how to ask for spiritual blessings when he wanted to. He requested these just as directly—"Create in me a clean heart O God" (Psalm 51). But surely allowing for such blatantly this-worldly prayers and worship opens the door to a slippery slope to the pernicious heresy that is the prosperity gospel that has taken hold across the globe, would it not?

"May there be no cry of distress in the streets!" How often will such a petition be raised by an unwed African American mother in Chicago while you are reading this book? Ought we to shush her and teach to pray for more "spiritual" blessings? Nowhere does reflexive recoil from health, security, and prosperity-focused petition flourish more readily than from those who enjoy a fair amount of both. Where a dearth of all three abounds, the need for an ostensibly more "spiritual" reading of such scriptures not only does not appeal to hearers of the Word, it would be rightly seen as preposterous were it suggested. Playing down the blatant divine interest in the material flourishing of the children of God proclaimed so often in the Bible is a luxury of the affluent. Now let us turn to shalom in the prophets and beyond.

6

Shalom in the Prophets and Beyond

Do not think that I have come to abolish the Law or the
Prophets; I have not come to abolish them but to fulfill them.

—JESUS THE MESSIAH OF THE JEWS (MATT 5:17)

As WE HAVE MADE forays into selective psalms with the vision of a three-
dimensioned relational shalom in our minds, we turn now to selected passages from the prophets. We begin with Jeremiah.

Jeremiah

Abandonment of the "promised land" component of the covenant between
Yahweh and the people of Israel finds no support in the book if Jeremiah.
Early in the book, the Lord's call for his scattered people to return to Zion
becomes a refrain: "Return, faithless, Israel, declares the Lord" (3:12). "Return, O faithless children, declares the Lord; for I am your master; I will take
you, one from one city and two from a family, and I will bring you to Zion"
(3:14). Myriad blessings await scattered Israel "If you return" (4:1).

The Lord's requirement that faithless Israel both repent from evil deeds
and actually return to Zion and embrace the regathering and resettling of
them into the place where he has made his name to dwell are not seen as
competing values or as potential spiritual enemies. They are friends. "Cir-
cumcise yourselves to the Lord; remove the foreskin of your hearts" (4:4).
The Lord's requirement is not to either return to Zion or just repent where
you are, but both/and. The blessing of the Lord shall comprise all three dimensions of shalom.

The Lord through his prophet declares his ongoing concern that all the stipulations of the covenant be fulfilled and that all of promised blessings be fully realized, including settlement into the promised land:

> Cursed be the man who does not hear the words of the covenant that I commanded your fathers when I brought them out of Egypt, from the furnace saying, Listen to my voice, and do all that I commanded you. So you shall be my people, and I will be your God, that I may confirm the oath I swore to your fathers, to give them a land flowing with milk and honey, as at this day." Then [Jeremiah] answered, "So be it, Lord." (11:3–5)

But the commitment of the Lord to that eventual resettlement of his people into the land of promise accommodated a temporary gathering and settlement of some of the people of Israel into that "foreign land," that land of exile, Babylon. In a letter from Jeremiah in Judah, the word of the Lord comes to the exiles:

> Thus says the Lord of hosts, the God of Israel, to all the exiles whom I have sent into exile from Jerusalem into Babylon: Build houses and live in them; plant gardens and eat their produce. Take wives and have sons and daughters; take wives for your sons and give your daughters in marriage, that they may bear sons and daughters; multiply there and do not decrease. But seek the welfare [*shalom*] of the city where I have sent you into exile, and pray to the lord on its behalf, for in its welfare you will find your welfare [*shalom*]. (29:4–7)

The use of *shalom* in this passage approximates well my own use of the term in this book. Shalom means nothing less than absence of hostility but it means much more. Its significance is far more positive than negative. It means to assert what is present more than what is absent. Shalom indicates a kind of overall character of lived human existence in community. And it indicates not just this lived human existence in community but its enjoyment—shalom is enjoyed; it is pleasurable to those who access its blessings. The admonitions to build houses and plant and eat and take wives and have sons and daughters and multiply are to be taken literally. But they are meant to convey more than the individual or the sum of any set of discreet actions such as those mentioned. These particular components of shalom serve to evoke the whole of life lived together before the Lord. The message is really all-encompassing—"Settle down and live your lives here for now. Enjoy life in all its ordinary, mundane, but also divinely intended relational dimensions. For thus I have made you to do from the beginning. Live in this world, with each other, before my face. Embrace this life as the blessing it still can be east of Eden."

The translation of *shalom* in the English Standard Version as "welfare" is apt. This word expresses the sort of all-encompassing scope of right relationships within a flourishing human community in prosperity that emerges again and again as the original and ongoing plan of the creator redeemer God for his children.

But what is not taught here is that place no longer matters in the Lord's redeeming work going forward. The exile remains punishment. The hope is not for habituation to the foreign land, but patient waiting for return to the promised land, to enjoy shalom there:

> For thus says the Lord: When seventy years are completed for Babylon, I will visit you, and I will fulfill to you my promise and bring you back to this place. For I know the plans I have for you, declares the Lord, plans for welfare [*shalom*] and not for evil, to give you a future and a hope. Then you will call upon me and pray to me, and I will hear you. You will seek me and find me, when you seek me with all your heart. I will be found by you declares the Lord, and I will restore your fortunes and gather you from all the nations and all the places where I have driven you, declares the Lord, and I will bring you back to the place from which I sent you into exile. (29:10–14)

The juxtaposition of the two experiences of welfare (*shalom*) are striking and intriguing. The first, the one in Babylon, is to be embraced immediately. The second lies in the promised future and shall occur in Zion. The Lord shall gather from all nations his scattered children and resettle them in Zion, where he shall "restore their fortunes" and where they shall be his people and he shall be their God. Though the better, more perfect, and ostensibly permanent shalom lies in the future, enjoyment of a temporary, provisional shalom is both possible and encouraged. The present shalomic possibilities bear the marks of the future shalom. They serve as foretastes, pointers, harbingers of what is to come. Settling for the Babylonian shalom is not allowed. To so settle would be to doubt the promise of the Lord, to diminish and distort proper enjoyment of the Babylonian shalom which is meant to include the hope of the better shalom to come. The Babylonian shalom is a shalomic way station along the path to the place of true shalom.

But on the other hand, setting ones hope upon the shalom to come does not require despising the way-station shalom the Lord provides to his exiled, sojourning people. Indeed, this preliminary shalom serves the coming shalom insofar as it demonstrates Yahweh's faithfulness to keep his promise never to abandon his people and his power to fulfill the promise of future shalom.

An illuminative use of *shalom* also occurs in Jeremiah 16. Here the prophet warns of the coming punishment of Judah to take place before Yahweh restores them. The character of the punishment is revealed: "I have taken away my peace [*shalom*] from this people, my steadfast love and mercy, declares the Lord" (16:5). Steadfast love (*khessed*) is the most dominant and in many ways the most characteristic feature of the divine character in his covenant relationship to his chosen people Israel. Again and again, throughout the Old Testament, *khessed* identifies the divine sort of love over against all other inferior and counterfeit sorts of love. *Khessed* or loyal love never ends; it never abandons the beloved; it stays with and keeps the beloved. The positive blessing of *khessed* love includes *shalom*. So what happens when the divine *khessed* is dialed back and *shalom* is denied to Judah?

> . . . thus says the Lord concerning the sons and daughters in this place, and concerning the mothers who bore them and concerning the fathers who fathered them in this land: They shall die of deadly diseases. They shall not be lamented, nor shall they be buried. They shall be as dung on the surface of the ground. They shall perish by the sword and by famine, and their dead bodies shall be as food for the birds of the air and for the beasts of the earth. (16:3–4)

When *shalom* is lost, what does such loss entail?

> No one shall break bread for the mourner, to comfort him for the dead, nor shall anyone give him the cup of consolation to drink for his father or his mother. You shall not go into the house of feasting to sit with them, to eat and drink. For thus says the Lord of hosts, the God of Israel: Behold I will silence in this place, before your eyes and in your days, the voice of mirth and of gladness, the voice of the bridegroom and the voice of the bride. (16:7–9)

As we saw in Zechariah 7–8, the conditions of *shalom* encompass something of the whole of life. Where the blessing of the divine *shalom* prevails, the three relational dimensions I have identified flourish: namely, the relationship between God's people and God, the relationship between God's people themselves before God, and the relationship between God's people before God in the place or the home in which God has settled them.

The features of *shalom* that prevailed prior to the fall remain features of *shalom*. After the fall, in the between time in which we live, *shalom* is only experienced partially, temporarily, in tastes and glimpses. As we see in Jeremiah 16, *shalom* takes on features surrounding comfort and honor associated with death and mourning unnecessary prior to the fall. Even after the fall, a *shalomic* divine blessing is both possible and desirable and the various extent of the granting and withholding of that *shalom* functions as a central tool of the Lord in his relationship to his people. Yahweh prompts desire for *shalom* among his people. The Lord reveals himself as and insists upon being known as the bestower and withdrawer of *shalom*. To God be the glory for the things he has done. What has he done? What does he continue to do? Promise to do? To be the Lord of *shalom*!

What was Jesus promising when he said to his disciples "Peace I leave with you; my peace I give to you. Not as the world gives do I give to you. Let not your hearts be troubled, neither let them be afraid" (John 14:27)? In Jeremiah and Zechariah and, I would argue, throughout Holy Scripture and throughout history, the three-dimensioned *shalom* I have identified is uniquely the blessing of the creator and redeemer of this world. And it is the characteristic blessing of the Lord as well—*shalom* in all its comprehensiveness and richness. Does Jesus promise this or some other *shalom*? One thing we know for sure. Gnostics and Marcionites and Manichaeans of various stripes are quick to reduce the "peace" promised by Jesus to something merely "spiritual," non-material. Maricon recognized that to pull this reduction off he needed to whack the Old Testament from the canon of Holy Scripture and to lop off large sections of the New Testament. Marcion's greatness as a heretic is partly grounded in his keen insight into the incompatibility between his hostility to the creator and the sort of *shalom* that smacks one in the face throughout the Old Testament. So, the Old Testament had to go.

"Ah!" we say, but clearly the sort of *shalom* Jesus credits the world with providing is just the sort of comprehensive and therefore materially inclusive sort I am advancing. Really? What of the man with his barns? He makes no mention of the relationship with the Lord or with others in is conversation with his own soul. He focuses exclusively upon what he thinks his wealth can provide to him. But he is deluded even there, because his wealth cannot keep him alive. Wealth is not evil but it is also not God and thus cannot provide proper enjoyment of the things it may be used to purchase, much less those dimensions of shalom that cannot be bought. The Old Testament sounds a warning to those quick to reduce Jesus' promised peace to some inner equanimity more in keeping with Buddhist aspirations than with the Lord of *shalom* we meet in Jeremiah's prophecy.

Joel

The unfaithfulness of the people of Judah and Jerusalem brings upon them the judgment of the Lord, bringing loss of the material prosperity the Lord had provided. Where once crops abounded, now locusts devour all vegetation and strip bark from the trees. The sweet wine that flowed freely is "cut off" from their mouths (1:5). The proper response to the Lord's punishment is lament and repentance with fasting in the midst of catastrophic famine: "Lament like a virgin wearing sackcloth for the bridegroom of her youth." "The fields are destroyed, the ground mourns, because the grain is destroyed, the wine dries up, the oil languishes. . . . Pomegranate, palm, and apple, all the trees of the field are dried up, and gladness dries up from the children of man" (1:8–12).

Should the people of God not have found gladness in the abundance once enjoyed but now ripped away? Is that the lesson the Lord means to teach? How might the people have avoided judgment? By despising the grain and the wine and the pomegranates while concerning themselves with "spiritual" matters instead? The Lord does deprive them of the pleasures of abundance they enjoyed and wished to go on enjoying in their sin. Does this divine depravation indicate that the material abundance actually has no place in the Lord's ultimate plans for his children and that it is high time they learned that this is so? Does the punishment serve the further purpose of beginning a weaning process by which the people of God learn to let go of such fleshly desires and pleasures—desires and pleasures that may have played some legitimate role in God's plans at an earlier, less mature stage of their development, their sanctification by the Lord but now must be left behind as a child leaves behind bicycle training wheels?

Apparently not. Joel admonishes the people, "Return to the Lord your God, for he is gracious and merciful, slow to anger, and abounding in steadfast love; and he relents over disaster" (2:13). What happens when the Lord "relents over disaster" in a new display of his *khessed*? The people are called into solemn assembly where they weep for their sins and are consecrated anew to the Lord. "Then the Lord became jealous for his land and had pity on his people." Then the Lord announces his plans: Behold. I am sending to you grain, wine, and oil, and you will be satisfied" (2:18–19). Oh no! Shouldn't the Lord rethink this plan? How often have his people presumed upon the Lord's goodness in the past and lapsed back into all manner of unfaithfulness? Again and again.

Yet the Lord remains steadfast along this course of material blessing: "Be glad O children of Zion, and rejoice in the Lord your God, for he has given the early rain for your vindication." The Lord heaps abundant blessing upon his people to vindicate the people and in doing so himself before the eyes of other nations. The great commission to evangelize all nations must await the resurrection of Jesus Christ, but witness to all nations through the Lord's chosen people begins with the call of Abraham. Yahweh, in his treatment of and dealings with his people, bears witness to the nations that he is the Lord of all. "Why should they say among the peoples, 'Where is their God?'" The Lord bears witness to himself among the peoples of earth when he punishes his people. But he reveals himself to the nations when he relents from punishment, displays his *khessed* in grace and mercy by heaping material blessing upon them: "Behold I am sending to you grain, wine, and oil, and you will be satisfied; and I will no more make you a reproach among the nations" (2:19).

The material blessing heaped upon Judah and Jerusalem provides to them much more than a simple lifestyle. However wise it surely is to keep our material desires and expectations in check—"give me neither poverty nor riches; feed me with the food that is needful for me" (Prov 30:8)—the witness of Holy Scripture makes it clear that the Lord is sometimes pleased to provide in great abundance. "[H]e has poured down for you abundant rain, the early and the latter rain, as before. The threshing floors shall be full of grain; the vats shall overflow with wine and oil. I will restore to you the years that the swarming locusts have eaten. . . . You shall eat in plenty and be satisfied, and praise the name of the Lord God, who has dealt wondrously with you. And my people shall never be put to shame" (Joel 2:23–27).

The Lord is not hesitant to restore his people to the materially abundant life they once knew, even though it was precisely when they enjoyed such abundance that they sinned. Is the Lord slow to learn his lesson about his people? No. He understands their propensity to sin all too well. He comprehends it perfectly. But what is also true is that material blessing is in fact an original, indeed a primeval blessing of the Lord fitted for his people to enjoy from the beginning. Redemption does not concede this material blessing turf one square inch.

What the Lord is going to bring about is not a people who, having matured spiritually, no longer need nor desire material blessing. He is going to enable his people to enjoy material blessing in the right way, receive the blessing with gratitude from his hand, make right use of the blessing of the Lord, and praise him in worship for his abundant mercy. And in this relationship in which the people receive aright the blessings of the Lord that then issue in proper worship, they truly come to know the Lord. How do we know these things? Because the Lord tells his people so: "You shall eat in plenty and be satisfied, and praise the name of the Lord your God . . . And you shall know that I am in the midst of Israel, and that I am the Lord your God and there is none else" (2:26–27).

Far from evidencing any hesitance or embarrassment about the appropriateness of the material blessing to come, these blessings are seen as vital to the revelation of the Lord to his people. Just as we know him wrongly apart from his punishment for sin, we know him wrongly apart from his propensity to bless in this way.

Are their people of the Lord who enjoy his abundant material blessing today? Could it be you and I? Are we something like or beyond "middle class" by Western standards? Are we aware that what passes for middling in twentieth- and twenty-first-century standards in the West makes us profoundly rich by comparison with virtually every person who has lived on this earth, including most of those who live on earth today? Do we believe in the Lord God almighty, maker of heaven and earth to whom Joel bears witness? By what or whose providence have we come to enjoy the highest standards of living in world history? From whose hand have such blessings come? From the father of lights from whom all blessings flow? The giver of every perfect gift? Talk about any middle-class existence in the West or in other lands where Western economic arrangements have been adopted in some measure and have seen similar historically unprecedented wealth production as some "simple lifestyle" is nonsense.

We're rich by any reasonable biblical or historical standard of comparison—richer indeed than any people who have ever lived. That this is so but little acknowledged plays a significant role in resistance by some evangelicals to shalom. Certain barriers against shalom depend much upon the denial or failure to recognize that the middle classes in the West are rich folk. We shall address this matter further in due course.

In any case, Joel bears witness to the inclusion of material and non-material, bodily and non-bodily dimensioning of the created order as equally claimed by the creator redeemer God as both spiritually dangerous and promising. Shalom rejects the either/or pitting of the proper so-called spiritual dimensions of life against the bodily and material dimensions of life. In sin, yes, every dimension of life as intended by the creator can be put to wrong use and can become a source of temptation and evil rather than the blessing it was in the beginning, has been periodically, and is still meant to be.

Micah

The ESV Study Bible: "The theme of Micah is judgment and forgiveness. The Lord, the Judge who scatters his people for their transgressions and sins, is the Shepherd-King who in covenant faithfulness gathers, protects, and forgives them." Ah! Such words are like scratching on a cocker spaniel's belly to one testing shalom by the words of Holy Scripture.

Zechariah

The prophet Zechariah made the return to the Holy Land from exile in Babylon during the reign of Cyrus around 538 BC. Returnees faced a grim existence in a devastated land and struggled to survive for many years. Hopes of a newly rebuilt temple at the center of a spiritual renaissance among the newly delivered people of God within a flourishing community were difficult to maintain. But maybe the people of Israel were meant to learn through the exile that where one lives does not matter anymore. Perhaps longing for the rise of a flourishing worshiping community in the land of Canaan conflicted with a new divinely inaugurated era in which every place is spiritually the same, spiritually neutral. Were the exiles wrong to imagine that they could not worship in a foreign land (Psalm 137)? Were they also wrong to long for—indeed, to pin their hopes upon—a restored, harmonious, and prosperous Zion? Speaking into the devastation of post-exilic Palestine, the Lord, through the prophet Zechariah, taught his people what to think about, what to care about, what to do, and what they had the firmest possible warrant to hope for because it is grounded in the Lord's own promise.

The following two extended excerpts from Zechariah 7 and 8 set forth a portion of this prophetic word of the Lord. They also exhibit beautifully and powerfully dimensions of the shalom I am contending for in this book:

> And the word of the Lord came to Zechariah, saying, "Thus says the Lord of hosts, 'Render true judgements, show kindness and mercy to one another, do not oppress the widow, the fatherless, the sojourner, or the poor, and let none of you devise evil against another in your heart.' But they refused to pay attention and turned a stubborn shoulder and stopped their ears that they might not hear. They made their hearts diamond-hard lest they should hear the law and the word that the Lord of hosts had sent by his Spirit through the former prophets. Therefore, great anger came from the Lord of hosts, "and I scattered them with

a whirlwind among the nations that they had not known. Thus,
the land they left was desolate."

    And the word of the Lord of host came saying, "Thus says
the Lord of hosts: I am jealous of Zion with great jealousy, and I
am jealous for her with great wrath. Thus, says the Lord: I have
returned to Zion and will dwell in the midst of Jerusalem, and
Jerusalem shall be called the faithful city, and the mountain of
the Lord of hosts, the holy mountain. . . . Thus says the Lord of
hosts: Behold, I will save my people from the east country and
from the west country, and I will bring them to dwell in the
midst of Jerusalem. And they shall be my people, and I will be
their God." (Zech 7:8—8:3)

Place still matters to the Lord. The promised land is still special to the
unfolding of redemptive history. Zion remains the place for which the Lord
is especially jealous because it is there especially, uniquely that he wishes to
place his name and dwell with his people. The Lord was with his people in
captivity. They had not been abandoned by their creator and redeemer God.
It was possible to worship him there. The Lord's claim is upon all that he
has made, including all peoples, not excepting Israel's Babylonian captors.
What Abraham Kuyper so eloquently proclaimed concerning the Lord Jesus
holds for the land of Babylon too: "There is not one square inch of this world
about which Christ does not say, 'Mine!'"

    But the universal claim does not imply uniform, undifferentiated value
and purpose for every parcel of earth, sky, or sea. The Lord is uniquely jealous for Zion precisely because of its crucial and unique place and function
in his plan of redemption.

    The place Zion is not sacred in itself. It is sacred because of the spe-
cial use made of it, including especially its designation as the divinely established home of his chosen people. There especially the Lord makes his
name to dwell, his word to dwell, his people to dwell. Thus the Lord makes
Jerusalem "the faithful city, and the mountain of the Lord of hosts, the holy
mountain" (Zech 8:3). There, on Zion, especially, the Lord makes himself
known, bears witness to himself for the sake of the whole world.

    The Babylonian captivity did not signal an end to the sanctification,
the sacralizing of particular places and spaces. It highlighted such sanctification as a permanent feature of the divine creation and redemption of
this world. But has not Jesus himself inaugurated a new era of geographical
indifference in his response to the Samaritan woman at the well—"the hour
is coming when neither on this mountain nor in Jerusalem will you worship
the Father. . . . the hour is coming, and is now here, when the true worshipers will worship the Father in spirit and truth" (John 4:21, 23). Do not

the lessons of the captivity include preparation for Jesus' ostensibly radical rejection of any differentiated valuing of particular places in the Christian era? The answer is no.

The word of the Lord illumines the character and conditions of shalom in his admonitions to his resettled people. Widowhood, orphanhood, sojourning, and poverty are all conditions of suffering brought on by the fall into sin. The people of God, in imitation of their Lord, do not turn a cold shoulder to those bearing such suffering. They do not teach such sufferers to ignore their suffering since the physical and material effects of their condition do not mater "spiritually." No, they are to show mercy by acting to relieve suffering in so far as they are able. That the Lord enables his children to bear up patiently in suffering and develops character in his children through suffering does not signal a transformation of suffering into not-suffering. Nor does sanctifying divine use of suffering make suffering a new "good" to be sought and spread around and rejoiced in the way true goods are. God does use hunger, disease, and death for good purposes but he calls his children to relieve them, not promote them. Sojourning is not the worst thing in the world. We are all sojourners now. But the sojourning is suffering and the goal of the sojourn we are on is to arrive once and for all at our home and to sojourn no more. While sojourning lasts, the people of God treat it as suffering to be mitigated where possible. True to the pattern throughout Scripture, scattering belongs to punishment and suffering. *Khessed* and mercy serve the redeeming activity of the God who gathers and settles the scattered ones (a pattern that shall continue in the New Testament). The promised gathering and settling of the formerly scattered and exiled ones opens up God's people to a sure hope of coming redemption.

When the gathering and settling of the formerly scattered and exiled ones is accomplished, what shall result? When such a plan is announced and, in effect promised, what expectations should then animate the hope of God's people? What does it look like when, as the Lord says, "they shall be my people, and I will be their God"?

> Thus says the Lord of hosts: Old men and old women shall again sit in the streets of Jerusalem, each with staff in hand because of great age. And the streets of the city shall be full of boys and girls playing in the streets. . . . Behold, I will save my people from the east country and from the west country, and I will bring them to dwell in the midst of Jerusalem. And they shall be my people, and I will be their God, in faithfulness and in righteousness. . . . I will not deal with the remnant of this people as in former days, declares the Lord of hosts. For there shall be a sowing of peace [*shalom*]. The vine shall give its fruit, the ground shall give its

produce, the heavens shall give their dew. And I will cause the remnant of this people to possess all these things. And as you have been a byword of cursing among the nations, O house of Judah and the house of Israel, so will I save you, and you shall be a blessing." (Zech 8:4–13)

Since elderly persons are included in this vision of things to come, is this a prophecy for the time between the times, east of Eden? Perhaps. Probably so. Whatever its historical horizon, this world or the next, the prophesy confronts us with a beautiful glance into shalom. The once scattered, exiled, wandering, and sojourning ones are gathered and settled into a peaceful, harmonious, loving community, the city of God. Sinners are reconciled with God and one another. They love each other. They share life with one another as the gift and blessing of their Lord whom they worship and to whom they give all glory. Shalom prevails—completeness, harmony, and prosperity. This shalom is essential to the blessing God's people enjoy and, as such, essential to their being a blessing to others, to the nations. The shalom bears witness to what forgiveness and reconciliation issue in on the other side. We are forgiven and reconciled for the sake of the restoration and more of the blessing we were made to enjoy from the beginning.

Between Testaments Reflections

Is there some attenuation of, alteration of, or transition away from affirmation of shalom in the Old Testament when we move to the New Testament? If so, surely the burden must rest with those defending such change. There is progression of revelation in history and Holy Scripture teaches that this is so and records such progression. Our Lord does new things and speaks new words. God once bore with the Gentiles with much patience but now calls all to repentance. The significance of the temple in Jerusalem has changed as Jesus predicted, just as he foretold its approaching destruction. So an argument against a fully orbed retention of Old Testament shalom in the New is by no means out of the question. But evangelical acknowledgment of the unity of the entire biblical witness, capped by Jesus' own claim that the Old Testament speaks of him, shifts the burden squarely on those insisting upon such a change.

The default expectation in comparison between the testaments should always be the discovery of their unity, not their discontinuity. Given such expectation, here are some features of the Old Testament shalom construed in terms of blessings and curses to which we should be alert in our reading of the New Testament: (1) prosperity as blessing—poverty as

curse; (2) security as blessing—insecurity as curse; (3) settlement as blessing—scattering as curse; (4) physical health as blessing; and (5) sickness
and death as curse.

Wholistic Spirituality

If we try to press contemporary linguistic patterns and categories onto our
reading of the Old Testament, one common convention threatens to distort
our understanding of these texts, namely, our use of the word "spiritual." In
at least two ways, our use of this term may pose a barrier to faithful reading
of the Old Testament. One is the use of "spiritual" to distinguish matters per-
taining to the non-bodily dimension of the human person from the bodily
dimension. Another is the use of "spiritual" to distinguish non-material, perhaps invisible realities from material ones. It is not that the Old Testament
writers did not recognize the reality of such distinctions or any significance
in such distinctions. They did. But they did not have a category of "spiritual"
to designate the non-bodily dimensions of the human person as those dimensions that mattered to the Lord or mattered most to the Lord. Likewise,
they did not work with some notion of the spiritual realm designating invisible realities that really mattered set over against merely physical dimensions
of reality that do not matter ultimately or that matter much less than the
non-material and invisible dimensions. Yet I fear that contemporary readers
of the Old Testament do in fact, to some significant degree, whether consciously or not, operate with such hermeneutical categories.

A more biblically compatible use of the word "spiritual," one that lets
us discern the shalomic message of the Scriptures, is let it designate all that
matters to our God. If God cares about something, if it matters to him, that
makes it spiritual, that means if should matter to us. Shalom obviously insists that the scope of divine concern extends to all that he has made and the
redemption likewise so extends. Such an affirmation of the universal scope
of divine concern and thus the universal scope of the "spiritual" does not
and must not imply a flattening or radical egalitarian notion of meaning and
worth. No. The scope of the spiritual encompasses hierarchies of value. But
hierarchical rank does not suggest non-essentiality.

Such a use of the word "spiritual" is usually compatible with the underlying assumptions and explicit teachings of the Old Testament concerning
the scope of divine concern. Thus, the Old Testament treats physical health,
material prosperity, and secure settlement into loving and flourishing communities as the blessings of God the creator and redeemer of Israel matter-
of-factly, not only without apology, but without betraying the slightest need

to explain or to apologize. Sins of the spirit and sins of the body are distinguishable but also of a piece. Virtues of the spirit and of the hands and feet are not the same but neither are they enemies or contrary species. They belong to the same *genus* of righteousness.

Pressure to dice up sin into fleshly and non-fleshly categories and dimensions, spiritual and non-spiritual categories, so that we can move quickly to emphasize the "spiritual," the "non-fleshly," is felt more by contemporary interpreters than by Old Testament writers or their audiences. The spirituality assumed, addressed, and nurtured by the Old Testament is wholistic. It assumes the comprehensive divine claim of the creator upon all that he has made and the wholistic scope of the ongoing and promised redeeming work of the creator.

The Old Testament strongly and explicitly acknowledges and address the sins of greed and avarice and pride and of unjust craving for and unjust discharge of political power. But correction of such sins involves no designation of the concerns for health, prosperity, and good governance as unspiritual. The corruption and pernicious use of an originally good dimension of creation does not negate its ongoing place in the shalom provided, promoted, and promised by God. What is needed is for sex and money and power to be put right, not put away.

We should discern in the Old Testament a pattern in which shalom in its fullness was lost with the expulsion from the garden of Eden. But we have also seen that, in spite of the fall and its consequences, the people of God are still, periodically and temporarily, blessed with approximations of a three-dimensioned shalom in the land east of Eden. The promise of the land is the promise of the experience of shalom in some measure. Punishment for sin results in the loss of shalom in whole or in part.

Various unsettled states always mark the disruption and loss of shalom in some measure. These states include being scattered, wandering, sojourning, and exiled. The divine *khessed* is displayed in many ways, but it always includes the actual bringing of shalom in some or all of its dimensions. And the promise of God to his people is always that of a fully-orbed and permanent shalom to come. I shall contend that shalom functions in the New Testament according to a parallel pattern.

But does my reading of the Old Testament support the notion of shalom as I have construed it? If and to the extent that it does, what should that portend for the New Testament if anything? The very words "old" and "new" would seem to encourage expectation of significance difference between the two "covenants" that comprise the Holy Scripture of the historic and global church. Yet it surely behooves us to remember that these two little three-letter words, "old" and "new," were appended to the *ex post facto* division and nomenclature of the two constituent volumes in question.

Condemnation of Maricon's rejection of the Old Testament need not and does not deny the reality and the significance of an intertestamental period. But that condemnation should nurture within us a reflexive expectation of and protectiveness for the unity of the two testaments. It should induce as well a concomitant suspicion of efforts to overdraw supposed differences between the testaments. The grounds for Marcion's rejection could hardly have been more profound or decisive—Jesus said he came not to destroy or to abolish the law, but to fulfill it. Jesus said that Abraham and Moses speak of him! The Old Testament was and remains the Bible of Jesus and thus also for his disciples. The default expectation of Christian reading between the testaments is to discover continuity, not the opposite.

But to the extent that development (not discontinuity in any fundamental sense) is identified in the passage from the Old Testament to the New, shalom, especially in its third dimension, seems to provide an attractive target for reinterpretation. Where such affinity for discontinuity between the testaments flourishes, the New Testament may become the great allegorizer and spiritualizer of the Old Testament behind many Christian pulpits and lecterns.

Folks happy to allow for the earlier stage of spiritual development among the faithful in the Old Testament imagine themselves free and even compelled to leave such material and physical fixation behind in the New—treasuring now "the things not seen" and counting "the things of this world as dung" as they believe they have been taught to do.

Perhaps attenuation of this-worldly concern, at least in some measure, does belong to the progressive revelation of our creator and redeemer. And perhaps such attenuation becomes acute at the transition between the testaments. But Marcion's condemnation and earlier resistance to the so-called Christian Gnostics should be heard as a trumpet blast of warning by the ancient and global church against all hermeneutical proclivities toward potentially anti-creation and anti-creator thoughts.

Affirmation of discontinuity between the testaments where the place of the material creation and the physical body are concerned should be forced to face a heavy burden of proof. The integration of material and non-material dimensions of both creation and redemption so obvious and prominent and unapologetically affirmed in the Old Testament should render challenges to it suspicious from the outset.

But so often the opposite instinct seems to prevail—namely, to allegorize or spiritualize otherwise "material" or perhaps "literal" readings of the Old Testament. The Song of Songs must be about something more, something higher, something more spiritual than the love between a man and a woman. Thus, even if it is about both, surely its mundane literal and physical meaning is instantiated in the text by divine inspiration as an accommodation to our reflexively earth-oriented, flesh-oriented tendencies as mainly or merely a means to the higher teaching about the Lord and his love for the church. Marcion and the Gnostics would be so proud!

I believe that shalom, in the fullest sense as I have understood it as taught in the Old Testament, survives in the New Testament. But how to prove it? How to test it? The test must include allowing the New Testament to assume its unique function as the now indispensable and supreme hermeneutical lens and judge of Old Testament interpretation. Jesus said the Old Testament speaks of him. He said that he is the Messiah of the Jews. Jesus warns, "Moses said . . . but I say . . ." (Matt 5:17–48). Jesus said he came to fulfill the law and the prophets. Jesus enforces upon his followers the necessity to interpret the Old Testament "through him," and not the other way around.

But in order to discern the interpretive expectations and opportunities indicated by Jesus's and the apostolic writers' relationship to and use of the Old Testament, we must also recognize the affirmation of the Old Testament as the word of God in the New Testament witness, including in the words of Jesus. Jesus is not only saying that the Old Testament, in the wake of his coming, may and must be read through him as the one to whom it bears witness, of whom it prophesied, in whom it finds its fulfillment. He is saying all of that, thanks be to God! But he is also saying that the Old Testament does *in fact* do these things.

The Old Testament shows itself the inspired world of God alongside the New Testament and, more concretely, alongside Jesus Christ, not by being transformed into something it was not until the incarnation, but as itself. The appearance of Jesus Christ does not make the Old Testament Holy Scripture. It reveals it as such. The eternal Son of God did not make the Old Testament the inspired, inerrant word of God by becoming incarnate, living a sinless life, dying an atoning death on the cross, rising from the dead, and ascending to the right hand of the Father with the promise to return. The Scriptures of the Old Testament were already the inspired, inerrant word of God. Jesus Christ affirmed that this had always been so. He did not cede authority or hermeneutical turf to the scribes and the Pharisees. He claimed it for himself and for the church insofar as she reads it through him.

So affirmation of the New Testament, and Jesus Christ himself in a special sense, as exercising unique hermeneutical priority over the Old Testament stands. But Jesus' affirmation of the Old Testament as the word of God does not enforce a one-way hermeneutic in which the Old

Testament can only be read through the lens of the New. In fact the "lens" analogy, though helpful and accurate for describing one means of reading the Old Testament, is inadequate. It does not comprehend the full scope of interpretive approaches warranted by the actual relationship that obtains between the Testaments given recognition that Jesus Christ fulfills the law and the prophets.

That relationship is not one in which the Old Testament is corrected by the New Testament. There is nothing whatsoever wrong with the Old Testament requiring a lens to correct. Right interpretation of a given passage of Scripture requires illumination, both by the Holy Spirit and by other passages from whatever testament the Spirit might employ! What is now ruled out is interpretation of any part of the canon *apart from* the revelation of God in Jesus Christ.

The interpretive landscape opened up by Jesus' claims about the Old Testament is very rich indeed. Consideration of Karl Barth's critique of Friedrich Schleiermacher's theology can help us comprehend it more fully. Barth affirmed Schleiermacher's attempt to make the doctrine of the Holy Spirit his point of departure rather than the word of God, as Barth had done. We need a theology of the Holy Spirit. Schleiermacher attempted it. He failed. But, Barth insisted, as long as Jesus Christ is at the center of any theology, any of the major Christian doctrines may and should be employed as points of departure, as fit vantage points from and through which to reflect upon the whole of the revelatory deposit in the canon of Holy Scripture. Think of the revelation of God as a multifaceted jewel with Jesus Christ, clothed with his gospel and all his benefits, at its center. Let the facets of the jewel be the great doctrines of the faith. The jewel may and ought to be viewed through every facet in order to observe every dimension of its brilliant and dazzling beauty.

The hermeneutical opportunities opened up by Jesus' claim upon the Old Testament present us with a multifaceted jewel, not a corrective lens. We can start anywhere, not just with the New Testament, and not just with the red letters in the New Testament—as long as Jesus Christ, clothed with his gospel, lies at the center of the jewel. The notion of letting passages "stand on their own," of some strict refusal to allow passages outside the particular historical and biblical context to intrude upon our reading, is ultimately unhelpful and potentially harmful. Where the Holy Spirit performs its illuminative task, every passage in the Bible illumines every other. Treating passages as threats to faithful interpretation of other passages is only apt at times because of the fall!

Believers do not have a relationship with the God of John 3:16. We have a relationship with the only true God, to whom *the whole Bible* bears witness. The attempt of the church is to hear the witness of the whole Bible all at once, over and over again, in its quest to know and love and obey and worship the one of whom it speaks. In some measure, this attempt always fails in the sense that we cannot take in all that it might tell us. If we never exhaustively know other human beings, including ourselves, how much more must we confess that the quest to know our God is never comprehensive, never finished, and thankfully so!

Happily, where a strong doctrine of the nature and authority of the Bible prevails, robust preaching occurs, and consistent Bible intake is maintained, something approximating this whole-Bible exposure, listening to many passages from both testaments actually flourishes.

Where such a wide-scoped, all-at-once hearing is attempted no matter how impossible, shalom survives, and the seemingly Gnostic-like marginalizations and dismissals and hostilities toward the material creation and physical bodies disappear like ghosts.

Still, areas of difference and development, if not discontinuity, between the testaments do confront us. One might be the matter of sacrifice, self-denial, and renunciation of the things of this world. To these matters we now turn.

Sacrifice and Shalom

That followers of Jesus Christ face the prospect of divinely required renunciation and sacrifice is clear in the New Testament. Obedience insures varying degrees of deprivation for every disciple up to and including the prospect of martyrdom. Lapses into forgetfulness of this foreboding reality requires periodic reminders from prophets raised up from the community of faith who rearticulate the radical and comprehensive claim of the Lord Jesus upon all who trust in him.

Christians from all over the world and across all denominational divides have heard in Dietrich Bonhoeffer's classic book on discipleship the faithful proclamation of truth—"When Christ calls a man, he bids him come and die." Cheap grace is counterfeit grace. Grace that accommodates the ministry of the word as a means of gain is a lie. Paradoxically, the true grace that comes to us through Jesus Christ costs us everything. True repentance repudiates every claim, even over, especially over, one's own life. Every other potential sacrifice, relinquishment, and repudiation that obedience may demand is included both explicitly and by the simple argument from the greater to the lesser. If the Lord may require my life, he may require that of my son, as Abraham learned, or my property or anything else. Jesus is the pioneer and finisher of our faith and we have not yet resisted evil to the point of death, at least not yet (Hebrews).

A hierarchy of value underlies the logic warranting such potential sacrifice, even of one's very life should obedience demand it. "For what will it profit a man if he gains the whole world and forfeits his soul?" (Matt 16:26). It is vital that *psyche*, translated here as "soul," refer to one's very life, body and spirit, or body and soul—not merely to the non-material dimension of human life. The gospel does not hold out the promise of or encourage any interest in gaining rather than forfeiting some ostensibly disembodied version of ourselves. What's at stake in discipleship is our whole person. Fear the one, Jesus said, who can cast body and soul into hell (Matt 10:28).

What values undergird Jesus' teaching? Jesus told the rich young ruler to sell his possessions and give them to the poor if he wanted to be saved. The hierarchy of value that underlies Jesus' command does not pit the value of God against the value of the life of the rich young ruler (Luke 18:18–30). Nor does it pit the value of God against the rich young ruler's possessions. Hmm? Why not? Should not *that* contrast in value, the one between God and everything not-God, including ourselves, serve as the default operative value hierarchy animating believers' decisions touching potential sacrifice and repudiation required by the obedience of faith?

Does not the value hierarchy between God and everything not-God underlie and justify such praise and worship such as, "You alone Lord, are my all in all; You alone are worthy of praise"; "All I need is Jesus!"; "I know all about the doctrine and the theology. Just give me Jesus. That's good enough for me"? Well, yes, but more needs to be said. Yes, the triune God, the Lord, the creator and redeemer of all, is more valuable than all. He alone sits atop the hierarchy of value. But the Lord is not just more valuable—he is uniquely valuable, uniquely worthy of praise—indeed of all praise, because praise for any value outside of him is due to him because he made it and sustains it and promises to redeem and sustain it eternally.

But when we say "just give me Jesus" the "me" is pretty significant, is it not? When we, prompted by the Scriptures, long to see Christ as "all in all" (Colossians) we are neither imagining nor longing for our own or other believers' absence from that condition, are we?

The hierarchy of value legitimizing the Lord's call for the rich young ruler to sell his possessions and give the proceeds to the poor is not between God and the rich young ruler or God and his possessions. It is between the rich young ruler and his possessions. He, the rich young ruler, is more valuable than his possessions. Again, "what will it profit a man if he gains the whole world and forfeits his *life*"? Accurate cost/benefit analysis demands forfeiture of the less valuable possessions in order save the more valuable life.

And yet the disciples balked at Jesus' imperative for the young man to divest himself of his possessions even thought they had left home and family to follow him. "Then who can be saved?" they asked (Luke 18:26). Was it because they had not been rich when they forsook home and family? But Jesus' response to their anxious query sheds crucial light on the way hierarchies of value function within Holy Scripture. This function in turn illumines vital dimensions of biblical shalom yesterday, today, and forever.

Hierarchies of value teach us the order in which things of value should be sacrificed—we should sacrifice what is of comparatively lower value in order to preserve or gain what is of comparatively higher value. That's the assessment Jesus invited the rich young ruler to make. But note well that the hierarchy operative here is of good things, not evil things. The rich young ruler is not being asked to give up adultery in order to be saved. He is not asked to give up ill-gotten gains, say some property illegally or immorally obtained.

Now for a vital piece of the puzzle. It concerns the paradox that lies at the heart of Jesus' imperative to the rich young ruler, divine calls for sacrifice of good things throughout the Bible, and especially the call to "lose [one's] life" to all would-be followers. Here it is—obedient sacrifice secures the thing sacrificed! Clench fisted clinging to good things, even our very lives, threatens and eventually, inexorably ensures their loss. He who saves his life will lose it, but "whoever loses his life for my sake will find it" (Matt 10:39). By divine design, according to his good creation, here we confront the deepest paradox that shapes the reality of human life on this earth. We are taught to relinquish, to let go of, to sacrifice, in order to secure, in order to receive back, what we give up. The giving up, the loss of the thing or person or place or possession involved is real, but temporary.

We are used to this paradox when it comes to our lives. The paradox is stated clearly and bluntly by Jesus himself and has secured for itself a permanent place in the preaching of the church across time and geography. But the pattern holds where other, lesser valuable goods than our very lives are concerned as well. The pattern was profoundly, chillingly, demonstrated in the divinely prompted but ultimately aborted sacrifice of Isaac by Abraham. In that case the sacrifice, Isaac, was received back in fairly short order, but the limited time frame should not obscure the devastating content of the Lord's command to Abraham. Søren Kierkegaard rightly teaches us to weigh more heavily the pain and foreboding that must have attended Abraham's preparation of the knife and the fire, and the three-day journey of father and son, the prepared implements of sacrifice in tow, and the mountain of sacrifice starring them in the face.

What was Abraham meant to learn from this truly horrible episode? And given that Abraham is held up to us in the New Testament as the model of the faith that saves, what are we meant to learn? We rightly understand that saving faith is not mere belief. Martin Luther called this mere belief, historical faith. Historical faith believes that the word of God is true. Such faith is essential and good. But it cannot save. Another element is necessary for such faith to become saving faith. Calvin also commented on the sort of faith that cannot save. He said it "flits in the brain" but cannot save anyone.

Luther identified the necessary additional element needed to render faith saving. Trust. Saving faith trusts the word of God and in doing so trust the one who speaks that word. There can be no trust of God apart from trust in his word. Trust leans. Trust relies. Trust depends.

Given saving faith's character as trust, it behaves in certain ways that illumine how faith and sacrifice are related. Since true trust relies, it must also risk. Luther said that the man who says he believes a boat can safely transport him from one port to another may be sincere, and may be said to exhibit belief. But only the one who hazards his life by boarding the boat and taking the voyage exercises faith. The first man believes something about the boat. The second man actually trusts the boat.

The risk-taking element of saving faith, the "hazarding" dimension, belongs to the character of the sorts of sacrifice the Lord requires of his people so often throughout Scripture. Why is this so? One reason is that the giving up of something valuable and good to the Lord acknowledges that all that we have, including our own lives, is a gift from his hand, and still belongs to him. When the Lord requires the sacrifice of an unblemished lamb upon an altar or divestment by the rich young ruler or Isaac by the hand of Abraham, he only requires of us what was always and remains his.

But now the paradox—obedient relinquishment of whatever the Lord requires turns out to be the path to its recovery. Lose your life—to save it! This pattern of relinquishing as the path to recovery and enjoyment does not reveal Lord as, in the end or over time or even periodically, stingy with the good gifts prepared for his children, including the gift of their very lives.

The pattern serves the recovery of shalom. Remember, shalom's three dimensions are cumulative and relational. Thus, the third dimension sums up and supplements the first two—the relationship between human beings with each other before God in the home prepared for them. Every element of the relational dimensions of shalom is pure bestowed gift and potentially blessing. But these bestowed gifts, including life itself, cannot be enjoyed as blessings except insofar as they are received, embraced, acknowledged, and used as the gifts from the hand of the Lord that they are. To the extent that we, in forgetfulness or defiance of their true character, try to seize and cling to and use and enjoy the gifts as though they belong to us, the gifts, instead of bringing blessing, become curses.

When the Lord requires sacrifices, renunciations, relinquishments of good things, his ultimate goal is not their permanent loss but their eventual and abundant recovery and enjoyment. He means to ensure that his gifts become blessings and not curses upon his children. Remember, we are not speaking here of the divine call to repudiate sin or evil as such, but to relinquish something good that can become or has already become a curse. Yes, the element of divine possession is involved. The Lord does assert his ownership of Isaac and lordship over Abraham in the call of Abraham to sacrifice Isaac. But the goal is that both prove to be the blessings they are meant to be. The lives of Abraham and Isaac are divine gifts with the potential to become blessings both to each other and to the world. But for that blessing to flourish fully, Abraham must relinquish Isaac into the hand of the Lord and receive him back as the pure bestowed gift he always was.

Exactly the same theological substance, dynamics, and goals are at work between Jesus and the rich young ruler. His sin was not that he was rich. Not at all. Abraham was rich and that was not a problem. Just as the Lord does not require sacrifice of a child from anyone except Abraham, Jesus does not require utter divestment and distribution from anyone except the rich young ruler. The prerogative Jesus asserts in the life of the rich young ruler parallels the prerogative the Lord asserts in the life of Abraham.

The interaction between Peter and Jesus following the encounter with the rich young ruler reveals that the pattern of relinquishment and recovery was indeed at work in that encounter. "Who then can be saved?" Peter asked. "See, we have left our homes and followed you." Jesus responded, "Truly, I say to you, there is no one who has left house or wife or brothers or parents or children, for the sake of the kingdom of God, who will not receive many times more in this time, and in the age to come eternal life" (Luke 18:26–30). Matthew and Mark have Peter say "we have left everything" and has Jesus include "lands" in the catalogue of recoverable relinquished goods (Matt 19:23–30; Mark 10:29). Note Mark's report of Jesus's words to his disciples: "Truly, I say to you, there is no one who has left house or brothers or sisters or mother or father or children or lands, for my sake, who will not receive a hundredfold now in this time, houses and brothers and sisters and mothers and children and lands, with persecutions, and in the age to come eternal life" (Mark 10:29–30).

Clearly the pattern of sacrifice in the sense of relinquishment of goods as the path to their recovery is present. The goods in this case belong to shalom. They are major components of the divinely intended settlement of his people into communities and families in possession of private property.

These passages alternately attract and repel certain contemporary evangelical sensibilities who favor a predominantly anti-wealth reading of them. They love the giving up of wealth of course, though none are calling for divestment by others or embracing it for themselves. They are able to make something of the relinquishment of family ties. One way or another they manage to stomach the promise of the reaping in the next world, though some feel it necessary to spiritualize that recovery. But oh how unwelcome are the three little words "in this time" employed by Mark and Luke. Better to stay more spiritual with Matthew! There one gives up hearth and home and kin with no hope of recovery until the eschaton. No temptation to cling to this-worldly treasures in the between time east of Eden.

But the words just sit there staring at us. They just won't go away—"in this time"—the prospect that relinquishment of home and wealth for the sake of the gospel may result in multiplied reaping of the same in this life. Why such recoil from many evangelicals?

I believe a complex stew of concerns, aversions, and unconscious instincts account for the reflexive inner disturbance and embarrassment this passage evokes from many an evangelical breast. That stew includes biblical teachings deemed inimical to a straightforward reading of the words "in this time." Predispensational readings of biblical eschatology emphasize that this world is on a downward trajectory. Evil is increasing and so is the trouble and suffering evil leaves in its wake. Does not history reflect that this is so? Does not the experience of most people confirm the futility of resting hopes for good things, for shalom "in this time"? Did not Jesus warn his followers, "in the world you will have tribulation" (John 6:33)? Has not our Lord warned us, "[do] not lay up for yourselves treasures on earth, where moth and rust destroys and where thieves break in and steal" so that hopes for anything like shalomic flourishing must rest on the world to come (Matt 6:19)? Did not the apostle Paul speak plainly enough that we are joint heirs with Jesus Christ "provided we suffer with him" (Rom 8:17)? Human experience in this world is mainly "trouble," right? That's what Jesus said his disciples could expect.

But the title of the book claims a place for shalom "today," "in this time," as does Jesus—shalom yesterday in the garden, tomorrow in the new heaven and new earth with the new Jerusalem at its center, but also shalom today, in this time. How can this be? Because shalom never for one moment ceases to be the will of the creator for human beings. Redemption is redemption not merely of human beings, much less of merely disembodied souls, but of the proper home of human beings, the whole creation that longs for the revelation of the sons of God that signals its own redemption. Just as our so-called spiritual experience only approximates what it shall permanently enjoy in the next world, so our whole experience, embodied, physical, and material, retains only the prospect of such approximation—as when one offers the cup of water to the thirsty or cares for sick or befriends the lonely or the outcast or works hard to provide for dependents. When we seek to provide a proper home for others, we imitate our heavenly Father and may boldly pray for his help.

The trajectory of history does not alter the biblical teaching that shalom, in all three of its relational dimensions, has not been utterly lost to us "in this time." We've already seen this spectacularly demonstrated in the Lord's blessing of his people in the Old Testament. The character of shalom remains the same no matter how much or little of it is allowed to those who experience it. Like the faith as of a grain of mustard seed that moves mountains, shalom, beheld in however slight a glimpse, sampled in however brief and miniscule a taste, is still shalom. Shalom, enjoyed however imperfectly and impermanently, is still shalom. The disjunction between the shalom periodically enjoyed "in this time" and that promised perfect and permanent shalom is great indeed, but the disjunction is between points on a continuum of shalom, not disjunction between species. It seems significant that Luke's gospel has long been deemed by the historic church the gospel to the poor.

Should not God want us humans gone so that he can be all in all? If Jesus bids us come and die according to a hierarchy of value, does that fact not argue for our own annihilation? No, because, as we have seen, the sacrifice envisioned, the relinquishment involved, paradoxically secures the thing hazarded for the sake of Jesus Christ, the gospel, and the kingdom.

When Jesus Christ is all in all the gifts of creation do not fall away, they take their proper place in three dimensioned shalom. The instinct to treat whatever is lower than something else on the hierarchy of value as a mere rung to traverse and leave behind or as an actual threat to true spirituality as we ostensibly mature beyond the need for the benefits they deliver is not biblical. The hierarchy of value informs, even determines a kind of order of sacrifice-ability, not an order of permanent repudiation. Where something ranks on the value hierarchy reveals nothing about its essentiality within the divine creation and redemptive purposes.

7

Gathered and Scattered

O Jerusalem, Jerusalem, the city that kills the prophets and stones those who are sent to it! How often I would have gathered your children together as a hen gathers her brood under her wings, and you were not willing! (Luke 13:34)

Where two or three are gathered in my name, there am I among them. (Matt 18:30)

—JESUS THE WOULD-BE GATHERER

A FREQUENTLY UNRECOGNIZED FEATURE of shalom confronts us in ways that parallel our observations concerning sin and obedience. That feature is settlement. Settlement contrasts with unsettlement, and scattering. Both an overarching pattern of divine activity and an embedded and repeated repetition of that pattern encompasses the biblical storyline from Genesis to the maps. The pattern is this—settlement, scattering, gathering, and resettlement. Shalom is characterized fundamentally with settlement. Unsettlement and scattering belong to divine punishment. Settlement is blessing. Scattering and unsettlement is a curse. Redemption gathers and settles and promises one day to gather and settle the children of God once and for all.

Acknowledgement and embrace of the biblical doctrine of gathering and settlement faces special challenges. These challenges arise partly because we live in the time between the times which, just as it is characterized by sin, so it is characterized by unsettlement. Obsession over a state of existence promised to us for the future but denied to us now seems to invite that universally repudiated habit of some who are so heavenly minded as to be of no earthly good. Another challenge to proper discernment of shalomic settlement in the time between the times is that we are explicitly told that we are in reality, now, in our time, *not settled*. We are in fact pilgrims on the way, resident aliens, in the world but not of the world, citizens of a better home not made with human hands. So, yes, settlement there but not here, right? In fact, given that our home is not here but there, surely pursuit of shalom here is ruled out, right? Shalom here means laying up treasure on earth where moth and rust corrupt, *nicht wahr*? A third challenge to proper emphasis upon shalom here and now is that movement, pilgrimage, sojourning, even scattering, the opposite of shalomic settlement, play such essential and central roles in the divinely orchestrated redemptive drama recounted in the Bible and now playing out in our own lives in this world just as the book of Acts depicts, foretells, and teaches us to expect. A final and arguably most troubling and therefore potentially most potent challenge is that pursuit of shalomic settlement in this world repudiates and abandons the missionary mandate of the Great Commission of our Lord—a mandate at the heart of which lies that word spoke to Abraham at Ur now expressed with supreme authority to every disciple of the risen Lord—not gather, settle, and stay, but emphatically, *go*!

These are formidable challenges indeed. And they shall have to be met if my contention that shalom deserves an exalted place in Christian attention in this world is to prevail. I believe a combination of three powerful factors conspire to obscure the place shalomic settlement actually occupies in Holy Scripture. First is that we do live in the between time on this fallen planet with nothing but fallen sinners where, Jesus warned, we should expect trouble, not shalom. Second is that we are told explicitly that we are pilgrims on this earth, sojourners, resident aliens, citizens of another world. Third, advance of the gospel demands movement, not digging in, sinking roots, and resisting all pressures to dislodge us.

Settlement First, Last, and in Between

But rather than addressing directly and in sequence the formidable challenges already noted or confronting the three powerful factors that tend to shape current evangelical reflection on settlement, I want to approach the question from the opposite direction—as though reflexively "movement"-focused or "scattered"-friendly readings of Scripture are in the hot seat and must prove themselves, and not the reverse. We could read the biblical narrative with a hair-trigger alertness to every seemingly settlement-unfriendly passage that, when encountered, lets loose with an "Aha! See, I told you!" But let us do the opposite. Read the Bible from Genesis to Revelation poised to spot any and every passage conveying even the slightest pro-settlement sentiment. When we do this, I believe, the pervasive biblical teachings about movement, pilgrimage, sojourn, resident alien status, not laying up treasure in this world, and longing for arrival at our eternal home are not lost. But their true meaning, their purpose, is uncovered, a meaning only visible when seen from the perspective of and set in juxtaposition with the equally pervasive emphasis upon divine settlement of his people.

Such shalomic reading contends that unsettled states of being arise one way or another because of the fall of humanity into sin and that redemption, among other things, restores humanity to a settled state of being. Punishment for sin in Eden resulted in expulsion from Eden. Punishment meant the denial of the divinely intended blessing of settlement into the paradisaical garden home, expulsion from it into a less settled state—one in which resettlement was sought. Punishment for the wrongful attempted settlement at Babel was the scattering of the offenders. Rescue of Noah and his family meant their gathering and temporary settlement, such as it was, in the ark, preserving them for resettlement once the flood waters receded.

The blessing of Abraham included the promise to make from his seed a great nation to be settled into a promised land flowing with milk and honey. Punishment of the people of God bought unsettlement and bondage in Egypt. Redemption brought deliverance with the hope of return and settlement in the promised land. Punishment for sin entailed relegation to wanderings in the wilderness instead of the blessing of settlement.

Fulfilment of the promise to Abraham required conquest and settlement in the land. Punishment brought the unsettlement of Babylonian exile. Forgiveness promised resettlement in Zion. Defense of settlement as a fundamental feature of divine blessing according to the witness of the Old Testament is more straightforward than in the New. Before we make the case that settlement remains an essential feature of redemption and divine blessing in the New Testament, a word about creation and redemption.

Creation and Redemption

Recognition of the place of shalomic settlement requires discernment of the complex but biblically demonstrable relationship between creation and redemption. What is that relationship? Creation teaches us what God intended and intends for his children yesterday, today, and forever. Redemption is the response of the creator to the threat to divine creation and creation purposes. Redemption arises because of sin and seeks sin's defeat and the reversal of its consequences yesterday, today, and forever. From this perspective redemption serves creation, not the reverse. The goal of redemption is a new creation. Creation lasts forever. Redemption ends as an ongoing divine activity. It lives on as an essential feature of memory and thus informs worship in eternity, but redemption as an ongoing activity ends with its successful redemption and perfection of the fallen creation. Shalom, including settlement into a divinely prepared and maintained home, is the result and goal of creation.

Redemption, in order to achieve the rescue, restoration, and renewal necessary for the new creation—the renewed and perfected and never to be lost paradise—makes the consequences of sin serve the reversal and defeat of those consequences. Expulsion is a step on the path toward reentry. Scattering paradoxically leads to regathering and settlement.

Yet, given the fall and its consequences, ought the children of God acquiescence to unsettlement and resign themselves to a scattered, shalom-deprived existence? Surely we must not set our hearts on shalom, or at least this dimension, the third dimension of shalom, here and now. To do so would be futile and potentially idolatrous, right? We must wait and hope for the coming shalom but not pursue it and count on it now, correct? Well, yes and no. Augustine's insight into the possibilities vis-à-vis sin might help us grasp a proper view of the possibilities vis-à-vis shalomic settlement east of Eden.

Augustine warns us that, in our time, in the between time, in this city of Cain, *non posse non peccari*, it is not possible not to sin. Therefore what? Stop prizing, expecting, and pursuing obedience? I didn't think so. Our Lord's sovereign providential governance of this world sees to it that even human sin is made to serve his redemptive purposes and the defeat of sin and its consequences. Exhibit A—the death of Jesus. But we ourselves follow our Lord as the repeatedly repentant ones. We do not sin on purpose in order to provide an opportunity for the Lord to make it serve redemption against its sin character. That the Lord turned Joseph's brother's intent to harm into blessing does not encourage more intended harm.

No, permanent shalom in all three of its dimensions is not possible in this life. But shalom continues to belong to the blessing of the Lord here and now if only in glimpses and tastes, and are to be received as such. Love for others still must include pursuit of provision for their settlement and not their wandering and scattering. God's power to keep and sustain us apart from full and permanent shalom does not undermine the permanent status of shalomic settlement as the blessing of God here and now just as is empowerment for repentance. That sin can distort the quest for either does not alter the fundamental reality. Fixation on repentance can morph into self-deceptive forms of works-righteousness and self-righteousness. Fixation on shalomic settlement can morph into an insidious prosperity gospel focus. That good things can be turned to bad by us sinners does not and ought not lead to a baby-out-with-the-bathwater eschewal of what the creator made good.

New Testament Gathering and Settling?

Should not faithful reading of the Old Testament produce in Christians the expectation that shalomic settlement would be similarly affirmed in the New Testament? I think so. Affirmation of shalomic settlement is pervasive in the Old Testament. Consistently, shalomic settlement is identified as a constituent component of divine blessing. Should not the notion that with the coming of the Messiah this component of blessing must cease to animate the hearts of the faithful come as bit of a surprise if not a shock? And yet, such readings of the New Testament are not unusual and acceptance of not only the loss of shalomic settlement but the inappropriateness of the pursuit of shalomic settlement is sometimes encouraged.

Why do such notions gain credence? Because many teachings in the New Testament seem to encourage them. For a time at least, Jesus had nowhere to lay his head. Jesus said a time was coming when no single, central place of worship would be needed. Believers are taught that their citizenship is not in this world. They are taught that they are pilgrims and strangers, resident aliens in this life, sojourners and exiles on this earth. So, cased closed. Forget about shalomic settlement here and now! Not so fast.

These and other New Testament warnings and admonitions against expectation of any permanent or perfect enjoyment of shalomic settlement are indeed prevalent in the New Testament. They must be taken with full seriousness. But they stand side by side in the New Testament with equally clear and profound affirmations of shalomic settlement. These voices must be heard as well.

The millennia of human history still growing east of Eden is a history of the continued distortion and disfigurement of what God made. Forgetfulness of Eden allows for the normalizing, even the spiritual glamorizing of conditions consequent upon human rebellion. A rich lexicon of post-Edenic realism grows up within the very word of God itself: sojourner, pilgrim, exile. Gathering, settlement, peace, harmony—the primordial marks of shalom—give way to a new prevalence of movement and dynamism—scattering, wandering, divine commissioning not to stay but to go. The eternal Son of God, the Lord and savior of sinners, won't stay still either. No wonder they asked "from where did he come?" and "where is he going?" Indeed, he was on the move and signaled that more and necessary and salutary movement was to come—"I am going" and "It is good for you if I go" and "I will come again."

The necessity of movement east of Eden is undeniable. So is the loss of shalom. So is the necessity of a new lexicon of movement related to the lost paradise behind us and the promised homeland before us. But the contention of shalom is that we have afforded the new conditions and the new lexicon a place it does not deserve. Namely as signaling the replacement of shalomic settlement in God's original purposes in creation with acceptance of unsettlement as the new and to-be-accepted condition of life east of Eden. If perfect and permanent shalomic settlement is impossible in this world, what place ought such settlement play in Christian expectation and aspiration?

Elusiveness of Settlement

However attractive some ideal of stability and harmony appears, however enticing its allure, does it not always and everywhere allude our grasp? However deeply such visions touch our longings, are they not bound to disappoint? In the end, do not such longings mock us and then punish us for clinging to such doomed dreams? Recall those pathetic future-focused musings over barns bursting with bounty by a man with only a few hours of life left. "Do not lay up for yourselves treasures here on earth," didn't Jesus warn (Matt 6:19)?

Have not mature human beings, from time immemorial, learned the prudence of a wise and distinctive detachment of the heart and mind precisely from the most precious things this life has to offer both animate and inanimate? To food and land and houses, yes, but also a sad and tragic but all the more real detachment from friend and spouse and child and even from our own lives? He who would save his life will lose it.

Does not the central place God gives to sacrifice teach us that sober, truth-illumined wisdom refuses to cling to, to set its heart upon, anything in this world? Does not divine approval of Abraham's knife raised and poised for downward thrust into Isaac's chest teach this? Love for God clings to no other but him, does it not? Did not the apostle Paul understand this? He counted everything so much rubbish and dung in order to gain Christ! And did not Jesus Christ himself follow the path of detachment in order to save and to provide the model his disciples left in this world were to follow?

Saving love prompted the eternal Son to let go of rather than cling to the very prerogatives of deity, including his settlement within the Godhead, where he enjoyed a complete and perfect and holy life in community with the Father and the Spirit. How much quicker ought we to spit on the whole of this fallen, distorted, corrupt, corruptible, and corrupting world we inhabit? However perfect in beauty, however conducive to and nurturing of human flourishing and human love and human joy was Eden—does not wisdom now, on this side of the flaming sword, east of that "Paradise" hear with prudent clarity the second word of Milton's classic title—"Lost"?

There is a very powerful logic to this whole train of thought. It sinks its hooks into the psyches of Christians and the church periodically. Not just among a few folks fresh from sobering encounters with the Preacher of Ecclesiastes, but from serious attempts to hear and obey the voice of God breaking forth from the whole of his written word. When this happens, a predictable array of values find emphasis and articulation and certain practices pop up here and there. World-denying and creation-denying vows of chastity, poverty, and obedience emerge, eschewing as they do the now-doomed "worldly" values of sex and marriage and money and power and authority. Separation from "the world" into cloistered enclaves ostensibly more conducive to prayer and sanctification commences. If maintenance of such enclaves requires subsidy from "filthy lucre" gained by others still mired in the mud out there "in the world," reflection on the contradiction of that embarrassing entanglement is kept to a minimum.

Yet world-denying and settlement-elusive rhetoric punctuates Holy Scripture. But what does it really mean? Where is it meant to lead? When it is taken with the greatest uncontextualized seriousness, it leads to Jonestown. When less so, it leads to monastic communities that pray and prize hermetic withdrawal of individuals within the community.

Scattering for the Sake of Settlement

But does the pattern of New Testament teaching really call for a radical break with the Old Testament affirmation of shalomic settlement as the blessing of God in this world? I do not think so. The episodic enjoyment of shalomic settlement in the Old Testament always fell short of Eden before the fall and of the promised shalom of the New Jerusalem. So shall such episodic enjoyment in the New Testament or, more particularly, in the post-Pentecost era in which we live. But shalomic settlement remains an essential component of divine blessing—an appropriate object of Christian expectation, aspiration, and petition in this world even as such expectation, aspiration, and petition open us sinners up to special temptations to sin. But such temptation attends every proper human aspiration, even those deemed purely "spiritual." Identification of how an otherwise healthy and divinely intended enjoyment of blessing has and may go wrong does not answer the question of how believers should view such enjoyment given the dangers.

One key verse that for some suggests abandonment of settlement as a fit concern for either God or his people is Jesus' announcement to the woman at the well that a day is coming in which neither at Jerusalem nor on Mount Gerizim shall God be worshiped (John 4:21). Rather, where two or three are gathered, there shall Jesus be in their midst and there shall they worship God in spirit and in truth. I shall revisit this important passage, but for now, shalom notes that what is envisioned is not a scattered, place-disinterested, settlement-disinterested state of affairs. Rather, Jesus is forecasting the fulfilment of his promise to build his church, which involves divine gathering of believers in specific places and settling them there.

Pentecost inaugurates a new epoch in the saga of divine redemption. The fulfillment of the promise to Abraham that his seed would become a blessing to the nations shall now enter a new and spectacular stage as the gospel is preached to all the nations. The fulfilment of this promise post-Pentecost, far from leaving shalomic settlement behind as a once necessary but now superseded and obsolete feature of divine blessing, shall see the multiplication of shalomic settlement revolving around the international planting of churches.

It is the contention of shalom that various sorts of movement common in the Bible are made necessary, one way or another, because of the consequences of the fall—either as punishment for sin or as necessary to the redemption that leads to eventual resettlement. This should be kept in mind when we assess their significance. Some of these movement words refer concretely to divine punishment—"expulsion," "scattering," "wandering," and "exile." "Exile" is included because of the movement to the place of exile. The Lord uses these shalomic-disruptive punishments for the redemptive good of his people. But this redemptive use in no way signals the replacement of the blessing of shalomic settlement with the blessing of unshalomic unsettlement. The Lord's word to the Babylonian exiles, as we have seen, is a case in point. In his mercy, the Lord does not call for the exiles to habituate themselves to unsettlement. Rather, the Lord calls them to, albeit imperfect and impermanent, provisional settlement in Babylon for the time being, and to hope for return to their true homeland in Zion. In the midst of shalom-deprived living, partial, impermanent, episodic divine affording of shalom constitutes the blessing of the Lord in the between time. And it has to be noted that the Lord through Jeremiah called for his people to repent and to set their hearts upon resettlement in the promised land.

Unsettlement in Pursuit of Settlement

Beside unsettlement resulting from punishment, voluntary sacrifice of shalom proves necessary to the redeeming work of the creator. The great act of such sacrifice occurred in the emptying (*kenosis*) departure of the second person of the Holy Trinity from the shalomic bliss of the Godhead in order to save sinners (Philippians 2). Sent from the Father, the Son sojourned and tabernacle among us through the incarnation, coming down from heaven to this earth and then up to the cross and down again into the depths of the earth to the place of the dead and then up again to earth and up again to the right hand of the Father with the promise to return for those given to him by his Father. Not much enjoyment of shalomic settlement being enjoyed here!

To what end did this sacrifice of shalom aim? Does Jesus' journey into the far country of this fallen earth establish unshalomic unsettlement as the newly sanctified ideal for the people of God? No. Jesus' refusal to cling to the prerogatives of his deity and "stay home" in the Godhead arises because our God is not only creator but redeemer from all eternity. The fall of humanity into sin together with its consequence, including the loss of shalom, shall not have the last word upon God's creation. God's creation and the original purposes for it shall be fulfilled, including shalomic settlement. That fulfillment requires redemption. That redemption requires temporary sacrifice and loss of intra-trinitarian shalom, if you will, in order to restore the shalom for which God's children were made. So redemption requires temporary loss of shalom by the Son of God (and the Father and Spirit too in distinct ways) in order to secure shalom forever. Thus, Jesus promises to go and prepare a place for those given to him by the Father and to return so that they can be together in that place.

In the time between the times, the followers of Jesus also are called to and have the privilege, the happy duty, to hazard temporarily their own partial and impermanent enjoyment of shalomic settlement for the sake of the shalomic settlement of others. Love does not tear down homes or treat the shalomic-nurturing dimensions of community with nonchalance, but blesses and encourages these as foretastes of the coming shalom.

Pilgrimage to a holy site also accords with our between time as time of lost and longed-for shalomic settlement. It confesses that one is no longer and not yet properly settled. The whole of existence in the between time is one of profound unsettlement. Therefore, I have to, I need to move. I need to go. Particularly shalom-affirming pilgrimages are those that journey to places where Yahweh made his name to dwell once upon a time—where he gathered and settled his people. In doing so the Lord's provisional and partial bestowal and maintenance of shalom upon his people both reminds them of that shalom from which they have fallen and been expelled and to which they are headed. Such provisional and partial enjoyments of shalom serve as foretastes and down payments of the shalom to come. And they justify and inform relative pursuit of shalom in the between time, especially shalom for others.

On its own, Eden suggests certain features of human existence as blessings, as "good" and "very good," as the divinely intended aim. But the full meaning of Eden needs help, as every part of Bible does, from the rest of the canon of Holy Scripture. With that help certain absences, silences in the Eden narrative, become significant. In Eden we find no hint of scattering or of pilgrimage; no need to travel; no suggestion of any need for another world, for citizenship in another world; no alienation of Adam and Eve from the creator prior to the fall, but also none from the physical world or from their own bodies.

8

The Place of Place

There is a town in north Ontario
With dream comfort memory to spare,
And in my mind
I still need a place to go.
All my changes were there.

—Neil Young, "Helpless"

Here I raise mine Ebeneezer;
Hither by Thy help I'm come
And I hope by Thy good pleasure,
Safely to arrive at home.

—Robert Robertson, "Come, Thou Fount
of Every Blessing"

"Istanbul." I admit it. I enjoy fielding the oft-posed questions that allow me to answer with such an exotic and even fearsome place name, "Istanbul." The uniquely carved wooden chess set purchased there, always on display in my office, prompts the vanity-serving inquiries, "Where did you get this?" "Where did this come from?" "Istanbul. Did you see *Skyfall*? I picked it up in that market. The one into which James Bond and his pursuer plunged their motorcycles in that crazy chase scene."

In cheekier moods, I sometimes skip "Istanbul" and instead reach back to that ancient and storied city's earlier name, the one it boasted before it fell to the Turks and to Islam, "Constantinople." When completely out of control, and more time on my hands I respond with the even more ancient "Byzantium."

The articulation of certain place names often prompts immediate involuntary reflection. Such names may stir deep emotion, even wonder. Kilimanjaro. Siam. Gettysburg. Selma. The Lorrain Motel. Dallas. Dachau.

From whence comes this power of place names to produce, spontaneously, so much in so many of our minds and hearts? Is universal susceptibility to the evocative power of place names and of the places themselves a good thing? What does this power suggest about the significance of place as such? Does God himself attach significance to certain locations on this earth?

That such might be the case is by no means obvious for many. Did not Jesus himself rebuff such a notion in his response to the woman at the well? She broached the controversy over the proper place for worship then agitating the already fixed but still heated division between Samaritans and Jews—on this mountain *or* in Jerusalem? Neither! For Jesus said to her, "Woman, believe me, the hour is coming when neither on this mountain nor in Jerusalem will you worship the father" (John 4:21).

So do particular places matter in particular ways or not? Or did particular places matter in Old Testament times but not since Jesus announced the coming destruction of the temple? If so, why? Can we know anything about God's thoughts and will regarding such matters?

Place Pertinence

Two place-interested trends in church development, missional strategy and the pursuit of church growth on both sides of the Atlantic invite fresh consideration of the place of place in the ways of God with us his children and with the church Jesus promised to build. The two trends I have in mind are the increased pursuit of (1) church mergers and (2) the establishment and development of multi-site congregations. Both trends confront, willingly or not, acute consideration of place, of geographic and strategic location.

Might Holy Scripture offer teaching, guidance, and theological insight to congregations considering or already far advanced down one or both of these newly preferred paths to the advance of the gospel? The answer is a resounding "yes." In fact, when we press the question of the place of place upon Holy Scripture we discover a deep, ancient, divinely articulated and enacted "theology of place."

This amazing, biblically imbedded theology impinges not just upon the narrower concerns attending church mergers and multi-site development, but upon the whole of God's activity from the creation of this world to the consummation of his redeeming purposes beyond this world. The inescapable place-consciousness stirred up by church merger and multi-site needs the guidance this theology provides. This embedded, largely unnoticed (and thus neglected) teaching sheds immediately relevant and urgently needed light upon the particular concerns raised where church merger and multi-site are concerned.

But the theology of place itself bears upon the whole of our existence before God. God is and means to be known, acknowledged, and worshiped as the maker, the sustainer—and sometimes the destroyer, but nevertheless!—the Lord of every place. In the following chapters I shall uncover and explore this theology of place embedded throughout the Bible, highlight its particular relevance to church merger and multi-site, and demonstrate key dimensions of its relevance for the church, and indeed for the whole human race.

Nowhere Else but Here

But first, back to Istanbul. The chase scene from the blockbuster movie *Skyfall* provides recent and widely shared connection to that ancient and still geopolitically important city. But my own treasured connection to Istanbul—a deeper, more substantive and emotional bond—centers on an ancient house of worship that stands a few blocks northeast of the famed Grand Bazzar. Haggia Sophia (Saint Sophia) constituted the center of orthodox Christianity for some nine hundred years. Saint Chrysostom (which means Golden Mouth) and Gregory Nazianzus, known and honored simply as the Theologian, both preached in the even more ancient church that once stood on the present site of Haggia Sophia.

There in Constantinople itself and not so far away, just down the road a piece really, at Nicea, at Chalcedon, and at Ephesus, what have proven to be the most enduring and essential components of Christian confession were hammered out by the ancient church—the doctrines of the Trinity and of the person of Jesus Christ. Here, within the wider sphere of Haggia Sophia—not elsewhere, but here—the church learned that to defend the teaching of God's Holy Word meant defending (against the teaching of Arius) the only true God who inspired that Word as one God in three persons and not otherwise. Precisely here, in present-day western Turkey, not elsewhere, the historic church satisfied and convinced itself that Bible-honoring witness to the incarnate Son of God confesses Jesus Christ as fully divine and fully human, one person in two natures, and not otherwise.

But does it really matter *where* these undeniably beneficent and momentous watersheds of consensual Christian confession emerged? These
things occurred, in God's providence, not just anywhere, but precisely here.
Should this matter to us today? If so how? Or how not?

No longer accommodating a living congregation, Saint Sophia now
functions as a museum and a pilgrimage destination for Christian believers. It stands witness to a bygone era during which the only true God once
"made his name to dwell" in a space now dominated, indeed overwhelmed,
by Islam.

This ancient church faces, just a couple thousand feet to its west, another house of worship, this one vibrating with activity, prayer, and worship galore—the also famous Blue Mosque. These days the many cash-flush
Western pilgrims emerging from the nave of Haggia Sophia tend to gaze at
but not visit this living center of Muslim vitality.

Instead they invest their limited time in Istanbul in careful, meticulous inspection of the now quiescent but formerly living site of historically
momentous, enduringly defining Christian development. They wistfully
ponder their own connection to and stake in that distant era as they examine the significantly eroded, partially dilapidated relic of a once profoundly
influential flourishing but now lost Christian community. A Christian community then situated at the center of global power in the only city on earth
where one can actually stroll from Europe to Asia and back again without
leaving town.

Haggia Sophia recalls, as no other still extant visible monument can,
events and decisions that six centuries later have proven to be vital to faithful Christian hearing of and confessing of the word of God. It also stands as
a concrete reminder and proof that on land now hostile to the name of Jesus
Christ, this same Jesus, the Son, once visibly wielded the "all power" given to
him by God the Father by doing exactly what he promise he would, namely,
build his church (Matt 28:18; 16:18).

But all this can be and surely should be studied and appreciated without traversing continents and seas, right? And yet the pilgrims continue to
stream forth not only to Haggia Sophia but to thousands of precisely and
less precisely locatable patches of ground around the globe; to the ruins of
churches throughout the world, and to carefully housed objects displayed
under buffed up glass that bear witness in their own unique ways to a history of the keeping of that promise made by the Messiah of Israel to future
apostle Peter at Caesarea Philippi some twenty centuries ago—"upon this
rock I shall build my church" (Matt 16:18).

Why do they come? Why must they come? They want to think and they
want to feel. They want to consider and they want to ponder. They want to

remember and be prompted to remember what they could not have experienced. As we shall see, this sort of intentional vicarious remembering is deeply biblical, expected by God, and beneficial to his people of all ages.

They want to recall the memories and experiences of others because, as followers of Jesus Christ, they have a stake in those memories too; they are connected to those "rememberers," they are made by God in Jesus Christ inheritors of a history they did not live through and so also of the cherished remembering of that history.

Some arrive at such remarkable sites as Haggia Sophia with fairly low or cloudy, inchoate expectations and then, unprompted, spontaneously, involuntarily, no one more surprised than they—when standing at the center of the complex itself, they think and feel something special, something anchored very specifically and very concretely, to this place and no other.

Why? Is this sort of pilgrimage justified? To be encouraged? Are we confronting here an alternately shallow and possibly dangerous sentimentalism, nostalgia, or borderline idolatry in relation to land or place or space? These and other dangers do indeed threaten the ones who wallow in reveries of historical memory and imagination. Such dangers arise not from any intrinsic perniciousness of the practice itself, but from the same source that mars and distorts so many other things and practices God made good—our sin.

Sex, marriage, parenthood, the consumption of food, buying and selling, and the list goes on. Oh what a mess we have made of these originally good institutions and relationships and activities. Yet God, in his refusal to let us his children sink into the abyss we have deserved, instead rescues, sanctifies, and redeems and gives us new life so that there, in marriage and child-rearing and buying and selling, the good God intended is again witnessed and enjoyed. So also with the ubiquitous biblical call for remembering and celebrating the place of place.

Bible Places Galore

Is it not striking how difficult, awkward, even impossible it is to speak much at all about the revelation of God in Holy Scripture, of the history of divine activity, of his words and deeds or of Jesus Christ himself without peppering our sentences with a plethora of place names? Eden, Babel, Ur, Canaan, Jericho, Carmel, Babylon, Galilee.

The word of God lays upon the people of God the happy duty of concerning themselves with a veritable conveyor belt of places made (permanently?) significant and precious by God. That significance is established first by the divine creation, then by God's preservation of all that he has made, then by the integral role God gives to place in the execution of his plan for his people. God then, as we shall see, requires the remembering of places that witnessed his speaking and acting. He expects this remembrance to provide content to the praises of his people and even language identifying the promised future.

God through his word thrusts before us, into our hearing and our imaginations, place names and geographical references ranging from rivers and mountains to wadis and wells. He directs the eyes of our hearts not only backward and downward as though place only mattered then and there and even perhaps here and now, but also forward—"I go to prepare a *place* for you" (John 14:2); "Then I saw a new heaven and a new earth" (Rev 21:1); "I saw the Holy City, the New Jerusalem coming down out of heaven" (Rev 21:2).

Why the pervasive and necessary orientation toward place and the remembering of place and the anticipation of place? Has not God seen to it? Were not God the Father and Son and the Holy Spirit in cahoots to render God's people virtually mute regarding himself, the history of his creative and redemptive activity, their own praise to him and hope in his promises without continuous reference to place?

But even if all this is so, what relevance does the undisputable historic significance of Jerusalem or even of Haggia Sophia have for the declining church on the corner considering merger with another congregation across town? Or what connection could the wistful recalling of Jesus' baptism in the river Jordon possibly have with the faded Polaroid snapshot of my own baptism at a now-dissolved church in South Carolina?

We shall have to establish whatever legitimate answers Holy Scripture makes possible to these and many other questions. But for now we forecast a bit of what we shall discover. The power and legitimacy of place is grounded in the deep, permanent significance God gives to all that he has made, including this earth (even though it is set for destruction!). God's creation of the earth, his sustaining of it, his providential use of it, his ownership of it, its goodness, his visiting of it, his tabernacling within it, his placing of us his creatures made in his image within it, his making of his name to dwell within it, his making it bear witness to himself, his glorifying of himself within it and so hallowing it—all make clear that place is important to God.

"Thy kingdom come, thy will be done on *earth* as it is in heaven," Jesus prompts us to pray (Matt 6:10). He promises, praise the Lord, to make us new and to give us new bodies. But he also promises to make "all things new," to make a new heaven and a new earth, a new Jerusalem.

God the Son takes on human flesh and comes to this earth and then goes to make a "place" for us. Yes, place matters to God and so must matter to us as well.

Just Stuff?

The biblical case for the importance God himself gives to place is very strong. As passage after passage has God and his people treating place with great importance, the message "place matters" becomes irresistible and overwhelming. We shall see also that the theological importance of place that emerges proves to be very deep, rich, and beautiful. Place turns out to contribute a major dimension of salvation, the Christian life here and now, and of the promised eternal life beyond this world.

Nevertheless, real resistance to the sort of value place deserves will have to be addressed. Opposition to acknowledgement of the importance of place, or of anything physical or material tends to pride itself as assuming a more "spiritual" posture toward this life than those who treasure and cling to this world. Those who take such a stance point to many passages in the Bible as support for their views.

The supposedly wrongheaded notion of the Babylonian exiles provides a case in point. The exiles (wrongly?) found it impossible at times to worship God in foreign land (Psalm 137). Did not the prophet Jeremiah warn against misplaced trust in the Jerusalem temple as a refuge of safety against the enemies of Israel (Jer 7:4)? What about Jesus' seemingly dismissive "You worship what you do not know" in response to the Samaritan woman's assumption that there must be a proper *place* to worship, either in Jerusalem (as the Jews insisted) or on Mount Gerizim (as she and her Samaritan community believed)? Instead, Jesus insisted, "the hour is coming, and is now here, when the true worshipers will worship the Father in spirit and truth . . . God is spirit, and those who worship him must worship in spirit and truth" (John 4:16–24).

Could there be a more definitive repudiation of the significance of place than this? The truckloads of place-valuing passages from the Old Testament notwithstanding, do not Jesus' words trump and supersede them? Does not this pointed response to the woman at the well belong to that same pattern of authoritative teaching of Jesus we confront in the Sermon of the Mount—"you have heard it said, but I say" (Matt 5:21–48)? Do we not confront in Jesus Christ the new Moses promised to the first Moses and proclaimed by the first Moses on the threshold of the promised land (Deut 18:15–20), the one greater than Moses and worthy of more glory? An

Old Testament promise fulfilled in Jesus Christ and explicitly proclaimed in the New Testament (Heb 3:1–3)? And must we not acknowledge in Jesus's words the signaling of a shift from a previous age in which place occupied a significant place in God's saving activity to a new world under a new covenant in which that significance is seen now as obsolete and, if clung to, spiritually dangerous?

Did not Martin Luther capture faithfully and beautifully Jesus' own teaching in his famous hymn—"let goods and kindred go, this mortal life also, the body they may kill, his truth abideth still" ("A Mighty Fortress Is Our God")? Was not the faith of Abraham made paradigmatic of the saving faith called for by the gospel of Jesus Christ? And was not Abraham's first demonstration of such faith his leaving, as the bidding of the Lord, his family and his land (Gen 12:1)?

How often do believers, fresh from the loss of houses or lands in the wake of fire or flood, articulate their faith with words such as, "It's just stuff. All that matters is that we are alive. We were spared." Do not such words strike us as in keeping with the teaching of the Bible and so as unassailable? Part of my task will be, not to repudiate all that such words express—such words are more reductive than simply wrong. But I shall attempt to demonstrate that words such as "just stuff" cannot, not by a long shot, comprehend the full teaching of Holy Scripture regarding the value God himself gives to place.

What we shall find is that, in the transition from Old Testament times to our time, God's *use* of place, of land—his territorial purposes, if you will—have indeed moved into a new but previously prophesied phase. But we shall also see that the value God places upon place and the purposes of God for place in his redeeming plans have not fundamentally changed. Indeed they have, if anything, only intensified and heightened. Any notion of a new devaluing of place, trumped as a new freedom *from* place to freedom *for* an ostensibly more spiritual posture toward this world and our own lives, will not stand biblical scrutiny. That this is so illumines not only church merger and multi-site but our lives in this world and hopes for the word to come.

In light of the central and permanent inclusion of place throughout the Scriptures, shalom calls for believing the Bible from Genesis to the maps. Shalom calls for reflection upon the need to provide maps as a necessary service to serious students of the word of God. Charts tracing historical periods and watershed turning points demarcating those periods need maps to depict more fully what the creator was up to all along. Does not the Bible rub our faces in places and the importance of places? Might not the tendency to minimize or even deny the significance of place arise from that old heretical Marcionite hatred of creation and the creator?

9

Shalom and Prosperity

> . . . the devil, the prince of the impious city, when he stirs up
> his own vessels against the city of God that sojourns in this
> world, is permitted to do her no harm. For without doubt the
> divine providence procures for her both consolation through
> prosperity, that she may not be broken by adversity, and trial
> through adversity, that she may not be corrupted by prosperity;
> and thus each is tempered by the other, as we recognize in the
> Psalms that voice which arises from no other cause, "Accord-
> ing to the multitude of my griefs in my heart. Thy consolations
> have delighted my soul." (Ps 94:19) Hence also is the saying of
> the apostle, "Rejoicing in hope, patient in tribulation."
>
> —AUGUSTINE OF HIPPO[1]

WHOEVER WISHES TO TRASH money as the enemy of the good must
love the Bible. What a treasure trove of warning and besmirching it provides. The anti-money talk reaches a crescendo of sorts in Paul's letter to
Timothy: ". . . they who will be rich fall into temptation and a snare, and
into many foolish and hurtful lusts, which drown men in destruction and
perdition. For the love of money is the root of all evil" (1 Tim 6:10, KJV).
Yes, we know that the King James Version gets the translation wrong. It
should read "the love of money is *a* root of *all kinds of evils*" (ESV; emphasis mine). But still, the indictment against money is sweeping, even
unique in all of Scripture, is it not?

---

1. Augustine, *Selected Writings*, 273.

Paul goes on to the set the love of money squarely against all things spiritual, all things good:

> For the love of money is a root of all kinds of evil. It is through this craving that some have wandered away from faith and pierced themselves with many pangs.
>
> But as for you, O man of God, flee these things. Pursue righteousness, godliness, faith, steadfast, gentleness. Fight the good fight of faith. Take hold of the eternal life to which you were called and about which you made a good confession in the presence of many witness. (1 Tim 6:10-12)

Did not our Lord himself set money in direct opposition to God? Did he not juxtapose them in mutually exclusive opposition and set before all would-be children of God an either/or choice? "No servant can serve two masters, for either he will hate the one and love the other, or he will be devoted to the one and despise the other. You cannot serve God and money" (Luke 16:13).

Money is treated as a unique threat to discipleship, a threat ranked with idolatry, but idolatry of a special sort. The right relationship with God we were created to enjoy, the first and primary and foundational dimension of shalom, faces a matchless foe among many foes in the temptation to the love of money, in the desire to be rich.

The whole Bible, including our Lord's own words, elevate the love of money to its own exclusive pedestal of perniciousness and malignancy. Money's lure is uniquely powerful, its attraction especially insidious, its temptation distinctively destructive. But why? Because of the scope and the substance of money's promises. Wealth promises so much, and what it promises encroaches on such a wide swath of exclusively divine turf. Money promises to deliver what only the Lord provides: health, security, comfort, peace—shalom. By doing so, money stokes our deepest desires. Jonathan Edwards spoke the truth—"to have a man's desire is to have the man."

Money wins from us much more than mere desire or unusual commitment—it wins us. We fall in love with money. Love produces commitment and loyalty. Nothing rules a person, nothing wins obedience and service like love. Powerful and cruel dictators who depend upon fear cannot compete with love where obedience and service is concerned. When we fall in love, we ponder how to please and obtain the beloved all day long and then we dream of the beloved in the night. She's our first thought upon waking, our last preoccupation when we drift into sleep, and she lingers in our unconscious with our permission.

Like no other potential source of human goods, money seems to hold out to us every or almost every component of deepest human longing and craving: power, health, security, provision of all necessities and luxuries. And unlike the protection and provision some wealthy and powerful person might promise, money seems to guarantee independence as well. We then can become patrons and creditors to others if we wish. What do we long for that money does not hold out to us? We serve money because it promises to serve us. And not only us but the ones we love as well. Goodbye student loans. Goodbye the fears of lacking resources for whatever health care might one day be needed. Goodbye worry. Hello safety, security, provision, and peace. Hello shalom! Goodbye obscurity and anonymity as well. Hello fame. Money will etch my name or anyone's name I want into limestone or marble (my choice) on a divinity school hall where full professors with tenure shall hold forth against the prosperity gospel! Surely that scenario will exonerate me, make up for my having slipped up, let may guard down, and let myself become rich.

But of course, neither our Lord nor the Scriptures condemn money or wealth as such. Quite the opposite. From Genesis to Revelation, money, wealth, and much that money and wealth provides is treated as the blessing of God. Though perhaps uniquely susceptible to idolatrous devotion that may wreck faith itself, the children of God are taught that money and wealth are to be recognized, acknowledged, and treated as the blessing of God—"You shall remember the Lord your God, for it is he who gives you the power to get wealth" (Deut 8:18). This is a foundational word of Holy Scripture about money and wealth and about much that can be purchased and secured (in a qualified sense of course) with wealth—that the Lord, in his wisdom and mercy, gives power for his children to obtain it. The first word, the foundational word, the more comprehensively controlling interpretive word about the gifts and blessings of the creator of heaven and earth is not negative but positive.

If we wish to know what marriage is, we start not with its destruction, distortion, abuse, misuse, or its abandonment, but with its original character and purpose in creation. The primordial state of a thing governs interpretation of its fallen condition, not the reverse. The better, more beautiful, and more true vow is to remain faithful to one's spouse, not to refrain from adultery. "Love, honor, and cherish till death do us part" is better than "I promise not to be bad." But, since in our rebellion against our creator, we have fallen into pernicious use of all the blessings, much ink is spilled in Scripture identifying, defining, examining, and denouncing pernicious use of the blessings in all their rich variety.

Affirmation of the primordial blessing status of the power to get wealth is striking in the Deuteronomy 8 passage. Paul sets the love of money against everything good and wholesome and appropriate to the life of a disciple in 1 Timothy 6. But Moses sets the divinely bestowed power to obtain wealth squarely into the heart of the relationship between God and his people. "You shall remember the Lord your God, for it is he who gives you the power to get wealth, that he may confirm his covenant that he swore to your fathers, as it is this day." What? How can this be? God gives his people the power to get wealth in order to confirm his covenant with them that he swore to their fathers? How much more of "spiritual" value and function can a blessing from the Lord attain than this?

Surely the New Testament must "interpret" the Old Testament here. And when it does, that gloss on the passage before us must surely result in a veritable negation of its straightforward meaning. It must. Otherwise how shall we refute and combat the prosperity gospel? How shall we not be compelled to admit that they were right all along?

We do believe in progressive revelation after all. Perhaps Moses could not see the dangers of greed and the idolatrous potential of the love of money as we do now. Oh, but yes he did. Moses not only knew well such dangers, he warned explicitly against them:

> Take care lest you forget the Lord your God by not keeping his commandments and his rules and his statutes, which I command you today, lest when you have eaten and are full and have built good houses and live in them, and when your herds and flocks multiply and your silver and gold is multiplied and all that you have is multiplied, then your heart be lifted up, and you forget the Lord your God, who brought you out of the land of Egypt . . . Beware lest you say in your heart, my power and the might of my hand have gotten me this wealth. (Deut 8:17)

If the danger of having wealth and gaining the benefits prosperity brings is so obvious and so great, why is the Lord himself providing the occasion for it? Why is the Lord mixed up with the bestowal of prosperity upon his chosen ones? Does the Lord himself lead his children into temptation and then have them pray that he not do so in the model prayer Jesus himself would eventually put into their mouths? Rather than settle his people into conditions of prosperity and plenty galore, why not establish them into a "simple lifestyle" instead?

Simple Lifestyle?

The short answer is that it has not pleased our God to establish anything like some ostensibly simple lifestyle as the standard optimum condition for spiritual flourishing. We are warned against seeking to become rich. But clearly it does please our Lord, according to his wisdom and timing, to bless his children with great material prosperity, when he so wills.

The simple lifestyle popular in much evangelical talk is without biblical warrant. It is an ill-defined, strained, self-serving, and (unwittingly?) hypocritical notion. Driven by the guilt of folks like myself who are, by any reasonable global and historic measure, rich, but having no plans to divest themselves of their possessions and distribute them to the poor, a theology of the simple lifestyle seems to provide a haven of acceptable middle-class living. It construes an acceptable simple lifestyle by identifying "the rich" somewhere a bit above where we are or hope to reach. But few who enjoy anything warranting the label "simple lifestyle" belong to noisiest anti-prosperity evangelical prophets.

People all over the world call us "rich Americans" and they are exactly right. I encountered this truism when I lived in Southeast Asia, where depths of poverty unknown in the United States prevail. But you can find similar schooling from better experts than yourself on the difference between poverty and riches just as well on any inhabited continent that strikes your fancy on the next mission trip. If you own a home, have car or two, heating and air conditioning, and especially if you have a dental plan—you are rich.

And oh! That hurts! Its intolerable! Something must be done. Something short of divestment. Something short of vow-taking and cloister-inhabiting. Something that lets me blast away at the heresy of health and wealth theology but somehow lets me keep exactly those benefits capitalism affords that separate me from the world's poor. Something that frees me up to furrow brow, pound pulpit, and protrude neck veins in full fulmination against the prosperity gospel without parting with much that matters to me.

It may well be that guilt plays a role in evangelical approaches to the subject of prosperity. But surely the proper hermeneutical course must not be to ram the whole Bible through the hermeneutical keyhole of Proverbs 30:8 as if it were a new *regula fidei*—"give me neither poverty nor riches."

Paul rejoiced that the Philippian church had demonstrated concern for his physical and material needs. But he feared that his rejoicing would be interpreted as a not-so-subtle complaint that he was in need at all. Not so, insisted Paul, for "I have learned in whatever situation I am to be content" (Phil 4:10–11). Leading up to the bombshell that the love of money is a root of all kinds of evil, Paul warns those who imagine "that godliness is a means of gain." Such folk are in fact deluded. The truth is that "godliness with contentment is great gain, for we brought nothing into the world, and we cannot take anything out of the world. But if we have food and clothing, with these we will be content" (1 Tim 6:5–8). Hmm. Food and clothing. Nothing more. Is this the material benchmark of the simple lifestyle commended to us? No shelter? Is this what the petition of Proverbs 30:8 entails and portends?

Must the "simple lifestyle" preachers give up air conditioning, mascara, fancy fountain pens, and especially those quintessential badges of affluence—dental insurance plans? Ought Pope Francis's little dashing Fiat be surrendered? Should Francis refuse costly preventative medical care, costly nutritional and vitamin supplements, and exorbitantly expensive surgeries needed to save his life? Should he renounce, for himself at least, all the truly luxurious benefits of modern health care unimaginable apart from the unprecedented wealth created by the capitalism he so reflexively indicts? I think that he should. Not because he names the name of Christ, but because he has taken the vow of poverty. Even better would be to renounce the vow and enjoy the benefits with a clear conscience.

Not far from my suburban domicile, homeowners' association fees of an upscale subdivision employ a bagpiper to roam the hills surrounding the stately homes of this cushy enclave. Of an evening, the Scottishly girded and skirted piper makes his rounds in haunting and majestic serenade. Should opposition to the prosperity gospel reach levels of intensity that would forbid residence in such a community and refuse tithes from an offender? The frequency and fervency of affluent evangelical decrying of the prosperity gospel suggests that some believe so.

But, ultimately, the common rhetoric against the prosperity gospel, though technically correct, tends to fall flat. It fails to hear the witness of the whole of Scripture and, for that reason, fails to faze Bible-thumping purveyors of the prosperity gospel or those who follow them. And it falls flat for keen assessors because the decriers themselves are rich. It falls flat because even if the theology of simple lifestyle was biblically defensible, and it is not, it would need prophets who practice what they preach rather than the physicians needing to heal themselves to render the rhetoric even potentially credible.

One problem is that the exaggerated, selective, and blind-spot-nurtured anti-money and anti-wealth talk issues disproportionately from rich Christians who do not know that they are rich at a time in history during which the Lord has seen fit to make more Christians rich than ever before. Never has the need for guidance on how to be rich been more urgent. The prosperity gospel highlights that need. But the anti-prosperity crowd has little too offer. It enjoys, clings to, and wants for its children and, I suppose, for the impoverished, the American Dream while all the while denying that this is so. It feels compelled to decry and foment against the American Dream and against America itself as, to borrow an apt phrase from John Calvin, a veritable "factory of idols." But Calvin understood that the idol factory lies within not outside of us sinners. We make idols of whatever lies to hand.

Shalom in the Earthly City?

Jesus' parable about the man and his barns illumines biblical teaching about wealth very well. It simultaneously gets wealth, since it is a blessing of God, off the hook, while exposing the human sin that stupidly and unnecessarily converts the Lord's blessing into a curse. When one brother asked Jesus to tell his other brother to "divide the inheritance" with him, Jesus said:

> "Take care, and be on your guard against all covetousness, for one's life does not consist in the abundance of his possessions." And he told them a parable, saying, "The land of a rich man produced plentifully, and he thought to himself, "What shall I do, for I have nowhere to store my crops?" And he said, "I will do this: I will tear down my barns and build larger ones, and there I will store all my grain and my goods. And I will say to my soul, 'Soul, you have ample goods laid up for many years; relax, eat, drink, be merry.' But God said to him, 'Fool! This night your soul is required of you and the things you have prepared, whose will they be?' So is the one who lays up treasure for himself and is not rich toward God." (Luke 12:15–21)

The sin of the man with the barns was not his prosperity. The clue to his sin lies in the little conversation he had with himself. There he forgot one of our Lord's favorite topics—our mortality. The Lord who speaks in the Bible provided plenteous preparation for the emergence of the great existentialists, whether atheist or Christian, with his obsession over death—how death hangs over the heads of us sinners like a Damocles sword. No sooner has he promised future blessings than he rubs our mortality in our faces, reminding us that our very lives are about as secure as grass or vapor—they fly away with the abandon of dandelion spores.

The man with the barns thought money could provide what only the creator and sustainer of this universe ever has or ever will—life itself and everything good about life. And since death stalks every living creature this side of the eschaton; since death's death, though forecast and certain, awaits the arrival of the next world, must not expectation of shalomic blessings await too? Mortality alone exposes the presumption that money can deliver what it sometimes seems to promise to individuals. But presumption of a secured and happy future for kingdoms and nations are equally foolhardy.

The shock of Alaric the Visigoth's sack of Rome in AD 410 helped to give birth to the first great systematic theological work to appear in the history of the church—Augustine's *The City of God*. From the standpoint of shalom it is both fascinating and affirming that this foundational Christian meditation centers around the comprehensive purposes of God in creation for his human creatures, just as does shalom. For Augustine, Christian hope in its fullest sense had to encompass the full scope of the creator's purposes in creation and the promises of redemption. That full scope finds its most apt expression not through examination of individual piety, or family worship, or missionary endeavor, but in the habitation of a city.

The sack of Rome, with its implications for the whole life of the inhabited world, invited the deepest and most comprehensive Christian reflection because it threatened to reverberate through every dimension of human life, through all three relational dimensions of shalom. That first dimension, between the children of God and God, though distinguishable from the second and third dimensions of shalom, is not separable from them because the scope of creation purposes of the God to whom we are related always encompasses the other two dimensions—that between the children of God themselves before their shared heavenly father, and their relationship with each other before God in the home he made for them. None of the three shalomic relational dimensions can reach fulfillment apart from the fulfillment of every other dimension.

It may be the case that God is at work day by day working inside of those who are his to advance them from one degree of glory to another (2 Cor 3:18). Thanks be to God! But it is not the case that this divine work, or any other ostensibly "spiritual" work touching the relationship of sinners to God and their relationship to each other before God can reach fulfillment in this life apart from the fulfillment of that third dimension of shalom—the one touching place, home, habitation, *civitas*.

From this vantagepoint, the shock Alaric's exploits delivered, not only to the many unbelieving citizens of the Roman empire, but to the great *Doctor Gratiae* in Hippo was appropriate. It would not have been more Christianly, more biblically "spiritual" to blow if off with a "who cares about Rome," we have another city that has foundations. Rather, the more appropriate response runs something like this—"Here we are in exile, sojourners through this vale of tears. Let us not set our hearts on the happiness afforded here but upon the happiness promised there. In the meantime, though, buoyed by the sure hope of the coming city, let us settled down as the sojourners we are, pray for the welfare of this Babylon, and receive with thanksgiving what shalomic blessings come from the hand of the builder of our coming homeland."

The trouble Jesus forecast for his followers in this world reverberates through every dimension of shalom, distorting and diminishing enjoyment of shalom, including enjoyment of that comprehensive flourishing of the whole of life with and before God in the home meant for us. That trouble reaches to and reverberates through kingly powers and governments and nations. And this matters because our God's purposes and claims extend to Caesars' realm. This earthly city, Augustine warns:

> . . . is often divided against itself by litigations, wars, quarrels and such victories as are either life-destroying or short-lived. For each part of it that arms itself against another part of it seeks to triumph over the nations though itself in bondage to vice. If, when it has conquered, it is inflated with pride, its victory is life-destroying; but if it turns its thoughts upon the common casualties of our mortal condition, and is rather anxious concerning the disasters that may befall it than elated with the successes already achieved, this victory, though of a higher kind, is still only short-lived; for it cannot abidingly rule over those whom it has victoriously subjugated.[2]

For Augustine, one crucial deficit of any shalomic enjoyment afforded in the earthly city is that it cannot last. But such deficiency does not turn a shalomic good into an evil or a matter of indifference.

> But the things which the [victorious] city desires cannot justly be said to be evil, for it is itself, in its own kind, better than all other human good. For it desires earthly peace for the sake of enjoying earthly goods, and it makes war in order to attain this peace; since, if it has conquered, and there remains no one to resist it, it enjoys a peace which it had not while there were opposing parties who contested for the enjoyment of those things which were too small to satisfy both. This peace is purchased by toilsome wars; . . . Now when victory remains with the party which has the juster cause, who hesitates to congratulate the victor, and style it a desirable peace? These things, then, are good things, and without doubt the gifts of God.[3]

---

2. Augustine, *City of God*, 481–82.
3. Augustine, *City of God*, 481–82.

Augustine boldly and unashamedly treats as a blessing of God the securing and enjoying through war "earthly peace for the sake of enjoying earthly goods." Oh how politically incorrect such an assertion falls, especially upon the early twenty-first-century ears of affluent evangelical elites busy simultaneously securing dental and retirement plans for themselves, decrying the prosperity gospel, and accusing those who vote for candidates they believe will pursue prosperity-friendly policies as captive to greed.

How can Augustine bring such unabashed affirmation of material prosperity and remain faithful to the many biblical warnings against money and the love of money? Augustine himself issued these warnings freely in his preaching. So what gives? What gives is that Augustine understood that the wrong use of a good, in this case money or general prosperity secured by the juster of two nations at war, does not transform the good into an evil. The sort of three-dimensioned shalomic blessing described in the book of Deuteronomy of the promised land or available to the people of God in Babylon, though temporary and falling far short of the coming shalom, remains the blessing of God to be received and enjoyed as such.

But, like all other divine blessings enjoyable in this world, we sinners prove able to receive them wrongly and to make bad use of them. For this reason, bestowal of such divine blessing not only opens opportunity for tastes and glimpses of the coming shalom, but also temptation to sin and even idolatry. Augustine again,

> These things, then, are good things, and without doubt the gifts of God. But if [recipients of such gifts] neglect the better things of the heavenly city, which are secured by eternal victory and peace never-ending, and so inordinately covet these present good things that they believe them to be the only desirable things, or love them better than those things which are believed to be better—if this be so, then it is necessary that misery follow and ever increase.[4]

However much warrant we think we find in the Bible or in the musings of great theologians for enjoyment of material blessings in this world, does not Jesus' own worldly poverty trump such prosperity-friendly readings of Holy Scripture? But was Jesus poor?

---

4. Augustine, *City of God*, 481–82.

Jesus Not Poor?

Wait! Of course he was! The Bible explicitly tells us so, does it not? And did not the apostle Paul love to slam the rich? Paul writes to the church at Corinth, a church populated by some rich folk, some of whom drew the apostle's rebuke for flaunting their wealth during observances of the Lord's Supper (1 Cor 11). Paul urges well-to-do believers to contribute out of their abundance to the poor believers in Jerusalem. He notes that the poor churches of Macedonia have already contributed out of their "extreme poverty" for the relief of their needy spiritual siblings back in Zion. Paul is prepared to wield the weapon of shame to extract participation in the collection of funds for the poor if he must.

Then, the apostle deploys perhaps the most compelling argument at his disposal to justify his plea, the *imitatio Christi* argument—"For you know the grace of our Lord Jesus Christ, that though he was rich, yet for your sake he became poor, so that you by his poverty might become rich" (1 Cor 8:9). This reasoning serves well the longstanding recognition of charity as a constitutive Christian virtue. But for affluent evangelicals bent on advance of a simple lifestyle, Paul's language here seems a bit problematic, to say the least.

Attempts to "spiritualize" such a text in order to strip it of its material implications strains credulity. As in the Old Testament, spiritual significance encompasses the whole of life, material and non-material. "Be warmed and filled" suffices not at all—only parting with cold hard cash satisfies the spiritual demand of charity, the happy duty of all believers, and especially of those the Lord has made rich.

So Jesus, who was rich, "became poor," and not only according to the apostle Paul. To would-be followers, Jesus provided this personal tidbit for their reflection: "Foxes have holes, and birds have nests, but the Son of Man has nowhere to lay his head" (Luke 9:58). Homeless? Was Jesus homeless? If so, that's pretty poor in my book and yours as well I imagine.

Words translated "poor" figure prominently throughout the Bible. The church has forever recognized the importance of poverty as a subject addressed repeatedly by the Lord God. But what meaning is conveyed to us when we read the word poor in the Bible? What do we mean by "the poor" when we speak of actual people? Most college students in America, even the sons and daughters of relatively affluent parents, live below the poverty line. Are they "the poor"?[5]

5. For what follows see Sowell, "Life at the Bottom," and also https://www.youtube.com/watch?v=oS-O6WDalug.

Also, many college graduates living together with other low-earning graduates and who will not be poor within five to seven years also live below the poverty line. Are they "the poor"?

What about single-mother-headed households living below the poverty line who eat three or more times a day, have a car and a mobile phone, a big television, and live in heated and air-conditioned apartments—are they poor? How do they compare, materially speaking, to the poor in Southeast Asia or the poor of whom Jesus spoke in his own day? What about the one billion who live on less than a dollar a day mainly in Asia and Sub-Saharan Africa? Okay, those folks are poor, no questions asked. But what definitionally elastic terms—poverty and the poor. And what an expansive semantic range the designation "the poor" comprises. Do affluent Christians holstering ready-to-draw hair-trigger denunciation against the prosperity gospel think such distinctions matter? Do they ponder them? Or is it enough to denounce the prosperity gospel and call for charitable generosity by Christians? Is Christian reflection about poverty exhausted once this denunciation and that call have issued forth? Ought Christian concern for the poor extend to consideration of how those in true material poverty might be actually delivered from poverty and join the ranks of charitable givers to the poor?

One complication of interpreting the words "poor" and "poverty" is the vast range of material conditions to which they frequently applied. Another is the variety people and material conditions and prospects for the future that may fit into one of these sorts of poverty and how long such folks tend to occupy that economic status. Most in America do not stay long in any sort of poverty.[6] Even the comparatively less poor of Americans rarely stay poor for much of their lives. Yet when those who have never been and never expect to be poor use the words "the poor" as in "God favors the poor" or "we should help the poor," they seem to be indicating a more or less permanent class of people, not an everchanging demographic. How helpful, how wise, how instructive are musings about the poor and poverty likely to be from such an ill-informed knowledge base?

The middle class is a far more stable category than "the poor" in America and in the West generally. Both "the poor" and "the rich" see far more turnover. The measure of poverty and thus those who are counted as "poor" for governmental purposes is itself arbitrary. The words "poor" and "poverty" have become bandied-about terms incapable of communicating much that is definite and even less that is meaningful in relation to New Testament

6. Sowell, "Life at the Bottom."

terminology. Contemporary usage mainly serves purposes related to the speaker's agenda rather than to convey any definite or shared meaning.

If the semantic range of the category designated by "poverty" or "the poor" is significantly wide in our day, and our own sloppy throwing about of the terms belie that diversity and range, how accurate is our reading of these words in the Bible and how might we possibly relate ancient meanings to contemporary usages? What meaning is conveyed to us when we encounter these words in Holy Scripture? What meaning is conveyed when we use these terms when we lead a small group Bible study or preach a sermon? It has become a fixture of evangelical political correctness that Jesus was born into and raised in poverty. Is this true? Was Jesus poor? And if so, for how long? And how poor for how long?

John Schneider and Martin Hengel, among others, contend that Jesus was born into and raised within a socioeconomic condition quite different from anything we think of as poverty now or was thought of as poverty then. If they are correct, that would seem to be a significant fact because it would mean that when Jesus spoke about "the poor" he was speaking about people other than himself and his immediate family. Justo Gonzales has demonstrated that Palestine in the first century was host to many who must be deemed "poor" by almost any reasonable historic or global standard.[7] But Jesus, Schneider and Hengel insist, belonged to none of these impover-ished groups; not to the homeless beggars, nor to other street beggars who had been orphaned at a young age and depended almost completely upon various intermittent sources of charitable aid. Nor did Jesus belong to the "working poor" of his day, comprised of day laborers and slaves. Nor did Jesus suffer in poverty among the *am haaretz*, "the people of the land," a peasant class mercilessly exploited by the many classes of property owners and lenders upon whom they depended.[8]

Nor, says Schneider, did Jesus belong to any of the upper classes, to the rich. Instead, Jesus was, contends Schneider, allowing for the impossibility of a simple transfer of contemporary economic categories to first-century Palestine, middle class for his time and place. If Jesus' "adopted father" Jo-seph was a *tekton* (traditionally translated "carpenter"), then he was born into a first-century middle-class subculture. And if Jesus himself was, as would have been usual, apprentice to Joseph and then a *tekton* himself, then he was himself middle class, at least until he entered upon his public min-istry, having set his face toward Jerusalem, and now "having nowhere to lay his head." The word *tekton* quite often designated not a carpenter working

---

7. Gonzales, *Faith and Wealth*, 72–75.

8. Schneider, *Good of Affluence*, 122–24.

with wood but a builder working in masonry with stone. Wood? Stone? Either way, first-century Palestine expert Martin Hengel argues, those skilled in such building were not poor:

> We should note first that Jesus himself did not come from the proletariat of day-laborers and landless tenants, but from the middle class of Galilee, the skilled workers. Like his father, he was an artisan, a *tekton*, a Greek word which means mason, carpenter, cartwright and joiner all rolled up into one (Mark 6:3).[9]

Furthermore, Joseph and Jesus' working years occurred during the progress of major building projects launched by King Herod in and around Galilee. As *tektons*, Joseph and Jesus, unless they were particularly incompetent *tektons*, likely provided an upwardly mobile middle-class lifestyle to their extended family.[10]

So was Jesus poor? Perhaps. But only for a while. For say three-ish years at the most. And if Jesus was genuinely "poor" during the three-ish years of his public ministry, he took on this poverty voluntarily not in order to glamorize either poverty or a simple lifestyle, but as an embrace of the full suffering that our sins deserved on the way to the epitome of suffering on the cross. And why did he do this? Again, not in order to glamorize the suffering of poverty, but in order to doom and eventually to kill all suffering, including the end of suffering, death itself. That is why he did not laugh or rejoice either when his friend Lazarus died or when he himself was about to die. In the first instance he wept and in the second he let loose with the cry of dereliction.

Suffering and death are not being "redeemed" in the sense of being transformed from an evil consequence of the fall into either a temporal or an eternal good on a par with love, joy, kindness, or divinely bestowed prosperity. Rather suffering generally, including the suffering of poverty and death, is made, against their fundamental character, to cooperate in its own demise. It is forced by sovereign grace to facilitate its situation into the crosshairs of the redeeming purposes of the creator where it shall be taken down once and for all. In the wonderful title of J. I. Packer's classic book, in the cross of Jesus, toward which he advanced full throttle from the inauguration of his public ministry, we see *The Death of Death in the Death of Jesus*. Yes, a relative counting of it all joy when trials and persecution come to believers in this life is made possible by the suffering and death of Jesus. But only because the grave could not hold him and thus cannot hold those

9. Hengel, *Poverty and Riches*, 26–27.

10. See Batey, *Jesus and the Forgotten City*; and Stambaugh and Balch, *Social World of the First Christians*, 92–94.

who are "found in him" not having a righteousness of their own. Lop off the end of the story in which suffering of all kinds, including poverty and death, is gone forever and no joy in trial and persecution remains.

Families of Jesus' class, like the middle classes of many historical eras, including ours, would not have been especially secure in their socio-economic rank. An injury or two to the skilled breadwinners could have smacked them down into poverty in a flash. But, again, like many middle class of our own day, they would have had much for which to be thankful in a material sense. And they would have been dependent upon expenditures by "consumers!" among "the rich" for their unpoor middle-class lifestyles, for which gratitude and praise to God was their happy duty. Do we even think of Jesus as having had a lifestyle? Yet he did. And he apparently had nothing to be ashamed of on that score. How dare he not have been poor! Yet, he was not.

Do we need Jesus to have been poor? Vow-of-poverty ascetics would seem to. But an informed understanding of Jesus' actual material circumstances seem to undercut the foundation of the two-level obedience that developed within Roman Catholicism on this score.

A full millennium before Martin Luther learned that experience, and especially suffering, makes a theologian, barbarians at the very gates of Rome schooled the bishop of Hippo. On August 24 in the year AD 410, Alaric and his Visigoths sacked the Eternal City, exposing the fragile precipice upon which any and all imagined citadels of human strength teeter this side of the eschaton. With the sack of Rome an experience-mediated education of Augustine commenced. As with Babel, the creator, sustainer, and judge of the whole earth snickers at the pretentious plans dreamed up by earthly monarchs, even imperial caesars (Psalm 2). Augustine's education continued and intensified over the twenty years he had left on this earth. A bit more time here would not likely have occasioned a reversal in his views. Within forty-five years Rome would fall.

So why get ourselves all wound up about some comprehensive, three-dimensioned, land-friendly, this-world shalom if the prospects for enjoyment of such blessings is so limited? Ought we not seek our teachers and prophets among the Christ-against-culture crowd H. Richard Niebuhr described for us a few decades ago? Do not Anabaptist or Amish pessimism about and withdrawal from this world offer more apt models of waiting and watching and bearing up in this valley of the shadow of death? Have not various millenarian doomsayers that spring up periodically and withdraw from society and wait for the end comprehended with more sober accuracy the real situation we all face? What about the seemingly irresistible attraction of the poor and outcast believers of every age toward the next world?

Are not they the Christians who really "get it"? Do not even rich Christians approximate such despairing of this world when, inevitably, their material resources fail to stop this world suffering from invading their lives? And they have so much farther to fall when Alaric knocks on their door!

The answer is that, in fact, the Christ-against-culture traditions do sound perennially relevant warnings against unduly optimistic views of what's possible in our between time. Where believers are few in number, are shut out of the corridors of governmental power and are unable to exert much or any cultural influence, the separatists and retreatists can often offer needed insights the church can use in such circumstances. They can sometimes salvage a little marginalized and threatened but still Christian culture and witness as a flickering wick amidst the strong winds of marginalization or even persecution from the wider culture and the political realm. Indeed, the separatists of old and the moderately retreatist voices in our own day do offer biblically informed insights and potential models for Christian faithfulness in the face of hostile social and political realities.[11]

But, however temporary, fragile, or incomplete the prospects for the material dimensions of shalom in this life, they remain divine blessings to be recognized as such. And, demonstrably, they remain matters of concern for our Lord who demonstrated his messiahship, not by making people sick but by healing them. And where James needed to warn and admonish those who imagined "be warmed and filled" an adequate response to those in need (James 2:16), and enjoyment of shalomic prosperity remained a possibility for the apostle Paul who "knew how to abound" (Phil 4:12).

In Holy Scripture we are confronted with the God who forbids his children from making their own material prosperity a priority but also from nonchalance regarding the prosperity of others. The biblical call for charitable generosity by the children of God toward the poor is the ancient consensual inheritance of the global church. But should Christian concern for the poor and Christian response to poverty include more than charitable generosity? Is it enough to settle for periodic and intermittent mitigation of the sufferings poverty visits upon its victims? Ought not the prospect of deliverance from poverty animate the desires of not-poor Christians upon the poverty stricken of their day?

More Than Generosity

This statement affirmed by the Gospel Coalition articulates much that shalom does while at the same time displaying a limitation that so often attends

---

11. See for example Dreher, *Benedict Option*.

evangelical statements addressing economic matters, a limitation shalom seeks to overcome:

> God created both soul and body, and the resurrection of Jesus shows that he is going to redeem both the spiritual and the material. Therefore, God is concerned not only for the salvation of souls but also for the relief of the poverty, hunger, and injustice. The gospel opens our eyes to the fact that all our wealth (even wealth for which we worked hard) is ultimately an unmerited gift from God. Therefore, the person who does not generously give away his or her wealth to others is not merely lacking in compassion, but is unjust. . . . The gospel replaces superiority toward the poor with mercy and compassion . . . Indifference to the poor and disadvantaged means there has not been a true grasp of our salvation by sheer grace.[12]

Shalom affirms every word of this statement. But is there something more that could be included, that should be included? Let us set beside this statement on Christian stewardship and generosity another one venture capitalist T. J. Rodgers (Cypress Semiconductor) shared with Dinesh D'Souza during a harrowing spin in Rodger's shiny new BMW:

> I keep hearing feed the poor, clothe the hungry, give shelter to those who don't have it. The bozos who say this don't recognize that capitalism and technology have done more to feed and clothe and shelter and heal people than all the charity and church programs in history. So they preach about it and we are the ones doing it.[13]

This from the same T. J. Rodgers who in 1996 blasted nun Sister Doris of the Sisters of St. Francis of Philadelphia, whose letter to Rodgers made him aware that the policy of her religious order, whose retirement portfolio included investments in Cypress, is "to withhold authority to vote for nominees of a Board of Directors that does not include women and minorities." Rodger's response, published in the *Wall Street Journal*, included, among many pointed chastisings of Sister Doris, the call for her to "get down off her moral high horse."[14]

Wow! What an awful person T. J. Rodgers must be! Surely Christians need not listen to this fellow on his own high horse trashing, of all people, the Sisters of St. Francis of Philadelphia. Whose next, Billy Graham? Martin

---

12. Quoted in Graybill, ed., *Stewardship Study Bible*, 635.

13. Quoted in D'Souza, *Virtue of Prosperity*, 124.

14. Rodgers, "Cypress CEO Responds."

Luther King Jr.? Jesus!? But what he says should grab the attention of Christians for one of the same reasons the statement by the Gospel Coalition should—because it addresses the plight of the poor. What the two statements share is concern for the plight of the poor. But the Gospel Coalition statement includes another concern completely absent from Rodger's retorts, namely, the focus on the necessity of individual generosity.

It should be no surprise that the church down through the ages has spoken with extraordinary clarity and consensus on this matter, because the Scriptures speak so consistently and emphatically—the triune God, who acts with amazing undeserved generosity towards us sinners, calls for his children to act with generosity towards others, especially towards those who are poor. The Gospel Coalition statement marshals its confidence in this biblical emphasis to buttress its strong insistence that followers of Jesus Christ must be generous with the material means at their disposal. If they do not, they show themselves blind to the conditions of their own salvation and unjust towards those for whom God is concerned and who would use them as instruments of his mercy on their behalf. Christian consensus about this line of interpretation across the centuries, across geography, and across traditions, rivals that of the doctrine of the trinity and of the person of Jesus Christ as fully human and fully divine.

Rodgers does not speak of generosity at all, neither God's nor man's. But he does speak pointedly and powerfully of a concern articulated in the Gospel Coalition statement. This concern also finds significant focus throughout the Bible. It is, to use the wording of the TGC statement, God's concern "for the *relief* of the poverty, hunger, and injustice." And though Rodgers does not speak of it, his words do impinge directly on TGC's insistence that "Indifference to the poor and disadvantaged means there has not been a true grasp of our salvation by sheer grace."

God's revealed concern for the plight of the poor fits like a hand in a glove with the ancient Christian call for individual and even corporate church and denominational charity toward the poor. But woe unto us if we miss a distinguishable concern embedded in the argumentation that reaches its crescendo in the unassailable mandate that Christians should be generous—namely that the poor *be helped*, that the poor move from being poor to not being poor. Would it be okay if the some of the formerly poor joined the cozy club of affluent Christians who are now charged themselves with the happy duty to help the poor out of their abundance?

Is anything known about how that might happen? Might the vaunted Christian "concern for the poor" clear a little space in its collective psyche to explore whether there exists any known and fantastically effective means for the lifting of hundreds of millions of people over multiple generations from poverty? What if the simplest answer to this question is "capitalism and free markets"? If that is the shortest answer, might Christians rejoice in the answer as a blessing from God for more than five minutes? Or must they transition with lighting speed to grieved hearts and minds over consumerism and greed, as though greed needed capitalism to flourish. And consumerism. What a badge of deeply felt Christian consternation that has become. And how do we make ourselves feel better? We read Wendell Berry. Or at least I do. And we feel partially cleansed because, even while I dirtied myself with a laptop computer, at least I could envision and approve of Wendell somewhere hacking away at his manual typewriter.

This relative, single-A-ball holiness-by-proxy mirrors the equally wrongheaded credit Roman Catholics give themselves—the two-tiered Christian obedience through which vow-less substandard disciples give themselves a little pat on the back for admiring and subsidizing the vow-takers cloistered in monastery and convent.

The truth Rodger's pointed words confront us with is that the main means by which human beings end up "not poor" has less to do with the generosity of other human beings than other factors. TGC acknowledges this in its strong recognition that even if we work hard for what we earn, the ultimate source for the fruit of our labors is the hand of a generous God. The Lord gives you the power to get wealth" (Deuteronomy 8).

Note that, historically, the means God uses to materially bless his people, to deliver them from poverty and into shalom-like prosperity, vary greatly and are by no means morally pristine. Cyrus. Pharaoh. Divinely empowered defeat of and deliverance from enemies. Yet the shalom achieved is not seen as thereby tainted. Indeed, God is please to display his sovereign power to hit straight with crooked sticks, using not only morally fallen human beings but even his enemies to achieve his desired end of shalom. And now the most spectacularly effective means to deliverance from poverty ever known flourishes in remarkable ways before our eyes—capitalism and free markets, the beneficiaries of which are you and I.

If you believe that the socialist policies advanced by a candidate would, if implemented, lead to significant increase in the number and percentage of people in poverty and so deprive them of shalom, ought that to be weighed along with other factors when Christians prepare to vote? How could it not weigh fairly heavily if seeing the poor helped must be a priority of believers because it is a priority of the Lord they served? Or is the relief of the poor or even deliverance from poverty only or mainly important because it provides the opportunity for "non-poor" believers to display generosity?

Shalomic Prosperity and the Prosperity Gospel

From the canon of Holy Scripture we can fill up two columns of material about wealth and material prosperity generally, one negative and one positive. Faithfulness to the biblical witness on this score calls for careful and serious reflection in order to do justice to both columns. In the negative column we are warned that money is a root of all kinds of evil. We are repeatedly admonished not to set our hearts on wealth and its promises. We must not take refuge for our souls in the fragile and fleeting delights material prosperity may provide. Only our God can truly serve as such a refuge. Only he can deliver on promises wealth seems to make to our hearts and minds. We are warned not to serve money. The temptation to do so is strong because money seems capable of delivering what Scripture insists only the creator and sustainer of the universe can—life, security, comfort, and happiness. We are also admonished not to be anxious about how we shall obtain the necessities of life that money can buy—food, clothing, and shelter. Not because these things do not matter or that they are not blessings of God, but precisely because they do matter, are blessings of God, and thus he promises to supply them.

This last item, "be not anxious," straddles the negative and positive columns. On the one hand it affirms material prosperity as the blessing of God to be acknowledged, counted on, received, and enjoyed from his merciful hand. On the other hand, the "be not anxious" insists that the focus, the aspiration, the longing, and seeking of the disciple must not rest upon material prosperity. Not only is the desire to be rich a danger and snare of the devil but even anxiety concerning basic bodily needs are enemies to true piety and display both a lack of trust in the Lord and disordered desire. The pursuit of the disciple must be for the kingdom of God, not mere physical or material flourishing.

Yet the "be not anxious" of the Sermon on the Mount does, along with the many passages we have identified throughout the canon of Holy Scripture, identify material goods as divine blessings. We are to seek the one who blesses, not these blessings. Yet we are to seek the one who so blesses knowing that he does bestow such blessings. And when such blessing are bestowed upon us or others, we are not to despise them, but to thank the giver of them, praise him, and enjoy the blessings as the gifts they are. We are to handle such blessings as good stewards, using what comes our way for the good of others, not just of ourselves, and with generosity toward those in need.

The rise of the prosperity gospel has rightly provoked prophetic denunciation from many evangelicals, especially from the affluent west and most prominently from affluent evangelicals in the United States of America. These evangelicals are the beneficiaries of the wealthiest nation in the history of the world by far. Yet they are not ascetics. They are not vow-takers. They are not divesting themselves of their wealth, nor are they calling upon others to do so. They are keeping their dental plans and 401Ks and 403Bs and doing what they can to help their children and grandchildren do the same. Is this okay? Is there hypocrisy here or some colossal blind spot that would benefit from some illumination?

Why such boldness and fervor against the prosperity gospel among affluent evangelicals? Perhaps the first answer to this question is that these evangelicals are serious students of the Bible and the Bible is squarely on their side. The Bible does not teach that our God's will is for his children to be always healthy and always rich in the world. Indeed disciples are warned that trouble, suffering, and persecution shall prove mainstays of Christian existence in this world.

Nor does our Lord count the enjoyment of health and wealth a mark of faithfulness among his children. So, given the Scripture's hostility toward the prosperity gospel and the spread of the prosperity gospel around the world, surely responsible evangelical defense of the gospel must include just the sort of prophetic repudiation we are seeing.

But the contention of shalom is that much current evangelical push-back against the prosperity gospel, though nurtured by faithful reading of Holy Scripture, will prove ineffective against the prosperity preachers and those who cling to their pernicious teachings. It cannot, and in fact should not prove effective, as long as it feeds itself upon only one stream of biblical teaching about health and wealth—the negative stream. And that is what it does. It pits its anti-prosperity and anti-health fixated trove of scriptures against the blatantly heretical promises of the prosperity preachers. But it fails to engage the vast trove of pro-health, pro-prosperity passages the prosperity preachers seize upon.

The more robust, the needed prophetic push-back against the prosperity gospel, must take their own preferred trove of scriptures away from them. The prosperity gospel preachers must be denied the haven they imagine these passages afford them. Accomplishment of this goal will require more that shouting "cross, cross!" and "suffering, suffering!" It requires taking with full seriousness that the goal of the cross is to end suffering, that believers must work to mitigate the suffering of others in this world, and that the Lord still is pleased according to his wisdom and timing, to bless materially and to heal and provide the means of healing to his children in this world. No prophetic denunciation of the prosperity gospel that cannot be as positive about health and wealth as the Bible is deserves its ineffectiveness in the face of what is in fact false teaching. We must step up our game by taking these pro-heath-and-wealth passages with due seriousness.

The battle here is not between Bible believers and Bible ignorers. Both sides are waving Bibles in the faces of their auditors and both sides have a heap of scriptures seemingly friendly to their deepest convictions. It is not enough for the anti-prosperity prophets to repeat over and over its own pet passages decrying the dangers of fixation upon money and health. We must stake our claim upon the health-and-wealth-friendly passages, which, as we have seen, are many. Those who follow the prosperity preachers read their Bibles, and that is a good thing. Evangelicals should make a bee line to their favorite passages and demonstrate that these do not support the prosperity gospel they have embraced.

But what they do support is a far more positive understanding of physical health and material prosperity as divine blessings than many affluent evangelicals are willing to admit and to celebrate openly. The irony is that these evangelicals are among the most affluent people who have ever drawn breath on planet earth. And they do not show signs of serious abandonment of the affluent capitalist society of which they are the beneficiaries. Even when they head to the third world to live as missionaries, as I and my family did, they are happy to receive support from the filthy lucre flowing from the proceeds of the affluent back in America to underwrite their ministries abroad.

Why this ironic and possibly blind hypocrisy? Let's speculate. Even if we fail to account for the irony, the failure to engage the pro-health and pro-wealth passages remains. It needs correction even if no one can quite nail down its causes. One possibility is that these evangelicals do not realize they are affluent. They may lack sufficient knowledge of the material conditions in which most people globally, historically, have lived and of those living on earth right now to recognize that by any reasonable standard, they are rich. So that's one possibility.

Another is that, being affluent, they, we, know firsthand the limits of wealth to provide what those who aspire to its acquisition believe it can deliver. America, like no other nation in history, is in a position to warn of the limitations of wealth to satisfy the human soul, because more folks here than anywhere else can say—"We sought it and got it, or were born to it, enjoyed it, and it disappointed." Perhaps a unique gospel-grounded stewardship and service to the global church emerges here. We American evangelicals are rich and are here to confess that it's not all it's cracked up to be. Well and good.

But woe to us if we, from our unrecognized but still all-too-real affluent perches, spurred on by only one substream of biblical insight, find ourselves saying, in effect, "be warmed and filled" to hundreds of millions who have yet to benefit from the poverty-destroying powers of capitalism. I suspect that guilt over evangelical affluence plays some role in the failure of anti-prosperity evangelicals to engage the pro-prosperity teachings of the Bible. If this is so, it also may help to explain why these evangelicals fail to recognize the inevitable ineffectiveness of the half-truth critique of the prosperity gospel they are dishing up. To the extent that guilt, whether recognized or not, fuels their anti-prosperity musings, their thinking drifts away from laser beam focus on demolishing prosperity teaching and more on spiritual self-help. Such self-help is needed, but the same streams of biblical teaching necessary for effective rebuke to the prosperity preachers are the same streams needed to make sense of their own guilt-ridden affluence; namely, teaching about material divine blessing and how to be affluent disciples of Jesus. If they are not going to divest and take vows of poverty, it might be advisable to open themselves to what the Bible has to say about such things. Attempts to somehow construe their affluent lifestyles as simple lifestyles are ludicrous and embarrassing. And the folks in the third world who flock to prosperity preachers especially would find such pathetic posturing laughable because it is preposterous. Seen from the perspective of the guilt-hypothesis, the fixation by the same evangelicals upon consumer culture and greed make sense. More than they are concentrated on an effective weapon against the prosperity preachers in the global south, they are trying to address their own material cravings here at home.

Among evangelicals, one voice sounds forth with much-needed insight on matters of money and poverty—that of Wayne Grudem. Grudem engages the scriptures prosperity preachers cling to, makes them his, and from them both repudiates the prosperity gospel while affirming material prosperity as the blessing of God and poverty as a consequence of the fall to be resisted.[15]

I suspect that a worrisome combination of factors animates the theologizing of the anti-prosperity evangelicals: (1) justified certainty that the prosperity gospel is a pernicious heresy, (2) neglect of major streams of biblical teaching in its prophetic opposition to the prosperity gospel, and (3) unrecognized guilt-inspired efforts to feel better about themselves while simultaneously fulminating against the prosperity gospel without divesting themselves of wealth or taking vows of poverty. One danger this mix of conviction and motivation poses is that it might minimize the gospel call to care for the poor. It might minimize the devastations of poverty that

15. See especially Grudem and Asmus, *Poverty of Nations*. But see also Novak, *Democratic Capitalism*; Rae and Hill, *Virtues of Capitalism*; Soto, *Mystery of Capital*; and D'Souza, *Virtue of Prosperity*.

only capitalism has ever significantly remedied for hundreds of millions of people and over multiple generations. And it might settle for charitable generosity to the poor rather than seek public policies that offer the promise of reducing the percentage of folk who are actually poor at a given time.

Prophetic denunciation of prosperity preaching may coincide with an unintended callousness for those yet untouched by the great dangers of consumerism that haunt the consciousness and disturb the Starbucks quiet times of affluent evangelicals who would spare them such difficulties. All the while these evangelicals are feeling really "spiritual" about themselves as they slurp up the last expensive dregs of that tasty Mocha Frappuccino.

Okay, I've gotten a bit cheeky here, but the never-have-been-poor and likely-never-shall-be-poor and the never-really-lived-and-worked-with-the-poor prophets to the poor may suffer some serious blind spots where the teaching of Scripture about poverty is concerned. They may unwittingly assume that the material benefits they have and are likely to continue to enjoy can be taken for granted, when in fact they are rare in history and are the products of capitalism and free markets (or at least relatively free). Only those who have benefited from such blessings tend to take them for granted. We who have so benefited should work diligently against the nonchalance about poverty only inexperience tends to muster and maintain. So how might the evangelical anti-prosperity crowd find illumination on such matters? Maybe another interest of theirs, racial reconciliation, can open a path to a better place where more of the Bible is heard.

The same community of evangelicals acutely disturbed by the prosperity gospel is also anxious to win African Americans to membership in the communities of faith where they worship and serve.[16] There are longstanding African American readings of both biblical testaments, but especially the Old Testament, as bearing witness to the God who delivers his children from actual physical bondage to freedom and prosperity in this world and the next. Pharaoh, Joseph, Moses, the Red Sea, the wilderness, and the promised land are in this world. African American Christians noticed such this-worldly divine deliverance from their first exposures to Holy Scripture reaching back to seventeenth-century indentured servitude in well-appointed Virginian households and in Carolina rice and cotton plantations.[17] Some of the spiritualizing and delayed-fulfillment-fixated hermeneutical instincts of evangelicals in recoil against the prosperity gospel seem incompatible with the this-worldly deliverance readings of the African American believers they so desperately wish to draw to their communities of faith.

16. On "white guilt" see Steele, *White Guilt*.
17. See Mitchell, *Black Church Beginnings*.

Where divine deliverance in this world is prized, as it is in African American preaching and theology (recall the title of Martin Luther King's famous little volume *Why We Can't Wait!*), comprehensive denunciation of Christian identification of health and wealth as divine blessings won't fly. But the new evangelical language of "the gospel for the city" and the clear insistence that redemption's scope includes the material creation may mesh nicely with black church theological foundations and instincts. But if it is wise, it will eschew the demonstrated bankruptcy of Marxist liberation theologies and learn to see the merciful hand of God in the spectacular lifting of millions out of poverty capitalism has achieved.

10

Shalom and Asceticism

Upon him was the chastisement that brought us peace, and
with his wounds we are healed.

—THE PROPHET ISAIAH (ISA 53:5)

There are eunuchs who have been so from birth, and there
are eunuchs who have been made so by men, and there are
eunuchs who have made themselves eunuchs for the sake of
the kingdom of heaven.

—JESUS AGAINST THE PHARISEES (MATT 19:12)

"FOR A BRIEF MOMENT, favor has been shown by the Lord our God," Ezra
declared to the Babylonians who returned with him to Judea and Jerusalem.
Yet despite such unearned favor and against God's command, Ezra learned
that "the people of Israel and the priests and the Levites have not separated
themselves from the peoples of the lands," but instead have and indulged in
"their abominations." In prophetic protest Ezra publicly fasted, tore his gar-
ment and cloak, and pulled hair from his head and beard and "sat appalled."
In this state and posture Ezra remained "until the evening sacrifice," as "all
who trembled at the words of the God of Israel" gathered around him.

At the evening sacrifice Ezra, in prophetic fashion, then prayed publicly to the Lord, his prayer cry to the Lord uttered also for the benefit of the
people of Israel. Ezra fasted, deprived himself in myriad ways, before the
Lord and the people. He went on to lead the people themselves to fast and
humble themselves before the Lord, calling them away from indiscriminate
and patently disobedient indulgence of their desires "among the peoples of

the land." But to what end? To the end that the people of Israel might embrace a life of fasting and non-indulgence as the center, norm, and goal of Yahweh's purpose for them? Was Ezra modeling ascetic discipline as the very heart of righteous living, one of self-denial and of bearing up? John Calvin would insist that the Christian life, at its very core, is one of self-denial. Was Ezra's fasting and prophetic, self-flagellant hair-pulling a reminder that no hope of this-worldly material prosperity should animate the expectations of Yahweh's pilgrim people?

Apparently not. Indeed, the shock of Israel's disobedience that prompted Ezra's ascetic impulse and action came from the opposite direction, so to speak. The people's disobedience threatened to squander and thus forfeit impending divine blessing—material blessing. Blindly but also repeatedly, the people Israel, and Adam and Eve too for that matter, tend to respond to divine blessing in ways that immediately put the blessing at risk. Listen to Ezra:

> . . . for our iniquities we, our kings, and our priests have been given into the hand of the kings of the lands, to the sword, to captivity, to plundering, and to utter shame, as it is today. But now for a brief moment favor has been shown by the LORD our God, to leave us a remnant and to give us a secure hold within this holy place. . . . Yet our God has not forsaken us . . . (Ezra 9:7–8)

And to what end has "God not forsaken [them]"? "[To] give [them] protection in Judea and Jerusalem . . . that you may be strong and eat the good of the land and leave it for an inheritance to your children" (9:9, 12).

The material blessing of deliverance from exile signaled for Ezra the possibility that Yahweh might relent in his punishment even more and allow at least for some proximate enjoyment by the people of a material prosperity sketched out by Moses in such dazzling fashion in his speech to the people in the Trans-Jordan.

Given the character of shalom as I have conceived it, it might seem difficult to imagine a more alien or unwelcome subject than asceticism. Surely asceticism must be rejected on principle if divinely intended shalom involves the flourishing and enjoyment of all three of its relational dimensions. Surely where such enjoyment is seriously affirmed and prized as the blessing of God, the self-conscious and deliberate denial of pleasures, the disciplined reigning in and constriction of desires themselves must prove enemies of shalom. But in fact, no, I shall contend that an ascetic component belongs necessarily and indeed, integrally, to both the Christian life here and now, and eternally to the life of the people of God in the coming new heaven and new earth. The relationship between ascetic practice and prosperity in Ezra provides a pointer toward a faithfully biblical comprehension of the relationship between these two seemingly incompatible biblical themes.

The word asceticism rightly evokes for us first of all the ancient, global, and rich history of monasticism. But for our purposes we must also include biblical and historical encouragement to self-denial, Christian discipline, and loving sacrifice as belonging to the history of asceticism. That Martin Luther repudiated vow-initiated, separatist, vocational monastic living but retained the practice of the Christian disciplines, stands as a sign that the church has always been confronted with the task of making sense of the shalomic substance of divine blessing and calls for self-denial and sacrifice, both of which are affirmed in Holy Scripture.

We have already confronted repeated and pervasive biblical affirmation of a three-dimensioned shalom which includes affirmation of material prosperity and physical health as prototypical divine blessings. But we must grapple with the seeming contradiction between shalomic blessings and pervasive divine calls for self-denial and sacrifice throughout Holy Scripture. Let us begin our examination of the relationship between shalom and asceticism by exploring Martin Luther's famously negative conclusions about the ascetic ideal.

Luther's Broken Vows

With more than three and a half decades of teaching and preaching behind him, Martin Luther still had more trashing of monks and monasticism in him that needed expression. Three days before he died, the great reformer preached for the last time. Taking Matthew 11:25–30 as his text, Luther held forth in Eisleben, the town of his birth—"Come to me, all who labor and are heavy laden, and I will give you rest." What beautiful and comforting words flow from the lips or our savior in this passage. Surely Luther could faithfully expound it without having to spew more venom at the poor monks and their vows and at the pope who approved of both. But no. Luther's well of invective against the ascetic class and their patrons ran deep.

On this occasion, Luther had his back up against what he viewed as a substitution by the pope of help the Lord provides to the faithful through baptism with the aid of merits stored up by monks:

> . . . the fact that God instituted baptism is a trifling thing to the
> pope and with him it soon became lost and impotent. In its place
> he created his shavelings, who wear cowls and tonsures; they
> are the ones who are going to save the world with their orders
> and monkery, so that anybody who entered an order possessed

a new and better baptism, by which not only he but also other people were to be helped if they wished to be saved. . . . So it is with our Lord God in the world; whatever he institutes and ordains must always be not only perverted but also reviled and discredited by the devil and his followers.[1]

Martin Luther's initial, growing, and enduring opposition to monkery matured into that contempt only familiarity produces. Of Protestant liberalism Karl Barth once said that the best defense against it is to take it in by the bucket-full. Don't withhold it from the eager beavers. That just makes them run after it more and more. Let them have their fill and they'll learn to despise it properly and forever.

Thus did Martin Luther earn his aversion to monasticism particularly and to asceticism more broadly. Massive intake resulted, eventually, in revulsion and then instilled a permanent inoculation against its lure and hyper alertness to its dangers. The effect is a bit like that of the Lord's quail provision to wandering Israel till it flowed from their nostrils. Luther's antipathy toward the monastery smacks of a deep-seated revulsion. It was personal. An earned bitterness courses through it. Familiarity breeds its own unique form of contempt. Contempt tends to distort perspective and veer into prejudice. But informed contempt may also yield penetrating insight. So let us let Luther spew a bit more venom about the monastics before we attempt to assume a less hostile posture toward the movement as whole.

Eventually Luther would doubt the legitimacy of a call to priestly or monastic celibacy. But even before such doubt emerged, he disdained vows of chastity with ample energy. The pope, for example,

> confirms that the servants of the divine Word should not let themselves be castrated, and yet he also prohibited them from having wives. The result of that can be seen: the priests become raging, burning devils and nothing but beastly fornicators. . . . Now we hear that the Lord Christ does not like this. St. Paul also says of this in 1 Corinthians 7:[9]: "It is easier to marry than to burn." . . . So it is whenever someone wants to modify or improve what God has made, it ends up becoming a real mess.[2]

Those who make themselves eunuchs spiritually "are chaste willingly and have the grace to remain a virgin voluntarily . . . yet not so as to make it into a service to God or an act of superiority." Of such aspiration to superiority through vows of chastity Luther explodes, "to hellfire with this! In the

1. Luther, *Luther's Works*, 51:385.
2. Luther, *Luther's Works*, 68:18.

papacy and in the monasteries we, too, abstained from women so that God would regard us as higher and better than Abraham and Isaac. It was for the sake of personal pride and righteousness that monks and nuns wanted to be higher and holier than other Christians in God's eyes."[3]

For Luther, self-denying sacrifice of an otherwise appropriate earthly pleasure can prove legitimate, but not if it believes the lie that such an action might serve God, who needs nothing from us and to whom we can contribute nothing. And not if it believes the lie that such ascetic acts have anything whatever to do with the justification of sinners. And not if one believes the lie that ascetic self-denial makes one superior to others. According to Luther, the "castration" appropriate to ministers of the word is the "castration of faith," which "enables you to serve the Christian Church, the Gospel, and your preaching office better."[4] Such sacrifice for the sake of the kingdom, the gospel, and others, abhors and eschews the error of "monks and nuns who, through the worthiness of their chastity, want to acquire and earn the kingdom of heaven—for that is given by Christ alone, and if it is given to us as a gift, we ought to accept it with thankfulness."[5]

For Luther, monastic life does not prove moral rectitude at all. Instead, the monasteries should be judged by the standard of loving service to others—"So even if I am a Carthusian or a monk and find that I am not helping my neighbor therein, I should break free from the order and help my neighbor."

Luther never tired of castigating all who wish to improve upon or aid the commandment of God by adding new commandments. The Lord said you should "Love . . . God with all your heart, and with all your soul, and with all your mind . . . and your neighbor as yourself" (Matt 22:37–39). Luther knows that obedience to this command is impossible without faith. But rather than allow the impossibility of the command to do its work and drive the would-be disciple to Christ and prayer, the pope comes along and adds to the command of God, calling for "praying the seven hours, fasting the long fasts, doing this and doing that."[6] When a layperson sins, works of penance are heaped upon him—"go to Rome, make a pilgrimage to this or that saint; he is to go barefoot, and do a lot of other things."[7] Where is the neighbor in need in all of this? It is not enough that the monks abandon help to others, now the pope prevents laypeople from good works.

3. Luther, *Luther's Works*, 68:18.

4. Luther, *Luther's Works*, 68:19.

5. Luther, *Luther's Works*, 68:19.

6. Luther, *Luther's Works*, 51:107–8.

7. Luther, *Luther's Works*, 51:107–8.

Against any escapist, neighbor-disinterested, or merit-fixated morality as had grown up on monastic soil, "Luther's new morality was not ascetic or unworldly. It was directed toward the world—not to transform it into a monastery but to let it remain the world and become what it was, God's good creation."[8] So "worldly" was this post-monastic Lutheran ethic that even St. Francis and his sixteenth-century spiritual progeny, who included ministry "in the world" as a major component of their monastic life, drew Luther's ire. Was such critique deserved?

In a life punctuated by many dramatic scenes, none quite compares with Francsco di Pietro di Bernadone's stripping naked and flinging of his clothes at the feet of his father as the Bishop of Assisi looked on. Thus Francis, in a radical act of abandonment to the sole care of the heavenly Father, renounced all of his personal possessions. From the eleventh century in Italy and southern France, the ideal of holy poverty enjoyed unprecedented appeal. Francis's renunciation marks a late and uniquely powerful reinvigoration of a tradition boasting roots reaching back not only to the eleventh century but on back to the year AD 422, when the thirty-year-old Symeon took up residence atop a twenty-square-foot pillar near Aleppo. Up to that pillar little sacks of food were hoisted by ropes and down from it small portions of human waste descended.

But do not ascetic forms of monasticism boast warrants reaching on back to the apostolic era itself and even into patriarchal times? Were not Jesus's instructions to "the Twelve" clear enough? "Acquire no gold or silver or copper for your belts, no bag for your journey, or two tunics or sandals or a staff" (Matt 10:9–10). Hadn't Jesus called the rich young ruler to divest and distribute his wealth to the poor (Matt 19:21)? It is good to recall that Francis Bernadone was born into a family of some means. And had not Jesus spoken approvingly both of those who are born and those who make themselves eunuchs (Matt 19:12f)?

But Franciscan "love of neighbor" failed to satisfy Luther's demands for "worldliness." The vow of chastity repudiates the creator who made sex and marriage good, put wine into the hopper of history to make the heart glad, and beer-brewing competence into German genes. Where in all this ascetic self-denial and sacrifice was enjoyment of divine blessings received from the hand of the creator?

Luther famously embraced the apostle Paul's recognition that "it is better to marry than to burn [with lust]" and turned that recognition against the monks, who, rather than heed the word of God, make fools out of themselves.

8. Oberman, *Luther Between God and the Devil*, 78.

The monks wanted to control the burning and evil lusts with
fasting, prayer, and the rosary, and wearing course clothing, but
these cannot put out the fire.

S. Jerome speaks in this case himself. "Poor fool that I
am—I did not lay myself in bed, but instead slept on the hard
earth and beat my chest with stones." . . . "Yet when I fell asleep,
I thought of nothing other than that I was at the song and dance
in Rome." Similarly, St. Bernard and St. Francis made children
and wives out of snow to lie beside in hopes of extinguishing
the burning. But that does not do it, for Christ, the best teacher,
lays no snares or other obstacles in our path. Instead he makes
[chastity] depend on the grace of God.[9]

Nothing evoked Luther's disdain for monastic vows so effectively as
did consideration of the mendicant or "begging" orders, which included his
own Augustinian tradition as well as the Franciscan order. Luther came to
view monkish begging not just as thievery but as grave-robbing.

. . . he told the story of a certain young monk who demanded of
a dying nobleman, "Sir, are you willing to give this and that to
the monastery?" Since the dying man was unable to speak and
could only give a sign by nodding, the monk said to the nobleman's son, "See, you notice that your father consents to giving
these things." Then the son asked his dying father, "Father, isn't
it your will that I hurl this monk down the stairs?" When the father gave the same sign the monk got what he deserved and was
thrown down the stairs. Such [deathbed] thefts of the monks
were enormous.[10]

Luther's distaste for mendicancy probably reaches back at least to age
fifteen when he had to beg for his keep as a schoolboy in Eisenach. Long
familiarity with the Franciscan beggars bred contempt for the practice. To
the Christian nobility Luther wrote,

One of the greatest necessities is the abolition of all begging
throughout Christendom. Nobody ought to go begging among
Christians. . . . It is not fitting that one man should live in idleness
on another's labor, or be rich and live comfortably at the cost of
another's hardship, as it is according to the present perverted
custom. St. Paul says, "Whoever will not work shall not eat."
God has not decreed that any man shall live off another man's
property, save only the clergy who preach and have a parish to

9. Luther, *Luther's Works*, 68:20.
10. Luther, *Luther's Works*, 54:281.

care for, and these should, as St. Paul says in 1 Corinthians 9, on account of their spiritual labor. And also as Christ says to the apostles, "Every laborer is worthy of his wage.[11]

Luther's disdain for begging and monastic dependence upon others for their upkeep was grounded in the conviction that an insidious hypocrisy flourished here. My own suspicion is that the ascetic ideals that have so often nurtured monastic thinking are themselves nurtured by ancient and unbiblical aversion to the body and to the physical world.

Some concoction of quasi-Platonic and heretical (Gnostic, Marcionite, Manichean) stew seems to always swirl somewhere beneath the surface of Christian thought, ready to bubble up and either subtlety or blatantly distort our reception of shalomic Bible teaching. The ancient pedigree and enduring power of new mixtures of such concoctions is impressive.

Part of the power derives from the seeming proximity of this anti-material stew with orthodox Christian teaching. Its denials and assertions can track quite closely with certain teachings in Holy Scripture. Anti-creation, anti-physical, and anti-material notions demonstrably at odds with the storyline of divine revelation can gain traction in the minds of sincere Bible-believing Christians through appeal to verses here and there when detached from their canonical contexts. What about the Nazarite vow? What about the biblical encouragement to fasting? What about the pervasive, direct, and serious warnings against the dangers of both money and preoccupation with one's own health and safety that punctuate Holy Scripture from Genesis to Revelation? What about the default assumption throughout Scripture that the motherload of divine blessings are reserved for the next word?

Attraction toward some form of ascetic defense against the love of money and the variety of evils to which it gives rise seems particularly, perhaps even uniquely, welcome in our time of widespread and multi-generational affluence, does it not? And surely no more impressive demonstration of serious acceptance of the anti-prosperity Bible teachings avails than that of a vow-taking entrance into a monastery or convent. But for Christians unwilling to take such a drastic step, some form of simple lifestyle theology appears to be the next best thing to actual divestment and withdrawal into cloistered obedience, chastity, and relative poverty. Next in line is to just hang on to the major benefits of capitalism and free markets but continue to talk a good game by going Gnostic in preaching and in small group Bible study settings and in public prayer without giving up much in the way of material goods. Luther saw hypocrisy in the monks who lived as well as they could off resources earned by others. Would contemporary monks

11. Luther, *Luther's Works*, 44:191–92.

draw from Luther the same charge? Does not the ascetics' "deprivation" remain suspect so long as it accesses the extraordinary advances in medicine and physical comforts paid for by the wealth creation of others? The pope receives the best care the world has to offer. So do the champions of the so-called simple lifestyle who are careful to define "simple lifestyle" upward enough to keep themselves within it.

So, what if we successfully expose some deep vein of hypocrisy, though perhaps unwitting and unrecognized, along the trajectory between ascetic vow-taking and simple-lifestyle-claiming? Where does that leave us? Is there no place for ascetic self-denial in Christian discipleship and holy living? Does not Luther-like repudiation of asceticism expose the church to a Pandora's box of fleshly desire leading in time to a full-blown prosperity gospel?

After his conversion to Christianity at the age of twenty-eight, Basil of Caesaera toured monastic sites of the eremitic type in Mesopotamia, Palestine, and Egypt. Though impressed in certain ways with this form of monasticism, Basil opted not to follow the eremitic path. Instead he pioneered cenobitic monastic living which emphasizes life in community. Benedict of Nursia, whose sixth-century Rule would exert unparalleled influence within Western monasticism and within the church generally, credited Basil's work as foundational for his own and encouraged all monks to learn from the Cappadocian father.

But why did Basil forge a new form of monastic practice rather than embrace the long-established eremitic standard? He noted among the eremitics a tendency for spiritual egoism, fleshly competition, and self-righteousness. He feared that major dimensions of the Christian life would find scant opportunity for nurturing and growth in eremitic settings:

> How will [the monk] show his humility, if there is no one with
> whom he may compare and so confirm his own greater humil-
> ity? How will he give evidence of his compassion, if he has cut
> himself off from association with other persons? And how will
> he exercise long-suffering, if no one contradicts his wishes.[12]

Very good questions rooted in legitimate concerns. Along the same lines, one might pose a few similarly rooted queries to those who practice cenobitic monasticism where vows of poverty, chastity, and obedience serve as prerequisites for acceptance. How shall a community confirm God's enabling power and mercy displayed in the marriage estate and in child-rearing where both are banned?

---

12. Quoted in Haykin, *Rediscovering the Church Fathers*, 109–10.

As a Protestant I feel no acute pressure to affirm practices or beliefs merely on the basis of their ancient pedigree and widespread practice, including the long-standing embrace of monastic forms of Christian living. On the other hand, when doctrines and practices do achieve significant affirmation by orthodox Christians across time, geography, and multiple cultures, it should give would-be critics pause. For that reason, I hesitate to suggest that all monastic practice involves some lapse into some sub-Christian or biblically unpalatable way of life for any believers anywhere or at any time. Perhaps certain contexts argue for such separation of Christian communities from society to a greater extent than usual. After all, the biblical imperative to "be separate" applies to the whole church, as does its flip side—"go ye" (2 Cor 6:17; Matt 28:19).

One of the more usual rationales advanced for the rise of and the need for the rise of monasticism in the fourth century was of this contextual sort. Nominal Christianity grew exponentially in the decades following Emperor Constantine's conversion to Christianity in year AD 312. In order to secure a place for the pursuit, practice, and display of serious discipleship, so the reasoning goes, monastics needed to take their vows, separate from the laxity loosed within the churches, and follow Jesus Christ in earnest. Really? I question such defenses of monastic life. But still, the impressiveness of monasticism's pedigree does give me pause.

Perhaps we can say that if there is a place for permanent monastic withdrawal from the world, the burden is upon those who assert such a place. Confronted with Scripture's teaching on shalomic blessing, the missionary mandate, loving service to the world by believers, the urgent need for evangelization and church planting, and for good works of mercy to those outside the church, permanent ascetic withdrawal should be put into the dock and required to defend itself. Certainly the history of such efforts makes it clear that spiritual dangers attending such withdrawal are every bit as serious and insidious as any one faces "in the world." The case for the monastery as affording some optimum or even superior context and environment for "spiritual" advancement is, to put it mildly, not proved.

Martin Luther contended that the renunciation entrance into the monastery demanded was child's play compared to that required by the return to the world. Withdrawal may smack as much of fleshly indulgence, as any available in the world. Retreat to the monastery can mean mooching off the hard-earned money of those compared to whom I may now be encouraged to think myself superior; running from my own on responsibility for and service to others in order to hunker down and concern myself with my own salvation—a salvation that in Jesus Christ is already won and which is meant to free me to concern myself with the needs of others. Withdrawal to the desert is as likely to arise from a selfish and cowardly cop-out as from anything recognizable as obedience to the call to Christian discipleship.

Sabbath Rhythms and Strategic Asceticism

Much more biblically defensible are patterns of Christian living that prize rhythms of separation from the world followed by re-entry, such as the rhythm the creator built into the garden of Eden and maintained east of Eden—the pattern of living from Sabbath to Sabbath. Let Sabbath-keeping serve as a weekly retreat and withdrawal from the world in service to, among other things, re-entry into the world to which we are called to witness and serve.

Embrace temporary or even permanent and strategic renunciations of and self-denials from alcohol, sex, social media, and food for the sake of embracing sanctification, being set apart, being sanctified. But not set apart from the world as such. Not being set apart from the world God so loved that he sent his only begotten Son. No. Where divine sanctification reduces to some notion of a progressive holiness-producing work within a person it falls short of the scope of sanctification taught in the Bible. Sanctification that exhausts itself in concern for one's personal relationship to God is a fraud. Sanctification that harbors visions of a personal holiness fit to preen upon a stage where one's moral purity might glitter before the dirty unsanctified world is an abomination, but in fact it has too often animated mangled "Christian" aspiration.

So what, then, does a fully orbed biblical sanctification entail? Yes, it demands a setting apart. It calls for a coming out from the world. But to what end? Divine sanctification sets apart unto *holy use*. Sanctification is not for display as such and certainly not for preening. Sanctification is for the sake of service. In proportion as concrete service to others initiates, nurtures, and propels ascetic practice and self-denying discipleship, it may win biblical approval and warrant pastoral approval as well. But whatever biblical and pastoral approval is won must also pass the shalom test. Whatever ascetic acts or practices are deemed appropriate, whatever self-denials commend themselves, they must not label divine blessings as curses, must not substitute divine blessing as the goal of creation and redemption with something else.

The father who denies himself otherwise God-bestowed goods and pleasures for the sake of securing commensurate goods and pleasures for his children or others imitates Jesus Christ who became poor to make others rich. The ascetic who abandons the world to live however meagerly off the resources earned by others and who sets his life beside those others as superior lives in disobedience to the Lord and opposition to the revealed purposes of the creator.

Embrace of Sabbath-to-Sabbath rhythms of "be ye separate" and "go ye" seem less exposed to the self-deceptions permanent vow-taking withdrawal from the world tend to invite. Discipline, self-denial, renunciation, and sacrifice must serve shalom, not the reverse. The history of monasticism has too often gotten this order backwards and still does.

The original upsurge of monasticism that resulted in the founding of the great orders responded to the rise of Christendom. Once it became fashionable and potentially profitable both socially and monetarily to join the church, many did. The church has always been "worldly" in that its composition has always consisted in nothing but sinners. But imperial favoring of the church saw the rise of a new, more powerful form of worldliness within its ranks with which the church had no experience. It is not surprising that some Christians disapproved of this, could not abide it and fled. But the more admirable response was surely from those who stayed "in the world" but as those "not of the world" and, at least relatively speaking, kept themselves "unstained by the world." As such they became candles in the darkness. They, empowered by the Holy Spirt still doing his Pentecost work, became his witnesses to the uttermost parts of the world. And these braver and stronger ones shared some of their earnings with those who preferred to stay on permanent spiritual retreat back in the monastery rather than to obey the Lord's mandate to go and make disciples. Harsh words, yes, but needed. To cover their weakness and cowardice, as Luther saw it, they developed a theology that made them the truly spiritual ones and led many of those back in the world to buy into this construal of what they were up to and to subsidize it. This helped to secure future funding for their abandonment of the mandate of the Lord to go and make disciples.

But alas, now let me tell you about my friend Francis the Friar, who has sent me a birthday greeting each year for more than two decades. He is a Franciscan living and working and doing ministry in Washington, DC. For more than half a century this gentle, dedicated, and precious follower or Jesus has truly served the poor in Puerto Rico and in the States. He bears witness to the Savior out in the world and expends himself in service to the needs of those "little ones" at the bottom of society most of us do not see, never become friends with, and for whom Christ died. And Francis has done these things as a vow-taking Franciscan. I thank God for him and I stand by the wariness for monasticism I have articulated as well.

The Ultimate Ascetic Act

The greatest love, the Lord Jesus taught us, is to "lay down [one's] life for his friends" (John 15:13). Who would dare contest such an assertion? When he spoke these words, Jesus had set his face toward Jerusalem where he would, in fact, lay down his life for those friends given to him by the heavenly Father, and to whom he was also both servant and Lord. Jesus also warned his followers that servants are not greater that their master, and if he himself, though servant of all, would be rejected and killed, such like should his followers expect.

Visions of the glories to be revealed animated Paul's hope and undergirded his boldness and courage as a witness to Jesus Christ (Romans 8). That glorious inheritance to come reached proleptically from its certain future fulfillment into Paul's own life and informed the meaning of the tribulations he bore and continued to face—we are "fellow heirs with Christ, provided we suffer with him" (Rom 8:17).

We cannot lay down our lives for Jesus Christ the way he did for us. He is the spotless Lamb of God slain from the foundation of the world by whose stripes we are healed. He died once for all. He is the one mediator between God and humanity whose death rips the temple curtain in two. His death atones for sins; not his own, but the sins of others—his friends' sins. His death truly brings life, resurrection life, to others. Our deaths, in whatever context, cannot achieve such results, cannot deliver such blessings—were not meant to.

But our sufferings and deaths may become witnesses to Jesus Christ. "Witness" is an important word throughout Holy Scripture. The only true God, the creator and redeemer of heaven and earth, deserves, desires to have, and sees to it the he receives witness to himself. Jonathan Edwards taught that insistence upon the glorification of God by the whole of creation is necessary to the fulfillment of the divine purpose in creation because God is the most important and most valuable and so the most worthy of praise. Everything in the universe owes its very life to him, the creator and Lord of all.

To bear witness to Jesus Christ, who is the divine agent of creation within the Godhead, is to acknowledge that God's worthiness for praise is grounded in his act of creation. To God be the glory for the things he has done. What has he done? He has created the heavens and the earth.

To point away from oneself to the creator and to say "He alone is worthy of all our praise" is to identify one of the two essential warrants for the worship of God. The second is to acknowledge him as the redeemer of all that he has made. Evangelism is born at Pentecost. Witness is primordial.

It flourishes from all eternity within the Godhead itself—issues forth from the works of Jesus Christ, from the lips of John the Baptist, and audibly from both the incarnate Son and the heavenly Father—first at the baptism of Jesus and again on the Mount of Transfiguration. Jesus said,

> If I alone bear witness about myself, my testimony is not true. There is another who bears witness about me, and I know that the testimony he bears about me is true. You sent to John, and he has born witness to the truth. Not that the testimony that I receive is from man, but I say these things that you may be saved. He was a burning and shining lamp, and you were willing to rejoice for a while in his light. But the testimony that I have is greater than that of John. For the works that the Father has given me to accomplish, the very works that I am doing, they bear witness about me that the Father has sent me. And the Father who sent me has himself born witness about me. (John 5:31–34)

To his disciples the risen but not yet ascended Jesus says, "You shall be my witnesses" (Acts 1).

The blood of martyrs bears witness to Jesus Christ as surely as did Abel's against his brother Cain from the ground east of Eden. The heart of Christian witness is to proclaim "He is the Christ" whether or not one pays for such witness with their blood, with their life. But witness may and often has brought suffering and death. As I write this, there is news of the release of evangelical pastor Andrew Brunson from a Turkish prison after spending two years incarcerated for preposterous charges of terrorism. Brunson has suffered much and could have easily met his death for his obedience to the call of Jesus to serve as his witness.

When Christian witnesses refuse to save themselves by denying their Lord, when as soldiers without material weapons they stand as sentries at their witnessing posts come what may, they engage in the worthiest, most biblically unassailable ascetic act imaginable. For they show that they know they are not their own. They acknowledge their lives as his possession, as his property, which he may require, which may have to be laid down because the witness must be maintained.

The designation of those who pay for their faith with their very lives as martyrs could hardly be more apt. That martyrdom was in the offing for Christian disciples was inevitable not only in retrospect but on the basis of Jesus' own warning in the long last discourse of the gospel according to John (John 14).

Paul applies a cost-benefit analysis that illumines both suffering precipitated by witness and the rationale and warrant for sacrifice—he reckoned that "the sufferings of this present time are not worth comparing with the glory to be revealed" to the witnesses (Rom 8:18). What the warrant and glory of martyrdom does not secure is the glamorizing of either martyrdom or suffering generally, even it if is brought on by Christian obedience. Such suffering is a bearing up undergirded by faith in the promise of the coming end to all suffering. Yes, Jesus came to die. But just once and never again.

There is a sort of triumphalism forever denied to the church adorned as the bride of Christ. The gratuitous character of life itself and of redemption from sin render a cocky, strutting church an abomination in the sight of God. Our divinely intended dependence upon our creator and redeemer makes impossible any warranted triumphant declarations from our lips. But there is a triumphalism appropriate to our God and also to the incarnate Son even as he made his way toward that great turning of the cheek Fredrich Nietzsche found so pathetic and abhorrent. Christianity for him was a pitiful, weak religion calculated by its founder to produce wimps like himself.

But Nietzsche was wrong. Jesus wins. Jesus defeats all of his enemies and rules from an exalted position of eternal kingship. "All power in heaven and on earth has been given to me" (Matt 28:18). Now that's a lot of power. Jesus just goes about the exercise and securing of power along a path unfathomable to Nietzsche and to the world. That the greatest victory over enemies and the securing of the greatest power forever could be secured, had to be secured, through a *kenosis*, through a humbling and a taking on of the form of a servant obedient to a sending father even to the point of death on a cross, seems preposterous. Even though Nietzsche would eventually go mad, his critique of Christianity is not really crazy; it is just blind.

We know now that power is demonstrated and secured in a downward plunge from heaven to earth and up to the cross and down into the place of the dead and then up again from the grave and on up to that permanent seat of power beside the Father. We do not know this because we finally figured it out through deep pondering. We know it because it has already occurred and has been announced in the gospel.

When Jesus stood before Pilate it was not long until he would cry out, "My God, My God, why have you forsaken me?" (Matt 27:46). And the beautiful and mysterious depths of that cry we may never fully plumb. But whatever it meant and means, it does not compete with, cancel, or attenuate one whit the triumphant meaning of this exchange: "So Pilate said to him, 'You will not speak to me? Do you not know that I have authority to release you and authority to crucify you?' Jesus answered him, 'You would have no authority over me unless it had been given to you from above'" (John 19:10–11a). The same Jesus who turns the other cheek and stretches himself out of the cross for the Jews and the Romans and the devil to do what they are capable of doing also lets us know that

> For this reason the Father loves me, because I lay down my life that I may take it up again. No one takes it from me, but I lay it down of my own accord. I have authority to lay it down, and I have authority to take it up again. (John 10:17–18)

No, Nietzsche did not get it, and it's no wonder because only the those taught by the Father know either Father or Son. But Nietzsche was not wrong to despise a powerless deity. He was just blind to the ultimate and sovereign divine power with which we are confronted in Jesus Christ. That power neither glamorizes suffering and death nor transforms suffering and death into eternal goods as such. The continuing significance of suffering love and dying love in eternity is precisely that the divine love enacted in Jesus Christ suffers and dies in order to end suffering and dying for the beloved forever.

Since God in love suffered and died to save and to redeem, the suffering and dying belongs to the divine glory, to his worthiness for praise. That is why in John's vision in Revelation has the lamb slain from the foundation of the world worshiped forever. What belongs to the divine glory belongs eternally. Jesus' wounds, though healed, remain visible as needed reminders both of whom it is the saints worship forever and whom are the worshippers, and what sort of divine love secured for them the happy duty of worship, what sort of loving triune God it is with whom they have to do.

The suffering and dying of Jesus secures a place in eternity, in memory, and in worship. He shall always be the lamb slain from the foundation of the world and we shall forever be the blood-bought sinners with faces forever free of tears. Suffering and death are forever banished from experience but retained in grateful and worshipful memory. Actual suffering? No. In the meantime, down here east of Eden, suffering and death remain our enemies—enemies to be fought, doomed enemies whose periodic setbacks in the time between the time predict and announce better what is to come than their continuing victories that seem to belie their own doom. So we fight disease and poverty and war and as soldiers of the captain who assures us that suffering and death's doom is sure. The empty tomb ensures that our labor in the Lord is not in vain.

We marvel at how our Lord makes suffering and death serve the final killing of suffering and death. But we do not run toward suffering and death for this reason and we work to mitigate and rescue others from suffering and death as, with the Lord's help, we are able. However fundamentally wrong is the prosperity gospel, the hostility toward suffering and death it harbors boasts deep justification in Holy Scripture. And when the chief opponents of the prosperity gospel among affluent evangelicals in North America or those they love face suffering, they tend behave much as do adherents of the prosperity gospel. No, they do not shame others who suffer as obviously lacking faith, but they do pray for deliverance from pain and suffering. For this they have nothing to apologize. What is lacking is sufficient attention to and integrative theologizing with respect to the vast trove of pro-health and pro-prosperity passages in Holy Scripture upon which prosperity gospel preachers seize. By not embracing the happy duty to make sense of these passages, we concede that vast textual turf to the very prosperity gospel reading we rightly reject and identify as pernicious. We also allow to stand in unnecessary tension a disjunction between our inadequate anti-prosperity preaching and teaching on the one hand and our behavior and prayers on the other.

Shalom does not accommodate glamorization of suffering, including suffering brought on by poverty—we could even say the suffering *of* poverty. Shalom also refuses to overly minimize the suffering poverty brings, especially by those who are not themselves suffering in poverty but living in affluence. Shalom affirms the contentment in want the apostle Paul claims as a wonderful work of the Holy Spirit. But shalom opposes any nonchalance by affluent believers confronted with the poverty and suffering of others.

Buddhism may accommodate indifference to poverty, but not Christianity. The goal of the Buddhist is to escape suffering. The root of suffering is desire. The quest of the Buddhist is not to satisfy desire but to extinguish it. Thailand is host to the purest variety of Buddhism on earth. *Geelate* is the transliteration of the word for desire in the Thai language. The Thai word for turning something off such as a light switch is *dap*. The goal of a Thai monk is to *dap geelate*.

The place of desire in Christian teaching is very different indeed. It shares with Buddhist teaching awareness that human desires pose profound dangers to healthy human life and often do lead to great and avoidable suffering. But here the similarities end. For Christians, dangers arising from human desire stem not from their mere existence but from their disorder. The prominent role the term "concupiscence" has played in the history of doctrine is instructive here. Concupiscence refers to disordered desire. But for Christians the healthy state of human flourishing is not one in which desires are extinguished but one in which they are rightly ordered. Disordered desire, not desire as such, prompted Eve's reach for the forbidden fruit and Adam's reception of that fruit from Eve's hand.

The title and subtitle to John Piper's famous book both captures well the place of desire revealed in Holy Scripture and sets faithful Christian teaching in stark contrast with Buddhist's radical rejection of desire: *Desiring God: Meditations of a Christian Hedonist*. How incompatible is such a title with affirmation of an ascitic posture towards life as somehow basic to Christian discipleship? Shalom affirms this title but also affirms that the desire for God must include God as the giver of all good gifts, and these include physical health and material wealth. The prayers and thanksgivings of affluent anti-prosperity evangelicals tend to demonstrate that they agree that this is so.

The mistake made by the prosperity preachers is not that they affirm health and wealth as blessings of God. It is that they affirm health and wealth as continuous and primary marks of faith among believers. It is that they allow for the direct pursuit of material wealth and physical health as primary and constituent aims of Jesus' followers. Thus, they cannot faithfully integrate Jesus' "be not anxious" admonition in the Sermon of the Mount. They bring little or no enthusiasm to biblical warnings that trouble, persecution, and suffering await believers in this world. They shut their ears against clear and consistent biblical encouragement to delayed gratification. The motherload of promised divine blessings await the arrival of the New Jerusalem.

Fundamentally, shalom stands against the prosperity gospel. But shalom calls for a fresh re-engagement with the favorite scriptures of the prosperity preachers, many of which we have reviewed in this book. Shalom calls for a quest to speak as positively about health and wealth as do these scriptures themselves. If we do this, we shall not only achieve greater faithfulness to Holy Scripture but shall develop a more effective critique of the prosperity gospel itself.

11

The Coming Shalom

Since the creation came into being at the beginning
through God's power, the end of everything that exists
is inseparably linked to the beginning.

—Gregory of Nyssa

Before Augustine (354–430), no real philosophy or theology of history existed. Historians told stories, recounted events, but seldom related the stories to an overarching meaning or purpose at work within history. If any philosophy of history did inform reflection upon history, its name, as Vernon Bourke has noted, is "fatalism."[1]

Augustine, spurred on by an array of theological convictions, developed a stunningly elaborate and deep philosophy of history. Since the triune God governs all that he has made with meticulous providence according to revealed purposes set forth in Holy Scripture, believers may, at least to some degree, discern the hand of God in the sweep of world history and in the trajectories of their own personal histories. John Calvin included history as one of the three forms of divine revelation among the works of God, *opera dei*.

That such discernment of divine activity was possible not only legitimized Augustine's *City of God*, but also his *Confessions*, in which he reflects upon his whole life from birth up through his conversion to Christianity. God's hand had to be at work in that history too. Given the Bible's clear teaching of the creator and redeemer's personal and powerful upholding and guiding of all of history—"not one [sparrow] will fall to the ground apart from your Father" (Matt 10: 29)—such discernment-seeking reflection

1. Bourke, ed., *Essential Augustine*, 220.

164

was both warranted and promising. The *Confessions* inaugurated and legitimized the genre of Christian autobiography.

The same biblical assertions that legitimized such reflection upon one's personal history also warranted spiritual pondering of the whole of history. As we have noted, the sack of Rome in AD 410 prompted just such pondering by the bishop of Hippo. More clearly than before, Augustine recognized in Scripture a profound limitation of warranted optimism regarding this world. He conceived of the movement of history between two cities, the city of Cain and the city of Abel, this earthly city we now inhabit and the eternal city, the city of God to which elect of all ages are headed. Woe to the one who seeks true happiness in this world, Augustine warned. Only in the next world shall the true happiness flourish and never cease.

Until then we are exiles and sojourners, headed to our true home, to a city that has foundations, whose builder and maker is God. In this world, in this between time of exile and sojourn, we can expect to endure all manner of trouble, just as Jesus said we would. No true and secure felicity, no reliable resting place, no permanent abode, and no fully orbed shalomic settling into enjoyment obtains. Only a fool sets hope here. For those who do, disappointment awaits.

Are shalomic hopes of the sort I have advanced compatible with such Augustinian pessimism regarding this fallen world we now inhabit? If the mother lode of divine blessing lies beyond this world, must not hope for enjoyment of an elaborate three-dimensional shalom of the sort I have described refer utterly to the next world? "Theology" David Dockery says,

> can help us recover the awareness that God is more important than we are, that the future life is more important than this one, and that a right view of God gives real significance and security to our lives. We will understand that happiness is the promise of heaven and that holiness is the priority here in this world.[2]

Isn't Dockery right? Yes, he is right. And Augustine is right. Whoever sets their hearts on promises to be fulfilled in the next world as though meant for this world falls into a snare, abandons biblical priories, and faces inevitable and unnecessary disappointment. Every follower of Jesus Christ does well to listen often to Jesus' words—"in the world you will have tribulation" (John 16:33). And indeed, our Lord bids us follow him, seek first the kingdom and righteousness, not run after our own happiness. Woe to us who waste time in doomed efforts to use God for our own enjoyment of this world's pleasures.

---

2. Dockery, *Southern Baptist Consensus*, 161.

But it is also the case that the witness of Holy Scripture and the experience of the church across time and geography make clear that the due pessimism and warranted limitation of expectation articulated by Augustine is not the only word to be said about this world. Indeed, Augustine himself, as we have seen, had other things to say, and not all of them utterly dark concerning what is possible in this life.

The prominence of movement and place in Augustine's theology of history is both conspicuous and meaningful. Exile and sojourn are seen as both unsettled conditions within which suffering abounds and as potential harbingers of shalom, not the opposite of shalom. The glance back at Edenic paradise not only provided content to eschatological hopes but windows into potential glimpses and tastes of the coming bliss east of Eden.

The great teachers of the church found in the opening chapters of Genesis not only or even especially what was, but clues to what lies ahead, harbingers of what is to come. The creation accounts in the Bible's first chapters, when read regularly and prayerfully, stirs not only or finally nostalgia for a paradise lost, but longing and sure hope for an even better home to come. They should illumine what we have lost, what is to come, and remaining extant vestiges of both provided according to the wisdom and measure and timing of the Lord.

In the mesmerizing repetitive cadence of "let there be" followed by "it was good" we meet a creator enjoying his homemaking. The divine joy reaches a kind of crescendo with the settling of the first couple into the home personally and meticulously fitted and prepared for them—"And God saw everything that he had made, and behold it was very good."

For how long did our first parents enjoy life together before their creator in the home prepared for them? What did memories of that time mean to them after expulsion from the garden? The good news of Jesus Christ includes the promise and thus the certain hope that what lies ahead for the children of God shall share more in common with the pre-fall than the post-fall between time—the valley of the shadow of death.

Do you have memories of times when the three dimensions of shalom were enjoyed comparatively more than at other times? The good news of Jesus Christ is that these times bear more faithful witness to the future that awaits you and those you love who belong to Jesus than do the worse times. It is actually true that "the sufferings of this present time are not worth comparing with the glory that is to be revealed to us" (Romans 8:18). But the shalom of the garden and the glimpses and tastes of shalom afforded east of Eden do invite such comparison.

Inevitably and prudently, Eden continued to animate the mind and aspiration of God's people even as they considered settlement east of Eden.

When Abram and Lot divided land between them in a quest to bring peace between them, Lot chose the land of the Jordan valley because it "was well watered like the garden of the Lord, like the land of Egypt, in the direction of Zoar" (Gen 13:10).

The Lord's prophet prompts remembrance of Edenic shalom because such remembrance provides a uniquely faithful and fit pointer to the coming redemption of all things. Possible glimpses, tastes, and approximations of the lost garden properly inform east of Eden aspiration. Isaiah declares a future for Zion in continuity, if not identity, with that primordial shalom that once flourished in Eden—"For the Lord comforts Zion; he comforts all her waste places and makes her wilderness like Eden" (Isa 51:3). To this earth shall Eden-like shalom come. Upon Eden-like shalom ought the hopes of God's people be set because the Lord who knows the end from the beginning has so promised. The earth's deserts shall be turned into Eden. The end shall be like the beginning.[3]

The climax of the divine vision of "things soon to take place" given to the apostle John is shalomic in substance and scale. The loud voice from the throne announces the fulfillment of a central covenant promise:

> Behold the dwelling place of God is with man. He will dwell with them, and they will be his people, and God himself will be with them as their God. He will wipe away every tear from their eyes, and death shall be no more, neither shall there be mourning nor crying, nor pain any more, for the former things have passed away." (Rev 21:3–4)

The "former things" that have passed away do not encompass everything that ever happened in the past. Such a truism requires no reminder from the Lord's herald. The "former things" refer to the entire universe in its fallen state. Like "walking according to the flesh" and its fruit in Galatians. Like "the world" in "love not the things of the world," "the former things" speak of human beings and their world sunk in sin and its consequences. These passages do not negate or compete with others such as Jesus' "for God so loved the world" (John 3:16) or Paul's "the whole creation groans" (Rom 8:22). The fundamental features of this world as created by God have not passed away and never shall pass away. The world in its rebellion and in its fallen state shall pass away. What the creator made he shall redeem and the redemption is underway. What the creator made is marked for rescue, restoration, and perfection. This ongoing and promised redemption warrants and calls for a chastened, sober, but biblically grounded hope for this world situated in the crosshairs of divine promises. The redeemable and

3. See Smith, *Isaiah 40–66*, 392 and n. 178.

thus to-be-redeemed world in all three relational shalomic dimensions has been preserved from obliteration by the creator who made it.

We have noted the essential physicality of the created order God called good, very good, and beautiful. We have acknowledged a distinction between non-material and material dimensions of this created order, but not an antagonism between these dimensions. Both belong to the good and beautiful creation. Both are dragged down with humankind as a result of Adam and Eve's sin. We have further observed and emphasized that humankind itself is part of creation. That this is so should produce a reflexive bias against any notion, such as Gnostics harbor, that devalues the physical generally or the human body particularly. Likewise, we should greet with wariness any suggestion that the saving deliverance brought and promised through Jesus Christ be understood along platonic lines as the liberation of some spark of the divine from the tomb of the body.

The early chapters of Genesis do not stand alone and cannot be understood apart from the entire context of the biblical canon within which the church receives them. But it is proper for the church to identify and take seriously these central affirmations about the created order within these uniquely significant passages standing at the very fountainhead of Holy Scripture. When we fail to do so, the temptation to embrace Gnostic readings of certain either ostensibly or actually material-negative passages skyrockets and meanders into distorted sweeping antagonism toward the material world and the physical human body.

We have also noted that in Eden we are confronted with the home-making purpose of creation itself and that the perfect and beautiful home fit for humankind consists of three major relational realities—that between God and his human creatures, that between human beings themselves before God (*coram deo*), and that between human beings (creatures!) and God within the rest of the created order, the heavens and the earth, the universe, which is the original and perfect and home fit for humankind. Nothing in the physical dimension of the created order is either alien to God's good and perfect purposes in creation or dispensable to that good purpose.

But, of course, we sojourners and exiles east of Eden have never experienced the multi-dimensioned, three-layered relational paradise enjoyed for a time by our first parents. The distortion and spoliation brought on by humankind's rebellion against the creator has penetrated each of these dimensions and layers within the wrecked home we now inhabit. The consequences of sin reach into every nook and cranny of our lives, physical and non-physical. The consequences of sin touch every dimension of the goodness, perfection, and beauty God made.

All of us were born into this fallen world, not into Eden. This vale of tears, not that lovely garden, is our home. For this reason, we might be tempted to neglect Eden as comparatively irrelevant to our present lives. After all, we live east of Eden, in this time between the times, in this valley of the shadow of death. Won't fixation upon a paradise lost only distract us from the pressing challenge of living in the fallen world we confront on a daily basis, even when we look into a mirror? Would not preoccupation with the first and lost paradise, like obsession with the promised but not-yet-available new heaven and new earth produce, according to the familiar adage, folks "too heavenly minded to be any earthly good"?

Since we sinners, though believers in Jesus Christ, manage to distort and misuse every good gift bestowed upon us by our wise and loving creator and redeemer, the promise of life beyond the grave will undoubtedly receive its share of misuse at our hands. But the promise stands and we have it as promise now because we need it as promise now. The church has recognized across the centuries that the revelation of life before the fall and the promise of life in the new heaven and new earth teach us that redemption involves more than but not less than restoration of the what was lost in the fall.

Exploration of what was lost offers clues of what is to come. Comparison between what was lost and what is to come reveal a complex relationship between the two states, including dimensions of continuity and discontinuity. Before expulsion from Eden and after consummation, human beings are set in a relationship of mutual interdependence upon each other in dependence together before their wise, loving, sustaining, and providing God. Before expulsion, God is knowable as creator. After consummation of the age, he is knowable as creator and redeemer and as such as redeemer from all eternity.

Jesus Christ is the spotless Lamb of God slain *before the foundation of the world*. Eden and the New Jerusalem confront us with both continuities and discontinuities. No marriage in the promised new home. No tears, nor pain, nor death to come. No possibility of a new fall. Augustine famously juxtaposed a set of crucial possibilities and impossibilities in order to illumine continuities and discontinuities between Eden, our time, and the coming eternal life promised to the children of God: before the fall, *posse peccari*, it was possible to sin; after the fall, *non posse non peccari*, not possible not to sin; in eternity, *non posse peccari*, not possible to sin. In Eden it was possible to obey. East of Eden, obedience is still possible, but not perfectly and not continuously. In the next world—obedience only awaits.

What good news! On the other side, God will have slammed the door on our future sinning! That this is so reveals that Edenic shalom was not perfect. In perfect shalom not only is sin never committed, it is divinely forestalled. We can note certain continuities within Augustine' *posse* juxtapositions. Sin is unwelcome everywhere and at all times but only needs resisting in Eden and in our time. Though resistance to sin in our time shall not prevail, the end of sin is certain and resistance to it through repentance and faith is commended not least as a precursor to the promised final victory.

In his wonderful little book *The Great Divorce*, C. S. Lewis provides an extended meditation on this world and the next. He also contrasts heaven with hell. His terminology differs from mine in this book. What Lewis calls "heaven" I call the "new heaven and new earth" and what Lewis calls "earth" I call "this world." With these differences of terminology in mind, let us explore some of Lewis's thoughts in light of the shalom I have explored in this book.

Lewis advises that, "If we insist on keeping Hell (or even Earth) we shall not see Heaven: if we accept Heaven we shall not be able to retain even the smallest and most intimate souvenirs of Hell."[4] Shalom affirms this axiomatic future orientation of the Christian toward the new heaven and the new earth with its awareness that our citizenship and inheritance is there, not in hell and not in this world.

Lewis continues, "But what, you ask, of earth? . . . I think earth, if chosen instead of Heaven, will turn out to have been, all along, only a region in Hell: and earth, if put second to Heaven, to have been from the beginning a part of Heaven itself."[5] Shalom also affirms Lewis's acknowledgment that some sort of proleptic enjoyment of the coming world is possible here and now. Shalom insists upon the impossibility of a radical rejection, repudiation, or even denial of the essential and permanent place of this world in God's purposes in both creation and redemption. Otherwise the promise of God for the redemption of the whole creation effected in the arrival of the "new heaven and new earth" becomes incomprehensible.

Lewis cautions that the bus trips to heaven recounted in *The Great Divorce* are fantasies that attempt to capture the utter antagonism, irreducible incompatibility between heaven and hell. And earth occupies a kind of ambiguous, indeterminate place between heaven and hell as suggested in the citation above. But the fantasy, in its attempt to comprehend heaven, must move not in the direction of the loss of matter towards an ostensibly more spiritual (where spiritual is understood to mean immaterial) habitation, but rather to a more perfect, permanent, brilliant, and luminous materiality. Surely in this direction lie more biblically faithful exegetical tools

4. Lewis, *Great Divorce*, vii–ix.
5. Lewis, *Great Divorce*, ix.

capable of better approximating and anticipating the scope of the promised redemption. Matter is to be "helped" not discarded. What the physical and material dimensions of the fallen world need are not dissimilar to the needs of the fallen non-physical and non-material dimensions—such as the power to trust the word of God and to love one's neighbor.

Differentiation between material and non-material dimensions of creation illumine its wondrous complexity and unsurpassed beauty. But radical reduction of the term "spiritual" to the non-material dimensions is unbiblical and wrong. In most cases, Christian employment of the word "spiritual" should designate "that about which God cares," and, as such encompasses all that he has made. Both material and non-material.

By keeping the "spiritual" character of the entire creation in mind while also recognizing that this earth and this life, as Lewis has attempted to teach us, is not hell but a borderland between heaven and hell, we can and should pursue a more faithful comprehension of the place of shalom in this world. To the extent that we do so, certain benefits should follow. Negatively, we should become better equipped to oppose the prosperity gospel by claiming their pet Bible passages for ourselves. Positively, we should be able to better integrate a biblical affirmation of this world as the target of divine redemption without imagining that it is yet our home.

Bibliography

Augustine, Saint. *The City of God*. Translated by Marcus Dods. Modern Library. New York: Random House, 1950.

———. *On Christian Doctrine*. Translated by D.W. Robertson Jr. Indianapolis: Bobs-Merrill, 1958.

———. *Selected Writings*. Translated by Marcus Dods et. al. Roger Hazelton ed. New York: Meridian, 1962.

Babcock, Maltbie D. "This Is My Father's World." Hymn 58 in *The Hymnal for Worship & Celebration*. Waco, TX: Word Music, 1984.

Barth, Karl. *The Doctrine of Creation*. Vol. 3, pt. 2 of *Church Dogmatics*. Translated by Harold Knight et. al. Edinburgh: T. & T. Clark 1959.

Batey, Richard A. *Jesus and the Forgotten City*. Grand Rapids: Baker, 1992.

Bonhoeffer, Dietrich. *Creation and Fall; Temptation*. Translated by John C. Fletcher et. al. New York: Macmillan, 1959.

Brown, Peter. *Augustine of Hippo*. Los Angeles: University of California Press, 1967.

Bourke, Vernon, J., editor. *The Essential Augustine*. Toronto: Mentor-Omega, 1964.

Dockery, David S. *Southern Baptist Consensus and Renewal: A Biblical, Historical, and Theological Proposal*. Nashville: Broadman and Holman, 2008.

Dreher, Rod. *The Benedict Option: A Strategy for Christians in a Post-Christian Nation*. New York: Sentinel, 2017.

D'Souza, Dinesh. *The Virtue of Prosperity*. New York: Touchstone, 2000.

George, Timothy. *John Robinson and the English Separatist Tradition*. Macon: Mercer University Press, 2005.

Gonzales, Justo L. *Faith and Wealth: A History of Early Christian Ideas on the Origin, Significance, and Use of Money*. San Francisco: Harper and Row, 1990.

Graybill, Stephen J., editor. *The Stewardship Study Bible*. Grand Rapids: Zondervan, 2009.

Grudem, Wayne, and Barry Asmus. *The Poverty of Nations: A Sustainable Solution*. Wheaton, IL: Crossway, 2013.

Haykin, Michael A. G. *Rediscovering the Church Fathers: Who They Were and How They Shaped the Church*. Wheaton, IL: Crossway, 2011.

Hengel, Martin. *Poverty and Riches in the Early Church*. Translated by John Bowden. Philadelphia: Fortress, 1974.

Irenaeus. *Against Heresies*. Translated by Alexander Roberts et. al. Anti-Nicene Fathers 1. Grand Rapids: Eerdmans, 1985.

Lewis, C. S. *The Great Divorce*. San Francisco: HarperSanFrancisco, 2001.

Luther, Martin. *Luther's Works*. Vol. 1. Translated by George V. Schick. St. Louis: Concordia: 1958.

———. *Luther's Works*. Vol. 44. Translated by James Atkinson. Philadelphia: Fortress, 1966.

———. *Luther's Works*. Vol. 47. Translated by James Atkinson. Philadelphia: Fortress, 1966.

———. *Luther's Works*. Vol. 51. Translated by John W. Doberson. Philadelphia: Fortress, 1959.

———. *Luther's Works*. Vol. 54. Translated by Theodore G. Tappert. Philadelphia, Fortress, 1967.

———. *Luther's Works*. Vol. 68. Translated by Kevin G. Walker. St. Louis: Concordia, 2014.

Louth, Andrew, editor. *Ancient Christian Commentary on Scripture: Old Testament*, vol. 1. Translated by Joel Scandrett et. al. Downers Grove, IL: InterVarsity, 2001.

Mathews, Kenneth. *Genesis 1–11:26*. New American Commentary 1a. Nashville: Broadman and Holman, 1996.

Mitchell, Henry. *Black Church Beginnings: The Long-Hidden Realities of the First Years*. Grand Rapids: Eerdmans, 2004.

Novak, Michael. *The Spirit of Democratic Capitalism*. New York: Madison, 1982.

Oberman, Heiko. *Luther Between God and the Devil*. Translated by EileenWalliser-Schwarzbart. New York: Doubleday, 1982.

Origen. *An Exhortation to Martyrdom; Prayer; First Principles: Book IV; Prologue to the Commentary on the Song of Songs; Homily XXVII on Numbers*. Classics of Western Spirituality. Translated by Owen A. Greer. New York: Paulist, 1979.

Pelikan, Jaroslav. *Christianity and Classical Culture: The Metamorphoses of Natural Theology in the Christian Encounter with Hellenism*. New Haven, CT: Yale University Press, 1993.

Rae, Scott, and Austin Hill. *The Virtues of Capitalism: A Moral Case for Free Markets*. Chicago: Northfield, 2010.

Rodgers, T. J. "Cypress CEO Responds to Nuns Urging a 'Politically Correct' Board Make-Up." Cypress Semiconductor, May 24, 2012. http://www.cypress.com/documentation/ceo-articles/cypress-ceo-responds-nuns-urging-politically-correct-board-make.

Ross, Alan P. *Creation and Blessing: A Guide to the Study and Exposition of Genesis*. Grand Rapids: Baker, 1998.

Schneider, John R. *The Good of Affluence: Seeking God in a Culture of Wealth*. Grand Rapids: Eerdmans, 2002.

Smith, Gary V. *Isaiah 40–66*. New American Commentary 15b. Nashville: Broadman and Holman, 2009.

Soto, Hernando de. *The Mystery of Capital: Why Capitalism Triumphs in the West and Fails Everywhere Else*. New York: Basic, 2000.

Sowell, Thomas. "Life at the Bottom." In *The Thomas Sowell Reader*, 16–17. New York: Basic, 2011.

Stambaugh, John, and David Balch. *The Social World of the First Christians*. London: SPCK, 1986.

Steele, Shelby. *White Guilt: How Whites and Blacks Together Destroyed the Promise of the Civil Rights Era*. New York: Harper Perennial, 2006.

Name Index

Alaric, 128, 135–36
Arius, 16, 115
Augustine of Hippo, 7, 24n, 25n, 106, 121, 128–30, 135, 164–66, 169

Babcock, Maltbie D., 14n, 71n, 173
Barth, Karl, 25, 49, 65, 95, 149
Balch, David, 134n, 174
Basil of Caesarea, 26, 154
Batey, Richard A., 134n
Benedict of Nursia, 154, 136n, 173
Bernard of Clairvaux, 152
Berry, Wendell, 139
Bonhoeffer, Dietrich, 36, 73, 96, 173
Bourke, Vernon J., 164, 173
Brown, Peter, 24, 25n, 17
Brunson, Andrew, 159

Calvin, John, 38, 49, 99, 127, 147, 164
Chrysostom, John, 115
Constantine the Great, 155

Doris, Sister of St. Francis of Philadelphia, 137
De Soto, Hernando, 143n, 174
Dockery, David S., 165, 173
Dreher, Rod, 136n, 173
D'Souza, Dinesh, 137, 143n, 173

Edwards, Jonathan, 122

Florovsky, Georges, 26
Francis I, Pope, 126

Francis of Assisi, 151–52, 157

Graybill, Stephen J., 137n, 173
Graham, Billy, 137
Grudem, Wayne, 143, 173
George, Timothy, v, ix, 14n
Gonzales, Justo, 133, 173
Gregory of Nyssa, 164
Gregory Nazianzen, 26, 115

Hamilton, Forest, vi
Haykin, Michael A. G., 154n
Hengel, Martin, 133–34, 173
Hill, Austin, 174

Irenaeus, 27, 28n, 173

Jerome, 152

King Jr., Martin Luther, 138, 145
Kuyper, Abraham, 88

Lewis, C. S., 170–71, 174
Lloyd-Jones, Martyn, 63
Louth, Andrew, 40n, 174
Luther, Martin, 30, 31n, 99, 120, 135, 148–55, 157

Marcion/marcionism, 16–18, 23–24, 28, 31–32, 49, 55, 62–63, 83, 93–94, 120, 153
Mathews, Kenneth, 40n, 174
Milton, John, 22, 41, 109

Made in the USA
Columbia, SC
11 March 2019